THE AMBIVALENT WELCOME

The Ambivalent Welcome

PRINT MEDIA, PUBLIC OPINION AND IMMIGRATION

Rita J. Simon
and
Susan H. Alexander

PRAEGER

Westport, Connecticut
London

Library of Congress Cataloging-in-Publication Data

Simon, Rita James.
    The ambivalent welcome : print media, public opinion and immigration / Rita
J. Simon and Susan H. Alexander.
      p.   cm.
    Includes bibliographical references and index.
    ISBN 0-275-94492-1 (alk. paper)
    1. American periodicals. 2. United States—Emigration and
immigration—Public opinion. 3. Public opinion—United States.
I. Alexander, Susan H. II. Title.
    PN4877.S56 1993
    304.8'73—dc20   92-32671

British Library Cataloguing in Publication Data is available.

Library of Congress Catalog Card Number: 92-32671
ISBN: 0-275-94492-1

First published in 1993

Praeger Publishers, 88 Post Road West, Westport, CT 06881
An imprint of Greenwood Publishing Group, Inc.

Printed in the United States of America

The paper used in this book complies with the
Permanent Paper Standard issued by the National
Information Standards Organization (Z39.48–1984).

10 9 8 7 6 5 4 3 2 1

Contents

Introduction: How the Print Media Have Covered Immigration

An earlier version of this book described how the leading magazines in the United States and the *New York Times* covered and interpreted U.S. policy vis-à-vis immigration from 1880 to 1980. The 100-year time span was chosen because it coincided with the advent of the "new immigrants," when the movement to restrict immigration gained ascendancy and when the first major restrictive pieces of immigration legislation were enacted.

In the period immediately preceding the Civil War, the Know Nothing movement had opposition to further immigration as one of its major planks. The large number of Catholic Irish immigrants did much to stimulate the movement's anti-immigrant position. Following the Civil War, the Know Nothing movement all but disappeared and the number of immigrants arriving in the United States kept increasing. By the 1870s, "new immigrants" was widely used to refer to persons arriving from southern and eastern Europe. "New immigrants" referred not only to their countries of origin, which differed from those of the earlier cohorts, but also to the types of people they were. For example, they were more likely to be Catholics than Protestants; they were not English speaking; they were, in the majority, not skilled craftsmen or farm owners. Physically, they had characteristics that set them apart from the natives more than the earlier cohorts of immigrants, and, also more than the earlier cohorts, they were city dwellers. They crowded together in the cities closest to the ports through which they entered.

While the Know Nothing movement receded into the background, other groups, movements, and political parties expressed consternation, anxiety, fear, and other negative reactions at the seemingly endless stream of new immigrants who kept arriving at the United States' doorstep. The major fears were that these "new types" would alter the quality of life in the United States; would lower the wage levels and standard of living of the U.S. worker; would increase the crime, illiteracy, and pauperism rates; and would lower the level of culture.They would overcrowd U.S. cities and make them dirty, ugly, and dangerous, and they would fragment U.S. values and loyalties.

These reactions led to the enactment of legislation that sought to restrict the number of persons allowed to enter the United States as aliens and to specify countries from which they could come. Such legislation began in the 1880s and culminated following the end of World War I with the Quota Acts of the 1920s. Restrictive immigration statutes were also enacted in the 1950s following the end of World War II, but other factors, including hundreds of thousands of refugees from countries taken over by Communist regimes, altered the U.S. policy of restrictionism and brought about legislation that admitted aliens into the United States outside existing quotas. The illegal entry into the United States of hundreds of thousands of aliens also caused reconsideration of U.S. immigration policy.

Although magazines are the major media source for depicting U.S. beliefs and opinions about immigration, national poll data on immigration have been included, going back as far as data are available (from the mid-1930s).

The present volume expands the range of this book from 1980 to 1990. The expansion is especially noteworthy because it includes a decade in which two major pieces of legislation bearing on the number and types of immigrants allowed to enter this country were enacted. Media coverage of the debate preceding passage of the immigration bills was extensive and provided useful insights into beliefs about how immigrants are beneficial or hurtful to U.S. society, as are the national poll data that are included for the 1980–1990 decade. An appendix describing the major anti-immigrant movements in this country has also been added.

Data on the number of immigrants who have been admitted from 1980 to 1990, their demographic characteristics, and the countries from which they came are also updated. The major provisions of the immigration laws that have been enacted in the 1980–1990 period are included. In sum, this volume portrays the tension, the ambivalence, and the confusion in U.S. beliefs, attitudes, perceptions, and policies vis-à-vis immigration.

We acknowledge with appreciation and thanks the help of Linda Ireland, Fannie Norwood, and Ari Radestsky.

I

A STATISTICAL OVERVIEW OF FROM WHERE AND WHEN IMMIGRANTS CAME, MAJOR IMMIGRATION LEGISLATION, AND PUBLIC OPINION DATA

Part I is the prelude to the major theme of this work — a description and interpretation of how some of the leading media in this country covered immigration to the United States. In Chapter 1, statistics are provided on the number of immigrants by country of origin from 1810 to 1990, along with their demographic characteristics. Data on refugees by country of origin and estimates of the number of illegals who have entered the country are also provided. Chapter 2 contains an account of the major immigration acts that have been passed from 1880 to 1990 and summaries of the major political party platforms on immigration from the mid-nineteenth century through the 1988 presidential election. Results of national poll data (beginning with the availability of such data in the 1930s) bearing on issues of immigrants and refugees are reported in Chapter 3, as are opinions about levels and sources of immigration, preferences for particular types of immigrants, and constraints advocated for limiting or expanding immigration.

1

Who Came When and from Where: A Statistical Overview

Some 55 million people have come to the United States since English immigrants established a settlement in Jamestown, Virginia, in 1607.[1] Between 1810 and 1989, 40.5 million people immigrated to the United States; this number does not include those who did not stay, so it is a net figure. The starting point for this analysis is 1810 because we lack accurate data prior to that time. Table 1.1 shows the increase in U.S. population by births over deaths and by excess of immigrant arrivals over departures between 1810 and 1989. We see that the big increase in immigrants began with the 1830s; reached its peak in the first decade of the twentieth century; declined to its lowest level during the 1930s; and rose again sharply in the 1950s, 1960s, and 1980s. Indeed, during the 1930s the United States lost more people through migration than it gained. Over 6 million people came to the United States between 1900 and 1910; after that, immigration fell to between 2 million and 3 million per decade because of the passage of restrictive legislation and the onset of the worldwide economic depression in the 1930s, followed by World War II.

For the first 150 years, between 1810 and 1960, the large majority of immigrants (more than 80 percent) came from Europe. Between 1961 and 1970 the European immigration began to decline and was superseded by people coming from Central and South America, Canada, and the Caribbean. European immigration declined even more sharply to 18 percent from 1971 to 1980 and to 11 percent from 1981 to 1989. Between 1971 and 1980, immigrants from the Western Hemisphere comprised 44 percent of the total U.S. immigration. Mexico, Cuba, and Canada were the major sources of Western Hemisphere immigrants. In the decades from 1971 to 1989, more people emigrated from Asia (33 percent), mostly from the Philippines, Korea, and China, than they did from Europe. The rest of the world — Africa, Australia, and New Zealand — accounted for about 2 percent of the immigration to the United States.

TABLE 1.1
Increase in U.S. Population by
Component of Change, 1810–1989
(thousands per decade)

Period	Total Increase	Natural Increase*	Net Arrivals**
1810–1820	2,399	2,328	71
1821–1830	3,228	3,105	123
1831–1840	4,203	3,710	493
1841–1850	6,122	4,702	1,420
1851–1860	8,251	5,614	2,593
1861–1870	8,375	6,291	2,102
1871–1880	10,337	7,675	2,622
1881–1890	12,792	7,527	4,966
1891–1900	13,047	9,345	3,711
1901–1910	15,978	9,656	6,294
1911–1920	13,738	11,489	2,484
1921–1930	17,064	14,500	3,187
1931–1940	8,894	9,962	−85
1941–1950	19,028	17,666	1,362
1951–1960	28,626	25,446	3,180
1961–1970	23,912	19,894	4,018
1970	2,617	1,812	353
1975	2,165	3,144	1,894
1980	2,582	1,622	960
1985	2,325	1,674	651
1987	2,367	1,685	682
1988	2,409	1,742	667
1989	2,505	1,822	683
Total	212,964	172,411	40,553

*Excess of births over deaths.
**Excess of immigrant arrivals over departures. Estimated natural increase and estimated net arrivals do not coincide precisely with total increase figures because of imperfect data for births, deaths, and immigration.

Source: Conrad Taeuber and Irene Taeuber, *The Changing Population of the United States* (New York, Wiley, 1958), p. 294, Table 91; U.S. Department of Commerce, Bureau of the Census, *Historical Statistics of the United States: Colonial Times to 1970* (Washington, D.C.: U.S. Government Printing Office, 1975), pp. 8, 49; Bureau of the Census, *Statistical Abstract of the United States, 1990* (Washington, D.C.: U.S. Government Printing Office, 1990), p. 9.

Table 1.2 shows the particular countries from which the immigrants arrived in the greatest numbers between 1820 and 1989 and the peak year for each nationality. Except for Ireland, from which the largest influx came prior to the U.S. Civil War, European immigrants from the four other largest-sending nations (Germany, Italy, Great Britain, and Austria-Hungary) all came in the three decades between 1880 and 1910.

TABLE 1.2
The Leading "Sender" States, 1820–1989

State	Total*	Peak Year
Germany	7,071,100	1882
Italy	5,356,000	1907
Great Britain	5,100,000	1888
Ireland	4,723,000	1851
Austria-Hungary	4,338,000	1907
Canada	4,270,000	1924
Russia	3,428,000	1913
Denmark	369,000	1882
Finland	33,000	1882
Norway	856,000	1882
Sweden	1,283,000	1882
Mexico	3,208,000	1989
Caribbean (including Cuba)	2,590,000	1988
France	783,000	1851
Greece	700,000	1907
China	823,000	1989
Poland	587,000	1921
Portugal	497,000	1907
Japan	455,000	1907
Philippines	455,000	1989
Turkey	409,000	1913
Netherlands	372,000	1882
Korea	611,000	1987
Vietnam	443,000	1984

*All totals have been rounded off.

Source: American Heritage (New York: Forbes, Inc., 1981), p. 55; U.S. Department of Commerce, Bureau of the Census, *Statistical Abstract of the United States, 1990* (Washington, D.C.: U.S. Government Printing Office, 1990), p. 10.

Every year between 1820 and 1930 (1922 is the sole exception), the number of male immigrants to the United States exceeded the number of female immigrants, and every year from 1930 through 1979, more women than men migrated to the United States. As shown in Table 1.3, slightly more men than women arrived in the United States in the 1980s.

A breakdown by the marital status of men and women who migrated to the United States from the 1970s through 1989 shows that more single men than single women arrived, but more married, divorced, and widowed women than men entered during those years.[2]

Most immigrants the world over and throughout history tend to be young people who come to start a new life. In the decade from 1951 to 1960, the median age of immigrants to the United States was 25.8

TABLE 1.3
Immigration to the United States by Sex, 1930–1989

Year	Both Sexes	Males	Females	Percent Female
1930-39	699,375	312,716	386,659	55.3
1930	241,700	117,026	124,674	51.6
1931	97,139	40,621	56,518	58.2
1932	35,576	13,917	21,659	60.9
1933	23,068	3,219	13,849	60.0
1934	29,470	12,101	17,369	58.9
1935	34,956	14,010	20,946	59.9
1936	36,329	14,775	21,553	59.3
1937	50,244	21,664	28,580	56.9
1938	67,895	29,959	37,936	55.9
1939	82,998	39,423	43,575	52.5
1940–49	856,608	332,317	524,291	61.2
1940	70,756	33,460	37,296	52.7
1941	51,776	23,519	28,257	54.6
1942	28,781	12,008	16,773	58.3
1943	23,725	9,825	13,900	58.6
1944	28,551	11,410	14,141	60.0
1945	38,119	13,389	24,730	64.9
1946	108,721	27,275	81,446	74.9
1947	147,292	53,739	93,523	63.5
1948	170,570	67,322	103,248	60.5
1949	188,317	80,340	107,977	57.3
1950–59	2,499,268	1,157,864	1,341,404	53.7
1950	249,487	119,130	130,057	52.2
1951	205,717	99,327	106,390	51.7
1952	265,520	123,609	141,911	53.4
1953	170,434	73,073	97,361	57.1
1954	208,177	95,594	112,583	54.1
1955	237,790	112,032	125,758	52.9
1956	321,625	156,410	165,215	51.4
1957	326,867	155,201	171,666	52.5
1958	253,265	109,121	144,144	56.9
1959	260,686	114,367	146,319	56.1
1960–69	3,213,749	1,427,308	1,786,441	55.6
1960	265,398	116,687	148,711	56.0
1961	271,344	121,380	149,964	55.3
1962	283,763	131,575	152,188	53.6
1963	306,260	139,297	166,963	54.5
1964	292,248	126,214	166,034	56.8
1965	296,248	127,171	169,526	57.1
1966	323,040	141,456	181,584	56.2
1967	361,972	158,324	203,648	56.3
1968	454,448	199,732	254,716	56.0
1969	358,579	165,472	193,107	53.9

TABLE 1.3, continued

Year	Both Sexes	Males	Females	Percent Female
1970–79	4,336,001	2,036,292	2,229,709	53.0
1970	373,326	176,990	196,336	52.6
1971	370,478	172,528	197,950	53.4
1972	384,685	179,715	204,970	53.3
1973	400,063	186,320	213,743	53.4
1974	394,861	184,518	210,343	53.3
1975	386,194	180,741	205,453	53.2
1976	398,613	184,863	213,750	53.6
1976	103,676	48,283	55,393	53.4
1977	462,315	216,424	245,891	53.2
1978	601,442	286,374	315,068	52.4
1979	460,348	219,536	240,812	52.3
1980–89	6,332,218	2,596,589*	2,563,800*	49.7
1980	530,639	N/A	N/A	N/A
1981	596,600	N/A	N/A	N/A
1982	594,131	287,874	284,576	47.9
1983	559,763	271,966	264,975	47.3
1984	543,903	274,896	269,007	49.5
1985	570,009	286,141	283,868	48.8
1986	601,708	300,777	300,931	50.0
1987	601,516	300,238	301,278	50.1
1988	643,025	324,521	318,504	49.5
1989	1,090,924	550,176	540,661	49.6

*Data for 1980 and 1981 not available by sex.

Sources: 1911–32: U.S. Department of Labor, *Annual Reports of the Commissioner of General of Immigration* (Washington, D.C.: U.S. Government Printing Office); 1933–77: U.S. Immigration and Naturalization Service, *Annual Reports of the Immigration and Naturalization Service* (Washington, D.C.: U.S. Government Printing Office, 1941–77); 1978–79 and 1989: U.S. Immigration and Naturalization Service, *Statistical Yearbooks of the Immigration and Naturalization Service* (Washington, D.C.: U.S. Government Printing Office, 1979 and 1990).

years; from 1961 to 1970 it was 25.2 years; from 1971 to 1980 it was 25.8 years; and from 1981 to 1989 it was 27.1 years.

Until the mid-1840s, farmers, followed by skilled craftsmen, were the largest occupational group to enter the United States. From the 1850s until the passage of quota legislation in the 1920s, unskilled laborers (including farm laborers) was the largest category. Following passage of the 1921 and 1924 Quota Acts (discussed in the next chapter), more skilled laborers and craftsmen arrived than did unskilled workers. Few immigrants arrived in the 1930s, and most of those who did come were professionals, clerical workers, and skilled craftsmen. From the 1950s to the present, U.S. immigration law has given preferential status to immigrants with special skills, and skilled craftsmen and professionals have been admitted in larger numbers than persons in any other occupational categories.

Table 1.4 summarizes the number and percentage of immigrants by major occupational groups for 1910, 1930, 1950, 1960, and 1970. The same pattern prevailed in the years between 1971 and 1978. Among the immigrants who stated an occupation, professionals and skilled craftsmen constituted the largest categories.

The chart below compares the occupational categories entered by immigrants who arrived in the United States between 1985 and 1987 with those of the U.S.-born population. The data show that immigrants are distributed at both ends of the occupational ladder.

Occupational Group	Percentage of All U.S. Workers (1987)	Percentage of Immigrants (1985–1987)
Managers and professionals*	24	25
Technical, sales, and administration	31	16
Production, craft, and repair	12	12
Operators and laborers	16	22
Service occupations	13	20
Agriculture	3	5

*Managers, executives, architects, engineers, doctors, teachers, and computer scientists

Source: U.S. Department of Labor, "The Effect of Immigration on the U.S. Economy," (Washington, D.C.: U.S. Government Printing Office, 1989).

REFUGEES

From the years following the end of World War II until the present, persons seeking to enter the United States as refugees have attracted a great deal of attention and have been the subject of considerable debate and legislation. Refugee acts from 1953 to 1989 have allowed some 1.75 million persons from Europe, Southeast Asia, and the Caribbean to enter the United States outside the quotas allocated to these regions. The Refugee Act of 1980, for example, provided for the admission of 168,000 Indochinese per year. Table 1.5 lists the numbers of refugees by country of origin from 1961 through 1989. Almost one-third came from Cuba alone. The next largest groups were from Vietnam, Laos, Cambodia, and the Soviet Union.

TABLE 1.4
Immigrants Admitted, by Major Occupation Group, Selected Years, 1910–1970

Occupation	1910 Number	1910 Percent	1930 Number	1930 Percent	1950 Number	1950 Percent	1960 Number	1960 Percent	1970 Number	1970 Percent
Total admitted	1,041,570	100.0	241,700	100.0	249,187	100.0	265,398	100.0	373,326	100.0
Occupation reported	781,568	75.0	136,106	56.3	126,325	50.7	122,557	46.2	157,189	42.1
Housewives, children, and others with no occupation or occupation not reported	260,002	25.0	105,594	43.7	122,862	49.3	142,841	53.8	216,137	57.9
Total reporting occupation	781,568	100.0	136,106	100.0	126,325	100.0	122,557	100.0	157,189	100.0
Professional, technical, and kindred workers	9,689	1.2	8,585	6.3	20,502	16.2	21,940	17.9	46,151	29.4
Farmers and farm managers	11,793	1.5	8,375	6.2	17,642	14.0	3,050	2.5	3,839	2.4
Managers, officials, and proprietors	14,731	1.9	4,620	3.4	6,396	5.1	5,309	4.3	5,829	3.7
Clerical and kindred workers	—	—	—	—	—	—	19,972	16.3	13,818	8.8
Sales workers	12,219	1.6	14,414	10.6	16,796	13.3	4,414	3.6	2,699	1.7
Craftsmen, foremen, and kindred workers	—	—	—	—	21,832	17.3	19,156	15.6	28,192	17.9
Operatives and kindred workers	121,847	15.6	32,474	23.9	19,618	15.5	14,979	12.2	18,430	11.7
Private household workers	96,658	12.4	29,073	21.4	8,900	7.0	8,173	6.7	10,479	6.7
Service workers, except private household	8,977	1.1	6,749	5.0	4,970	3.9	8,812	7.2	9,272	5.9
Farm laborers and foremen	288,745	36.9	13,736	10.1	3,976	3.1	3,914	3.2	4,332	2.8
Laborers, except farm and mine	216,909	27.8	18,080	13.3	5,693	4.5	12,838	10.5	14,148	9.0

Source: U.S. Department of Commerce, Bureau of the Census, *Historical Statistics of the United States, Colonial Times to 1970* (Washington, D.C.: U.S. Government Printing Office, 1975).

TABLE 1.5

Immigrants Admitted as Permanent Residents under Refugee Acts, by Country of Birth, 1961-1989

Country of Birth	1961–70	1971–80	1981–88	1989
Total	212,719	539,447	831,968	84,288
Europe*	55,914	71,858	104,053	18,348
Austria	233	185	314	26
Bulgaria	1,799	1,238	893	126
Czechoslovakia	5,709	3,646	6,681	646
Germany	655	143	589	108
Greece	586	478	908	185
Hungary	4,044	4,358	3,486	588
Italy	1,198	346	264	44
Netherlands	3,134	8	10	—
Poland	3,197	5,882	26,144	3,842
Portugal	1,361	21	19	—
Romania	7,158	6,812	23,274	3,338
Spain	4,105	5,317	615	37
Soviet Union	865	31,309	39,858	9,264
Yugoslavia	18,299	11,297	278	23
Other Europe	3,561	818	722	127
Asia**	19,207	210,683	603,474	56,751
Afghanistan	—	542	18,196	2,606
Cambodia	—	7,739	103,697	5,648
China	5,300	13,760	7,093	502
Indonesia	7,658	222	1,280	77
Iran	—	364	29,957	8,167
Japan	554	—	—	—
Kampuchea	0	—	—	—
Korea	1,315	65	114	4
Laos	0	21,690	121,107	12,033
Thailand	—	1,241	21,835	4,347
Vietnam	5	150,266	28,033	21,883
Other Asia	4,375	1,538	2,312	346
North America	131,955	252,633	105,190	6,740
Cuba	131,448	251,514	100,454	5,245
Other North America	507	1,038	975	222
South America	121	1,244	1,537	175
Africa	5,486	2,991	17,668	2,268
Other	36	38	46	5

*Through 1970, Turkey included in Europe; thereafter, included in Asia.
**Includes Taiwan.

Source: U.S. Immigration and Naturalization Service, *Annual Reports of the Immigration and Naturalization Service* (Washington, D.C.: U.S. Government Printing Office, 1979 and 1989).

ILLEGALS

Illegals in the post–World War II era (undocumented immigrants, persons who entered the country illegally) have aroused the most controversy and have been the source of the most hostility on the part of the U.S. public and among members of Congress. The largest single group of undocumented aliens come from Mexico. The fear that thousands, even millions, of undocumented Mexicans are going back and forth across the border unnoticed by U.S. sentries has been the subject of congressional debate, media publicity, and public outcry.

As noted in Table 1.2, 3,208,000 Mexicans were reported to have immigrated to the United States between 1820 and 1989. The peak year within that time span was 1989. In the four decades since 1950, approximately 2,300,000 Mexican immigrants have entered the United States legally. In its 1979 and 1989 annual reports, the U.S. Immigration and Naturalization Service provided the following data on the number of illegal Mexican aliens who were apprehended in the United States from 1965 through 1989. Estimates concerning the ratio of those who enter the United States and are not apprehended to those who are caught vary from a conservative two to one to six or seven to one.

Year	Apprehensions of Illegal Aliens from Mexico
1965	55,300
1966	89,800
1967	108,300
1968	151,700
1969	201,600
1970	265,500
1971	348,200
1972	430,200
1973	576,800
1974	710,000
1975	680,000
1976	781,000
1977	714,179
1978	772,797
1979	776,671
1980	670,634
1981	725,696
1982	725,696
1983	1,010,745
1984	1,128,833
1985	1,146,211

Year	Apprehensions of Illegal Aliens from Mexico
1986	1,361,401
1987	1,093,621
1988	908,405
1989	808,732

NOTES

1. William J. Bromwell, *History of Immigration to the United States*, 1856, estimated that the number of passengers of foreign birth who arrived in the United States from the end of the Revolutionary War to 1819 was 250,000.

2. U.S. Immigration and Naturalization Service, *1989 Statistical Yearbook of the Immigration and Naturalization Service* (Washington, D.C.: U.S. Government Printing Office, 1990).

2

Major Immigration Legislation and Political Party Platforms, 1880–1990

MAJOR IMMIGRATION LEGISLATION

The period from 1880 to the mid-1960s is characterized by historians as the restrictionist era in U.S. immigration policy. Prior to the 1880s there were movements within the United States, such as the American Party, the Know Nothing Party, the Ku Klux Klan, and the American Protective Association, that favored restrictions on immigration and strongly recommended limitations and exclusion of certain groups of immigrants on the basis of racial and religious characteristics. Beginning with the 1880s and particularly with the passage of the Chinese Exclusion Act (1882), Congress began to take an active part in the administration and control of immigration. The Chinese Exclusion Act, which suspended entry of Chinese workers for ten years and barred all foreign-born Chinese from acquiring citizenship, marked the first time in U.S. history that a group of people were excluded because of their national characteristics.[1] Three years later, in 1885, Congress passed the Foran Act, which prohibited the recruitment of unskilled laborers by prepaid passage and advance contracting. In 1888, Congress ordered the deportation of all alien contract laborers within one year of entry.

In the two decades between 1896 and 1917, Congress grappled with literacy requirements as a means of restricting immigration. From 1896 until 1910, four literacy bills were debated in the Congress and passed in one of the houses. Between 1910 and 1917, Congress passed and sent to the president three literacy acts, each of which was vetoed by a president. In 1907 Congress established the Dillingham Commission to study the relationship between literacy, deviance, and the types of aliens who were likely to make the best citizens. Finally, in 1917, over a presidential veto, an Immigration Act was passed that required proof on the part of aliens over 16 years of age that they were able to read and write in some language (their native language, English, or any other). Those who could not meet those requirements were sent back. The same act also barred Asiatics (defined as persons from India, Indochina, Afghanistan, Arabia, and East India) from entry. This ban had nothing to do with literacy; it was added to the Immigration Act of 1917.

After more than two decades of debate, study, and law making, literacy tests turned out not to be effective barriers to immigration. The numbers of immigrants did not decline, nor was there a change in the countries of origin of the immigrants. It was the lack of effectiveness of the literacy requirements that led Congress to adopt another criterion for restricting immigration: national quotas.

The Johnson Act of 1921, known as the Quota Act or the Immigration Act of 1921, introduced the system of national quotas. The quota was determined as a percentage of the number of immigrants from the country in question at a designated census. The Quota Act limited the annual number of entrants of each admissible nationality to 3 percent of the foreign born of that nationality as recorded in the U.S. Census of 1910. It also set a limit on European immigration at 350,000. The Quota Act had been vetoed earlier by President Woodrow Wilson; when Warren Harding took office, he signed it into law.

Quotas were established for countries in Europe, the Near East Africa, Australia, and New Zealand. No quotas were imposed on immigrants from countries in the Western Hemisphere.

In 1924, the year the 1921 Quota Act expired, Congress passed another National Quota Act, named for its cosponsors, the Johnson-Reed Act. This time it set national quotas at 2 percent of the 1890 population. The Quota Act of 1924 also provided that beginning July 1, 1927, the quota limit would be 150,000, allocated on the basis of the estimated national origin distribution of the population of the continental United States in 1920. That portion of the 1924 act was postponed twice, but it finally became effective on July 1, 1929. The act also barred from entry all aliens who were ineligible for citizenship.

In the first two decades of the twentieth century, Congress passed various other pieces of restrictionist legislation that limited groups on the basis of political activities and ideologies and of medical histories. Anarchists and epileptics, for example, were excluded by these measures.

The period between 1929 and 1939 saw little legislative action, largely because there was so little immigration during those years. In 1932, immigration reached its lowest level since 1831; in fact, more people were leaving the United States than were entering. The worldwide depression was the major reason.

During World War II, in response to the labor shortage that the war created, Congress established a Bracero program, which permitted the entrance on a temporary basis of foreign agricultural laborers from Mexico, British Honduras, Barbados, and Jamaica. The Chinese Exclusion law was repealed.

Immediately following the end of World War II, Congress passed a War Brides' Act (1946), which admitted approximately 120,000 alien wives and children of U.S. servicemen on a non-quota basis. Two years later it passed a Displaced Persons Act, which admitted 280,000 people over a two-year period. Regular immigration quotas were mortgaged at 50 percent each year for as many years as it would take to pay back the number of immigrants admitted under this act. In 1950, still retaining the mortgage principle, an additional 415,000 displaced persons were admitted over the next two-year period.

The Immigration and Nationality Act of 1952, sponsored by Senator Pat McCarran and Representative Francis Walter, was the first major piece of immigration legislation since the 1921 and 1924 Quota Acts. The McCarran-Walter Act changed the formula for the computation of annual quotas from any country to one-sixth of 1 percent of the number of persons of each national origin in the United States in 1920. It limited immigration from the Eastern Hemisphere to 150,000 per year, but no ceilings were placed on Western Hemisphere immigration. The law removed racial barriers to immigration and naturalization. It broadened the definition of those classes of aliens subject to exclusion and deportation, and it expanded and strengthened provisions for the exclusion and deportation of other classes of aliens. It established preferences for skilled workers and for relatives of U.S. citizens.

The Hungarian uprising in 1956 sparked the passage of the first of a series of refugee acts that have continued until the present. In 1956 Congress allowed 21,000 Hungarian refugees to enter without regard for limitation quotas. In 1960, following the success of Fidel Castro in establishing a communist regime in Cuba, the United States passed the Migration and Refugee Assistance Act, which facilitated the admission and resettlement of more than 600,000 Cuban refugees into the United States. In 1964 Congress ended the Bracero program it had inaugurated in 1942.

The Hart-Celler Act of 1965 eliminated national origins as a basis for selection of immigrants to the United States. Instead, it established an annual limit of 170,000 aliens who could enter the United States as immigrants and a per-country quota of 20,000. Not included in the 170,000 figure were potential immigrants from Western Hemisphere countries. This act set a ceiling of 120,000 on immigration from the Western Hemisphere, thus allowing for the admission of 290,000 immigrants per year. The act established a system whereby immigration visas would be distributed according to a seven-point preference list that favored close relatives of U.S. citizens and those with needed occupational skills. Countries in the Western Hemisphere did not have a per-country quota. The act also broadened the definition of "refugees" to include not only people who were victims of political and religious persecution but also people who were victims of natural calamities. It established other categories of exclusion: people suffering from mental illness and drug and alcohol addictions; people who had physically contagious diseases; criminals, prostitutes, and subversives; and some 20 other different types of aliens.

The 1976 Immigration and Nationality Act extended the per-country limitation of 20,000 to the Western Hemisphere. In 1978, the act was amended to combine the ceiling for both the Eastern and the Western Hemispheres for a worldwide total of 290,000 immigrants per year.

The 1970s also witnessed the passage of legislation for the admission and resettlement of refugees, mainly from Southeast Asia, the Soviet Union, and Cuba. In 1975 the Indochinese Refugee Resettlement Program was enacted, allowing more than 200,000 Indochinese refugees to enter. In one piece of legislation, the Refugee Act of 1980, the United States established an overall policy vis-à-vis the admission and resettlement of refugees to the United States. "Refugees" were defined in accordance with the United Nations Convention of 1951 as persons outside their homeland who were unable or unwilling to return because of persecution or fear of persecution. The act created the office of U.S. Coordination for Refugee Affairs and the office of Refugee Resettlement in the U.S. Department of Heath and Human Services to coordinate international and domestic refugee programs and to arrange for effective absorption and resettlement of the refugees. The act assumed a normal flow of 50,000 refugees per year. It permitted the president, in consultation with Congress, to increase the annual allocation. In 1980, the level was set at 230,000 admissions.

The Immigration Reform and Control Act was passed in 1986. The major objective of the act was to reduce illegal immigration. It forbade employers to hire illegal aliens and established a public information and regulatory apparatus that helped employers comply with the law and detected and punished violators. It also established an enforcement apparatus to ensure that employers would comply with the laws banning discrimination in hiring on the basis of national origin or citizenship and an appeal process that would give persons who might suffer discrimination a channel for redress. A temporary program for legalizing undocumented immigrants who could demonstrate continuous residence in the United States as of January 1, 1982, was also created.

In November 1990, Congress passed the most liberal immigration bill since the first Quota Act of 1921 was signed into law. After considerable disagreement between the House and the Senate, a compromise on the number of immigrants admitted per year was reached. The House version would have increased immigrant visas to almost 1 million per year; the Senate version would have limited them to about 630,000. The compromise enacted into law will admit some 700,000 immigrants during fiscal years 1992 through 1994. Beginning in 1995, the act (P.L. 101-649) provides for a permanent annual level of at least 675,000 immigrants. The act establishes a three-track preference system for family-sponsored employment-based, and diversity immigrants. It raises employment-based immigrations from 54,00 to 140,000. It provides undocumented Salvadorans with protected status for a limited period of time, and it reverses the grounds for exclusion and deportation that have been controversial since their enactment in 1952.

POLITICAL PARTY PLATFORMS ON IMMIGRATION

In 1831, a political party issued a platform prior to a presidential election for the first time. At its convention in Baltimore, the National Republican Party began the practice that has since been adopted by all major political parties and has been in effect for every presidential election.

The first time the immigration issue appeared in a political platform was 1848.[2] The antislavery Free Soil Party included as one of its resolutions a plea that "the soil of our extensive domain be kept free for the hard pioneers of our own land and the oppressed and banished of other lands seeking homes of comfort and fields of enterprise in the new world."[3] Between 1848 and 1936, immigration appeared in at least one of the major party's platforms in every presidential campaign. Because our focus is on the period from 1880 to 1990, we turn to that period.

In 1876 the Democratic platform contained a long statement on Oriental immigration which read:

[The party] deplores the errors and omissions of the government that have exposed our brethren of the Pacific Coast to the incursions of a race not sprung from the same great parent stock, and in fact now by law denied citizenship through naturalization, as being neither accustomed to the tradition of a progressive civilization nor exercised in liberty under equal laws. We denounce the policy which thus discards the liberty-loving Germans and tolerates a revival of the coolie trade in Mongolian women imported for immoral purposes, and Mongolian men held to perform servile labor contracts, and demand such modifications of the treaty with the Chinese Empire, or such legislation within Constitutional limitations, as shall prevent further importation or immigration of the Mongolian race.[4]

On the same issue, the Republican platform said: "It is the immediate duty of Congress to fully investigate the effect of the immigration and importation of Mongolians upon the moral and material interests of the country."[5] The 1876 race marked the first time that either of the two major parties, the Republicans or the Democrats, issued a statement about Chinese immigration.

In 1880 the Democratic platform urged amending the Burlingame Treaty to allow no more Chinese immigration except for purposes of specific travel, education, and foreign commerce. The Republican platform included the following plank:

> Since the authority to regulate immigration and intercourse between the United States and foreign nations rests with the Congress of the United States and the treaty making power, the Republican party, regarding the unrestricted immigration of Chinese as a matter of grave concern under the exercise of both these powers, would limit and restrict that immigration by the enactment of such just, humane, and reasonable laws and treaties as will produce that result.[6]

The 1884 platform of the Democratic Party stated its opposition to

> The importation of foreign labor or the admission of servile races, unfitted by habits, training, religion or kindred, for absorption into the great body of our people, or for the citizenship which our laws confer. American civilization demands that against the immigration or importation of Mongolians to these shores our gates be closed.[7]

The Republican Party's platform denounced the importation of contract labor, whether from Europe or Asia, as an offense against the spirit of American institutions and pledged to sustain the present law, restricting Chinese immigration, and to provide such further legislation as is necessary to carry out its purposes.[8]

In 1888 the Democratic Party continued advocating "exclusion from our shores of Chinese laborers." The Republicans declared their hostility to the introduction into this country of foreign contract labor and of Chinese labor, claiming "they are aliens to our civilization and our constitution, and we demand the rigid enforcement of the existing laws against it and favor such immediate legislation as to exclude such labor from our shores."[9] These sentiments were echoed by the Prohibition Party and the American Convention Party.

The Democratic Party in 1892 continued to advocate against Chinese immigrants. The platform stated,

> We heartily approve all legitimate efforts to prevent the United States from being used as the dumping ground for the

known criminals and professional paupers of Europe, and we demand the rigid enforcement of the laws against Chinese immigration, or the importation of foreign labor, to degrade American labor and lessen its wages; but we condemn and denounce any and all attempts to restrict the immigration of the industrious and worthy of foreign lands.[10]

The Republicans favored the enactment of more stringent laws and regulations for the restriction of "criminals, paupers, and contract immigration."[11]

In 1896 the Democratic Party's platform declared, "We hold that the most efficient way of protecting American labor is to prevent the importation of foreign pauper labor to compete with it in the home market."[12] The Republicans took essentially the same position and announced,

For the protection of the quality of our American citizenship and of the wages of our workingmen against the fatal competition of low priced labor, we demand that the immigration laws be thoroughly enforced, and so extended as to exclude from entrance to the United States those who can neither read nor write.[13]

In the election campaign of 1900, the Democrats returned to the theme of Chinese exclusion. The party favored "the continuance and strict enforcement of the Chinese Exclusion Law and application to the same class of all Asiatic races."[14] The Republicans outdid the Democrats and advocated more effective restriction of the immigration of cheap labor from all foreign lands.

In 1904 the Republican platform applauded the attitude of President Theodore Roosevelt and the Congress in regard to the exclusion of Chinese labor. The Democratic platform made no reference to immigration. Four years later, in 1908, the Democratic Party platform contained a strong restrictionist plan, which read as follows:

We favor full protection, by both National and State governments within their restrictive spheres, of all foreigners residing in the United States under treaty, but we are opposed to the admission of Asiatic immigrants who cannot be amalgamated with our population, or whose presence among us would raise a race issue and involve us in diplomatic controversies with Oriental powers.[15]

The Republican Party platform was silent on the immigration issue.

A new third party entered the campaign of 1912 and was the only party to offer a proimmigration position. The Progressive Party's platform contained the following statement:

> Through the establishment of industrial standards we propose to secure the able-bodied immigrants and to his native fellow workers a large share of American opportunity. We denounce the fatal policy of indifference and neglect which has left our enormous immigrant population to become prey of chance and cupidity. We favor governmental action to encourage the distribution of immigrants away from the congested cities, to rigidly supervise all private agencies dealing with them and to promote their assimilation, education and advancement.[16]

Not since the period prior to the Civil War did any of the major parties express such positive sentiments toward immigrants.

The Democratic Party's platform did not contain a plank on immigration in 1912, and the Republican Party stayed on course. Its platform contained the following statement: "We pledge the Republican Party to the enactment of appropriate laws to give relief from the constantly growing evil of induced or undesirable immigration, which is inimical to the progress and welfare of the people of the United States."[17]

By 1916 the Republican Party had adopted some of the sentiments expressed in the Progressive Party platform of 1912. It said,

> We reiterate the unqualified approval of the action taken in December, 1911, by the President and Congress to secure with Russia, as with other countries, a treaty that will recognize the absolute right of expatriation and prevent all discrimination of whatever kind between American citizens whether native born or alien, and regardless of race, religion or previous political allegiance. We renew the pledge to observe this principle and to maintain the right of asylum.[18]

That statement is the first time a party platform mentioned the right of asylum. Remember, however, the year was 1916, and rumblings were already heard from czarist Russia that suggested that revolution was in the air and exiles would be a likely by-product.

For the second presidential campaign in a row, the Democratic Party failed to include a plank on immigration in its platform.

By 1920 the Democratic platform returned to one of its favorite themes: the exclusion of Orientals. It said,

> The policy of the United States with reference to the non-admission of Asiatic immigrants is a true expression of the judgment of our people, and to the several states, whose geographical situation or internal conditions make this policy, and enforcement of the laws enacted pursuant thereto, of particular concern, we pledge our support.[19]

Although the Republican Party's platform was also restrictionist, its rhetoric was more positive. It described the necessity for maintaining a high standard of living for U.S. laborers and justice for both aliens and citizens. Its plank read as follows:

The standard of living and the standard of citizenship of a nation are its most precious possessions, and the preservation and the elevation of those standards is the first duty of our government. The Immigration policy of the United States should be such as to insure that the number of foreigners in the country at any one time shall not exceed that which can be assimilated with reasonable rapidity, and to favor immigrants whose standards are similar to ours.

The selective tests that are at present applied should be improved by requiring a higher physical standard, a more complete exclusion of mental defectives and of criminals, and a more effective inspection applied as near the source of immigration as possible, as well as at the port of entry. Justice to the foreigner and to ourselves demands provision for the guidance, protection and better economic distribution of our alien population. To facilitate government supervision, all aliens should be required to register annually until they become naturalized.

The existing policy of the United States for the practical exclusion of Asiatic immigrants is sound, and should be maintained.[20]

The Democratic platform of 1924 contained the same rhetoric and substance of previous campaigns. It pledged to maintain "our established position in favor of the exclusion of Asiatic immigration."[21] The Republican Party had a long plank on immigrants, which declared,

The unprecedented living conditions in Europe following the World War created a condition by which we were threatened with mass immigration that would have seriously disturbed our economic life. The law recently enacted [the reference is to the 1924 Quota Act] is designed to protect the inhabitants of our country, not only the American citizen, but also the alien already with us who is seeking to secure an economic foothold for himself and family from the competition that would come from unrestricted immigration. The administrative features of the law represent a great constructive advance, and eliminate the hardships suffered by immigrants under emergency statutes. We favor the adoption of methods which will exercise a helpful influence among the foreign born population and provide for education of the alien in our language, customs, ideals and standards of life. We favor the improvement of naturalization laws.[22]

The platforms of the Democratic and Republican parties vis-à-vis immigration in 1928 were similar. The Democrats said, "Laws which limit immigration must be preserved in full force and effect, but the provisions contained in these laws that separate husbands from wives and parents from infant children are inhuman and not essential to the purpose or the efficacy of such laws."[23]

The Republicans stated,

The Republican Party believes that in the interest of both native and foreign born wage earners, it is necessary to restrict immigration. Unrestricted immigration would result in widespread unemployment and in the breakdown of the American standard of living. Where, however, the law works undue hardships by depriving the immigrant of the comfort and society of those bound by close family ties, such modification should be adopted as will afford relief. We commend Congress for correcting defects for humanitarian reasons and for providing an effective system of examining prospective immigrants in their home countries.[24]

The 1930s was a decade of negative immigration. In 1932 the Democratic Party platform carried no mention of immigration. The Republican platform reminded the voters that it was the party that passed the Quota Acts of 1921 and 1924.

The restriction of immigration is a Republican policy. Our party formulated and enacted into law the quota system, which for the first time has made possible an adequate control of foreign immigration. Rigid examination of applicants in foreign countries prevented the coming of criminals and other undesirable classes, while other provisions of the law have enabled the President to suspend immigration of foreign wage earners who otherwise, directly, or indirectly, would have increased unemployment among native-born and legally resident foreign-born wage-earners in this country. As a result, immigration is now less than at any time during the past one hundred years. We favor the continuance and strict enforcement of our present laws upon this subject.[25]

For the first time since 1848, neither of the two major parties mentioned immigration in its platform of 1936. The Republican Party made a passing reference to immigration in its 1940 platform when it declared, "We favor the strict enforcement of all laws controlling entry of aliens. The activities of undesirable aliens should be investigated and those who seek to change by force and violence the American form of government should be deported."[26] The Democrats remained silent on the topic.

During the 1944 presidential campaign, with the United States at war, neither the Republicans nor the Democrats included an immigration plank in their platforms.

The presidential campaign of 1948 marked a switch in the Democratic Party's position on immigration from exclusionist vis-à-vis Orientals and restrictionist vis-à-vis everyone else to a moderately positive stance. That year also marked the appearance of an immigration plank after a 20-year absence. In 1928 the Democratic Party platform favored the preservation of all restrictions except for the uniting of husbands and wives and parents and infant children. The 1948 campaign, then, is the watershed for the Democratic Party's position vis-à-vis immigration. The party announced,

> We pledge ourselves to legislation to admit a minimum of 400,000 displaced persons found eligible for United States citizenship without discrimination as to race or religion. We condemn the undemocratic action of the Republican 80th Congress in passing an inadequate and bigoted bill for this purpose, which law imposes un-American restrictions based on race and religion upon such admissions.[27]

The Republican Party maintained its silence.

For the Democratic Party, the 1952 plank on immigration was a continuation of its position in 1948. It stressed the need to admit refugees from communism and from war-torn Europe.

> Solution of the problem of refugees from communism and overpopulation has become a permanent part of the foreign policy program of the Democratic Party. We pledge continued cooperation with other free nations to solve it. We pledge continued aid to refugees from communism and the enactment of President Truman's proposals for legislation in this field. In this way we can give hope and courage to the victims of Soviet brutality and can carry on the humanitarian tradition of the Displaced Persons Act.[28]

The platform also discussed internal security. It stressed that "subversive elements must be screened out and prevented from entering our land." It concluded by pledging,

Continuing revision of our immigration and naturalization laws to do away with any unjust and unfair practices against national groups which have contributed some of our best citizens. We will eliminate distinctions between native-born and naturalized citizens. We want no "second-class" citizens in free America.[29]

Not since 1940 had the Republican Party included a plank on immigration in its platform. In 1956 it broke its silence and gave support to

An immigration policy which is in keeping with the traditions of America in providing a haven for oppressed peoples, and which is based on equality of treatment, freedom from implications of discrimination between racial, nationality and religious groups, and flexible enough to conform to changing needs and conditions. We believe that such a policy serves our self-interest, reflects our responsibility for the world leadership and develops maximum cooperation with other nations in resolving problems in this area. . . . This Republican Administration sponsored the Refugee Relief Act to provide asylum for thousands of refugees, expellees and displaced persons. . . . We believe also that the Congress should consider the extension of the Refugee Relief Act of 1953 in resolving this difficult refugee problem which resulted from world conflict. To all this we give our wholehearted support.[30]

The Democrats in 1956 also included a rather long statement about immigration, which started out, "America's long tradition of hospitality and asylum for those seeking freedom, opportunity, and escape from oppression, has been besmirched by the delays, failures and broken promises of the Republican Administration." It then went on to say how different the Democratic Party is from the Republican Party on these issues, how much fairer it is, and how much more committed it is to immigration.

We favor eliminating the provisions of law which charge displaced persons admitted to our shores against quotas for future years. Through such "mortgages" of future quotas, thousands of qualified persons are being forced to wait long years before they can hope for admission. We also favor more liberal admission of relatives to eliminate the unnecessary tragedies of broken families. We favor elimination of unnecessary distinctions between native-born and naturalized citizens. There should be no "second class" citizenships in the United States.[31]

Immigration was a major issue in the 1960 presidential campaign. The Democratic platform supported adjusting immigration, nationality, and refugee policies to eliminate discrimination and to enable members of scattered families abroad to be united with relatives already in the United States.

The national-origins quota system of limiting immigration contradicts the principles of this nation. It is inconsistent with our belief in the rights of man. The system was instituted after World War One as a policy of deliberate discrimination by a Republican Administration and Congress. The revision of immigration and nationality law we seek will implement our belief that enlightened immigration, naturalization and refugee policies and humane administration of them are important aspects of our foreign policy.[32]

The Republican Party's platform shared many of these views:

Immigration has historically been a great factor in the growth of the United States, not only in numbers but in the enrichment of ideas that immigrants have brought with them. This Republican Administration has given refuge to over 32,000 victims of Communist tyranny from Hungary, ended needless delay in processing applications for naturalization, and has urged other enlightened legislation to liberalize existing restrictions.
    Immigration has been reduced to the point where it does not provide the stimulus to growth that it should, nor are we fulfilling our obligation as a haven for the oppressed. Republican conscience and Republican policy require that the annual number of immigrants we accept be at least doubled; obsolete immigration laws be amended by abandoning the outdated 1920 census data as a base and substituting the 1960 census.[33]

Thus, by 1960, both major parties included strong proimmigration planks in their platforms. The Republicans favored admitting more immigrants than did the Democrats. The Republicans advocated repeal of the legislation that they had been most instrumental in passing only eight years earlier over President Truman's veto: the McCarran-Walter Act.

In 1964, the Democratic platform reminded voters of its position on immigration in 1960:

We proposed to adjust our immigration, nationality and refugee policies to eliminate discrimination and enable members of scattered families abroad to be united with relatives already in our midst. The national-origins quota system of limiting immigration contradicts the founding principles of this nation. It is inconsistent with our belief in the rights of men. The immigration law amendments, proposed by the Administration, and now before Congress, by abolishing the national-origin quota system, will eliminate discrimination based upon race and place of birth and will facilitate the reunion of families. The Cuban Refugee Program begun in 1961 has resettled over 81,000 refugees, who are now self-supporting members of 1,800 American communities. The Chinese Refugee Program, begun in 1962, provides for the admission to the United States of 12,000 Hong Kong refugees from Red China.[34]

The Republican Party's plank was much briefer. It said, "we pledge immigration legislation seeking to reunite families in continuation of the 'fair share' refugee program."[35]

After 1964 and through 1980, the Democratic Party did not include a plank on immigration in any of its platforms. In 1968 the Republicans said,

The principles of the 1965 Immigration Act — non-discrimination against national origins, re-unification of families and selective support for the American labor market have our unreserved backing. We will refine this new law [Hart-Celler Act] to make our immigration policy still more equitable and non-discriminatory.[36]

The Republicans reiterated much of the same notion in 1972 but added their support for the selective admission of the "specially talented" and "pledged to increase their efforts to halt the illegal entry of others."[37]

Neither the Republicans nor the Democrats included a plank on immigration in their 1976 and 1980 presidential platforms.

After a 20-year hiatus, the Democratic Party's 1984 platform contained the following position on immigration: "Our nations outdated immigration laws require comprehensive reform that reflects our national interests and our immigrant heritage. Our first priority must be to protect the fundamental human rights of American citizens and aliens."[38] It stated opposition to "employer sanctions designed to penalize employers who hire undocumented workers . . . and identification procedures that threaten civil liberties as well as any changes that subvert the basic principle of family unification."[39] It also stated opposition to "bracero," a guest worker program as a form of legalized exploitation.[40] Additionally, the platform promised that the Democratic Party would work to ensure that the Refugee Act of 1980 was complied with. "The party will provide the necessary oversight of the Department of State and the INS so as to ensure that the unjustifiable treatment visited upon the Haitian refugees will never again be repeated."[41]

The Republican Party's 1984 platform acknowledged the important and positive role that immigrants have played in U.S. history but then went on to state its central message:

We affirm our country's absolute right to control its borders. Those desiring to enter must comply with our immigration laws. Failure to do so not only is an offense to the American people but is fundamentally unjust to those in foreign lands patiently waiting for legal entry. We will preserve the principle of family reunification. With the estimate of the number of illegal aliens in the United States ranging as high as 12 million and better than one million more entering each year, we believe it is critical that responsible reforms of our immigration laws be made to enable us to regain control of our borders. The refugee problem is global and requires the cooperation of all democratic nations.[42]

Once again, in 1988, the Democratic Party platform did not contain a plank on immigration. The Republican platform included much the same message that appeared in its 1984 platform.

We welcome those from other lands who bring to America their ideals and industry. At the same time, we insist upon our country's absolute right to control its borders. We call upon our allies to join us in the responsibility shared by all democratic nations for resettlement of refugees, especially those fleeing communism in Southeast Asia.[43]

NOTES

1. In 1902 the Chinese Exclusion Act was renewed for an indefinite term. That term ended in 1943, when, in the midst of World War II, with China as a major ally, the ban was lifted. The Gentlemen's Agreement with Japan, which served to exclude Japanese from entrance to the United States as immigrants, was signed in 1908.

2. E. P. Hutchinson, *Legislative History of American Immigration Policy 1798–1965* (Philadelphia: University of Pennsylvania Press, 1981), p. 624.

3. Ibid.

4. Ibid.

5. Ibid.

6. Ibid., p. 625.

7. Ibid., p. 626.

8. Ibid., p. 627.

9. Ibid.

10. Ibid.

11. Ibid., p. 629.
12. Ibid.
13. Ibid.
14. Ibid., p. 630.
15. Ibid., p. 631.
16. Ibid., pp. 631–32.
17. Ibid., p. 632.
18. Ibid.
19. Ibid., p. 633.
20. Ibid.
21. Ibid., p. 634.
22. Ibid.
23. Ibid., p. 635.
24. Ibid.
25. Ibid., pp. 635–36.
26. Ibid., p. 636.
27. Ibid., p. 637.
28. Ibid., p. 638.
29. Ibid., p. 639.
30. Ibid., p. 640.
31. Ibid., p. 639.
32. Ibid., p. 641.
33. Ibid., pp. 641–42.
34. Ibid., p. 642.
35. Donald Bruce Johnson, *National Party Platforms: 1960–1976, Vol. II* (Urbana, Ill.: University of Illinois Press, 1978), p. 760.
36. Ibid., p. 760.
37. Ibid., p. 764.
38. *Democratic Party Platform* (Washington, D.C.: National Democratic Party Headquarters, 1984), p. 37.
39. Ibid., p. 37.
40. Ibid., p. 38.
41. Ibid.
42. *Republican Party Platform* (Washington, D.C.: National Republican Party Headquarters, 1984), p. 48.
43. *Republican Party Platform* (Washington, D.C.: National Republican Party Headquarters, 1988), p. 36.

3

Public Opinion on Immigrants: National Polls, 1937–1990

This chapter reports national poll data about U.S. public opinion toward immigration policy and immigrants from the late 1930s, when such data were first collected, until 1990. By "public opinion," we mean the aggregate of views people hold regarding matters that affect or interest the community.[1] Connecting that definition with the data referred to in this chapter, a more precise interpretation emerges, namely, the verbal responses that a representative sample of adults in the United States have made to questions about important issues affecting immigrants and immigration policy.

The typical sample size for national polls is between 1,500 and 2,000 respondents. Pollsters claim that with a sample that size, there is a 0.95 probability that the results obtained are no more than three percentage points off the figure that would be obtained if every adult in the country were interviewed. They also claim that it would be extremely expensive and time-consuming to increase substantially the sample size and that the reward for doing so would be minute.

Most of the polls reported in this chapter have been obtained from the Roper Public Opinion Research Center at the University of Connecticut in Storrs, Connecticut, and from *Public Opinion in America: 1936–1970*.[2]

Starting with the 1930s, we examine public opinion when the United States was experiencing its worst economic depression and when the conflict that was to become World War II had already broken out in Asia and Europe. It was also a period of strong isolationist beliefs and policies. The United States did not join the League of Nations when it was organized following World War I, even though Woodrow Wilson, the wartime president, had been one of its major architects and proponents. A residue of bitterness remained as the result of the failure of almost all of the U.S. wartime Allies to pay back the loans extended to them during the war, a widely shared belief that the United States had been dragged into an essentially European conflict, and a feeling that we benefited not at all by the Allied victory.

As the prospects for war increased in the 1930s, warnings were heard from Congress, other public officials, and leading journalists that the United States should not be misled and allow itself to be involved in another European or Asian conflict. National polls conducted in 1937, 1939, and 1941 showed that not only did the public express dislike for the prospect of involvement in a future war but also many respondents believed the United States' entry into the previous major conflict had been a mistake. The following items and the public's responses illustrate that position.[3]

Do you think it was a mistake for the United States to enter the World War?

Year	Yes	No	No Opinion
1937	64	28	8
1939	59	38	13
1941	39	42	19

If another war like the World War develops in Europe, should America take part again?

March 1937   No — 83 percent

Should we send our army and navy abroad to fight Germany and Italy?

September 1939   No — 84 percent

In 1937, Adolf Hitler had been chancellor of Germany for four years, but the Anschluss with Austria had not yet been made and German troops had not occupied foreign soil. By December 1940, most of Western and Central Europe were under Nazi control, France had been defeated, and the height of the German blitz over Britain had occurred a few months before, in the fall of 1940. The Hitler-Stalin nonaggression pact was still in effect, and the Eastern front was peaceful. In 1941 almost as many Americans thought our entry into World War I had been a mistake as did those who thought it was not. Approximately one in five did not have an opinion on the matter. During the two years in which Germany invaded Poland, Britain and France entered the war, France fell, and Germany invaded the Soviet Union, there was no significant alteration in the U.S. public's willingness to become involved again. As shown in the poll results below, in October 1941, two months before Pearl harbor, 79 percent said that if given the opportunity, they would vote to stay out of the war.[4]

If the question of the United States going to war against Germany and Italy came up for a national vote within the next two weeks, would you vote to go into the war or stay out?

Stay Out	Percent
May 1940	86
January 1941	88
October 1941	79

Predictably, the first items about immigration to appear on national polls in the 1930s asked about people who were forced to leave Nazi Germany and seek refuge. In May 1938 the public was asked:[5]

What's your attitude toward allowing German, Austrian, and other political refugees to come to the United States?

Response	Percent
Encourage, even if we have to raise immigration quotas	5
Allow them to come, but do not raise quotas	18
With conditions as they are, we should keep them out	68
Don't know	9

Although most respondents did not favor admitting refugees, there were some divisions on this issue. When responses were broken by the economic categories "rich-prosperous," "upper middle," "lower middle," and "poor," 30 and 29 percent of the rich and upper middle respondents answered "encourage" or "allow them to come," compared with 15 percent and 22 percent of the lower middle and poor respondents. Similarly, 43 percent of the respondents who were professionals encouraged or would have allowed them to come, compared with 15 percent of the factory workers. The respondents' sex and age made no difference on this item.

In January 1939, after Germany had annexed Austria and invaded Czechoslovakia, the following item appeared on a national poll.[6]

Should we allow a large number of Jewish exiles from Germany to come to the United States to live?[7]

No — 71 percent

If you were a member of the incoming Congress, would you vote yes or no on a bill to open the doors of the United States to a larger number of European refugees than are now admitted under our immigration quota?

No — 83 percent

Immigration policy and immigrants did not receive much attention in the national polls during the years the United States was at war. We found only one item on the topic: in September 1944, the public was asked to state its preference for different types of people rather than for numbers or quotas.[8]

Here is a list of different groups of people. Do you think we should let a certain number of each of these groups come to The United States to live after the war, or do you think we should stop some of the groups from coming at all?

Nationality	Allow (percent)	Stop (percent)	No Opinion (percent)
English	68	25	7
Swedes	62	27	11
Russians	57	33	10
Chinese	56	36	8
Mexicans	48	42	10
Jews	46	46	8
Germans	36	59	5
Japanese	20	75	5

Italians did not appear on the list. The two groups that enjoyed the lowest support were the major enemy nationalities, with the Japanese faring much worse than the Germans. Mexicans and Jews were clustered together below our wartime allies, the Russians and the Chinese. The neutral Swedes were second only to the British, who enjoyed the double advantage of having the correct racial-ethnic characteristics and of being an ally during the war.

Shortly after the war was over in December 1945, President Truman directed U.S. consulate offices in Europe to give preference to displaced persons within the existing quota stipulations. One month later, in January 1946, the public was asked:[9]

Should we permit more persons from Europe to come to this country each year than we did before the war, should we keep the number about the same, or should we reduce the number?

Response	Percent
More	5
Same	32
Fewer	37
None at all	14
No opinion	12

Slightly more than half of the respondents favored admitting fewer persons than we did before the war or admitting none at all. Only 5 percent would increase the numbers, and 32 percent favored keeping things as they were before the war. Respondents with a college education were more likely to favor admitting more or the same number of immigrants than were persons with a high school or grade school education (49 percent versus 40 or 34 percent).

Seven months later, in August 1946, the public's opinion on U.S. responsibility to European refugees was polled.[10]

There are still a lot of refugees or displaced persons in European camps who cannot go back to the homes they had before the war. Which of these four statements comes closest to what you think this country should do about these refugees?

Response	Percent
1. We should admit all of these refugees who are well and strong to the United States, no matter what other countries do.	10
2. We should take only our share of these refugees and insist that other countries do the same.	43
3. There are still too many here now and we should not admit any more at all, but we should help to get them settled elsewhere.	23
4. They are a problem for the European countries to worry about, and we should let those countries handle the problem.	17
5. Don't know	7

Once again, the more prosperous and more educated respondents were more likely to favor admitting at least "our share" of refugees. For example, 57 percent of the "rich" said they would be willing to take "our share," as opposed to 29 percent of the "poor"; 59 percent of the college educated respondents, as opposed to 27 percent of the grade school educated, were willing to take at least "our share" of refugees.

In the June and August 1946 polls, the following question was asked:[11]

Would you approve or disapprove of a plan to require each nation to take a given number of Jewish and other European refugees based upon the size and population of each nation?

Response	June (percent)	August (percent)
Approve	37	40
Disapprove	48	49
No opinion	15	11

In November 1947, people were asked if they would vote "yes" or "no" on a bill in Congress to let 100,000 selected European refugees come to this country in each of the next four years in addition to the 150,000 immigrants now permitted to enter each year under the present quota.[12] Seventy-two percent said they would have voted "no." Here again, the more educated and the richer respondents were more likely to vote in favor of more immigration. Sex and age made no difference.[13]

Respondents' Economic Status	Yes (percent)	Respondents' Education	Yes (percent)
Rich	31	College	34
Upper middle	23	High school	16
Lower middle	17	Grade	10
Poor	12	None	14

As the decade of the 1940s came to a close, as the Cold War gained in intensity, and as the Eisenhower administration took over, another dimension was added to the refugee problem: a growing number of East Europeans either did not want to return to their homelands because their country had been taken over by Communists or were running away from the Communist regimes under which they had been living. The Cold War, coupled with the feeling that the United States was a nation of immigrants, added fuel to the argument that this country had a special humanitarian contribution to make in resolving the postwar problem of displaced persons.

In 1953 President Eisenhower asked Congress to pass a law that would admit 240,000 of those refugees into the United States over a two-year period. When the issue appeared on a national poll, 47 percent said they approved of such a law and 48 percent disapproved; the remaining 5 percent had no opinion. Predictably, there was more support for the president's proposal from the more educated and more prosperous respondents. The following figures describe the differences by socioeconomic status.[14]

Economic Level	Approve (percent)	Education	Approve (percent)
1 (highest)	67	College graduate	70
2	58	College (one–three years)	58
3	49	High school graduate	51
4 (lowest)	40	High school (ninth–eleventh grade)	40
		Grade school	44

Shortly thereafter, another poll carried this item:[15]

In general, do you think the United States is letting too many immigrants come into this country or not enough?

Response	Percent
Not enough	13
About the right number	37
Too many	39
Don't know	11

Officially, the limit was still 150,000 per year. The large majority of the more prosperous and more educated divided their responses between "not enough" and "too many" (70 and 66 percent), as opposed to the less educated and less prosperous, 80 and 72 percent, of whom believed "too many" or "about the right number" were being admitted.

In the midst of the U.S.–USSR Cold War diplomacy, the Hungarians opted to test Soviet power and, indirectly, the United States' willingness to support nations within the Soviet sphere if they sought greater political autonomy. One of the by-products of the Hungarian revolt, which was defeated by direct Soviet intervention with troops and tanks, was thousands of refugees who escaped from Hungary and could not safely return to their homeland. Almost all of the Hungarian émigrés wanted to come to the United States. The U.S. public was asked the following question in a November 1956 Gallup poll.[16]

Five thousand refugees from Hungary are being admitted to the United States. If you have room would you be willing to have one or more of the refugees from Hungary stay in your house for a few months or until such a time as this person could be on his or her own?

Fifty percent said they would be willing to have a refugee live with them, 35 percent said they would not be willing, and 15 percent did not know. Referring to those 5,000 refugees, the public was asked a month later:[17]

Do you feel that the United States is letting in too many refugees from Hungary, about the right number, or not enough?

Response	Percent
Not enough	11
About right	48
Too many	34
Don't know	7

Perhaps because only 5,000 people were involved and because those who were admitted would not be eligible for citizenship, more people thought the number was too small or about right than complained that it was too many.

A year after the 5,000 Hungarian refugees were admitted, the public was asked how they felt about giving them permanent status.[18]

Under the present immigration laws, the Hungarian refugees who came to this country after the revolt last year have no permanent residence and can be deported at any time. Do you think the law should or should not be changed so that these refugees can stay here permanently?

The responses were evenly divided: 42 percent favored changing the law and 43 percent opposed a change. The other 15 percent had no opinion.

Between the time of the Hungarian refugee crisis and when the next groups of refugees sought asylum, the U.S. public was asked whether they would be willing to allow any refugees to enter and settle permanently in the United States. The question posed was:[19]

There are an estimated 15 million refugees in different parts of the world. These people have been forced to leave their home countries or have fled for various reasons. Are you in favor of or against allowing any of those refugees to come to the United States to make their homes?

Sixty percent said they would favor admitting some (the matter of how many was not asked), 31 percent were opposed to admitting any, and 9 percent did not know or did not answer.

Four years after the 5,000 Hungarian refugees were allowed to enter the United States, the first wave of the anti-Castro, middle class, professional Cubans sought asylum in the United States. From the time the first boat load landed until the exodus was over, some 600,000 Cubans settled in the United States, mostly in Miami.

In 1965 Congress passed the Migration and Refugee Assistance Act (popularly called the Hart-Celler Act), which placed ceilings of 170,000 immigrants from the Eastern Hemisphere and 120,000 immigrants from the Western Hemisphere and limited each country to 20,000 immigrants. Another 17,400 was set aside for refugees from all over the world. When he signed the bill at the base of the Statue of Liberty, President Lyndon Johnson said:[20]

This bill is not a revolutionary bill. It does not affect the lives of millions. It will not reshape the structure of our daily lives, or add importantly to our wealth and power. Yet it is still one of the most important acts of this Congress and this Administration. For it repairs a deep and painful flaw in the fabric of American justice. . . . The days of unlimited immigration are past — but those who come will come because of what they are — not because of the land from which they sprang.

In July and August 1965 the Gallup poll included three items about immigration policy. These questions appeared at a time when the United States was not responding to a crisis, that is, refugees were not waiting to be admitted on grounds of political asylum or religious persecution or because of devastating economic conditions in their country of origin. Thus, the public's responses at this time may reflect more long-term, detached views on the issue. The three items were:[21]

Should immigration be kept at its present level, increased, or decreased?

Response	Percent
Increased	8
Present level	39
Decreased	33
Don't know	20

Do you think the United States immigration policy should or should not have provisions for admitting people who escape from communism? ·

Response	Percent
Should	64
Should not	23
No opinion	13

The current immigration law restricts the number of persons coming from some countries more than others. This is called the "quota system." Would you favor or oppose changing this law so that people would be admitted on the basis of their occupational skills rather than on the basis of the country they come from?

Response	Percent
Favor	51
Oppose	32
No opinion	17

The Hart-Celler Act, passed in 1966, did away with the national origins quota system, about which the public was polled in the third item above. We see in response to the second item that refugees from communism fared better than refugees who sought asylum from nazism and fascism in the 1930s and early 1940s. Of course, economic conditions in the United States were much better in 1965 than they were in the late 1930s, and the United States had been through almost two decades of the Cold War.

In the decade of the 1970s, more than in any other period since the 1920s, the United States was concerned with immigration policy. The issue was thrust into the limelight as a result of four major factors: the defeat of South Vietnam by North Vietnam; erratic changes in Soviet policy, whereby it opened and then closed, or partially closed, its doors to Jews and other ethnic groups (Volga Germans and Armenians) who wanted to emigrate; Fidel Castro's willingness to allow Cubans to leave their island and make their way to the United States; and the illegal movement across the border between Mexico and the United States, with hundreds of thousands of Mexicans entering the United States. The U.S. government responded more positively to the first three factors than it had at any time since immigration restrictions were introduced in the 1920s.

Regarding the South Vietnamese who were evacuated to the United States at the time the Communists were about to enter Saigon and the thousands who left in small boats after the Communists gained control, the U.S. government passed legislation that aided their evacuation and helped them resettle in the United States. The first refugee act allowed for the entry of 7,000 Vietnamese per month; in the summer of 1979, President Jimmy Carter doubled that number to 14,000. However, most Americans did not support their government's actions on this issue. For example, in 1975, when the fall of Saigon was imminent, the U.S. public was asked if these South Vietnamese were evacuated, should they be permitted to live in the United States.[22] Fifty-two percent said they should not be permitted to live in the United States, 36 percent said they should, and 12 percent had no opinion. For the first time, age was an important factor in distinguishing responses. Fifty-six percent of the respondents under 30 years old (between 18 and 29) favored allowing the South Vietnamese to live in the United States, as opposed to 34 percent of the respondents who were between 30 and 49 years old and 25 percent of those who were older. Age was a significant factor in many of the public controversies of the 1960s and 1970s. The slogan "don't trust anyone over 30" gained widespread support, and the anti–Vietnam War and civil rights movements were led and supported by college-age youth and other persons under 30.

Shortly thereafter, a Harris poll asked: "Do you favor or oppose 130,000 Vietnamese refugees coming to live in the United States?"[23]

Forty-nine percent opposed, 37 percent favored, and 14 percent were undecided. Forty-eight percent of the college-educated public favored having the Vietnamese come to the United States, compared with 26 percent of those who had completed only grade school and 32 percent of those who had finished high school.

When the issue was posed in personal terms, for example, "Would you, yourself like to see some of these people come to live in this community or not?"[24] 48 percent said they would like to see some of these people come to live in their community, 40 percent said they would not, and 13 percent had no opinion. Fifty-nine percent of the college-educated population and 58 percent of those with family incomes of $20,000 or more favored this point, as opposed to 37 percent of the high school–educated and 40 percent of those with family incomes of less than $5,000.

During the same period, the late 1970s, another group of people were leaving their homeland, getting into boats, and making their way to the United States. They had a much shorter distance to go before they landed on U.S. soil. The thousands of Cubans who arrived off the coast of Florida in 1978 were granted refugee status like the Cubans who had come almost two decades earlier, but, unlike the Cuban refugees of the 1960s, many of the recent arrivals were not middle class and were not members of the professional and business community. Many came from rural areas, were poorly educated, and lacked urban occupational skills. When the U.S. public was asked whether the U.S. government should permit these Cubans to come and live in the United States, the responses looked like this: should, 34 percent; should not, 57 percent; don't know, 9 percent.[25] More Americans opposed than supported their government's action. The division of opinion for and against admitting the Cubans matched that reported for the Vietnamese almost exactly.

A May 1980 Gallup poll asked the following general questions about refugees and the obligation of the United States to them:[26]

Some people say that the U.S. government should permit persons who leave other countries because of political oppression to come and live in the United States. Others say that the federal government should halt all immigration until the national employment rate falls below 5 percent. Which point of view comes closer to the way you feel — that political refugees should be permitted to immigrate to the United States, or that immigration should be halted until the unemployment rate in the United States drops?

Response	Percent
Allow immigration	26
Halt immigration	66
Not sure	8

Respondents on the lower rungs of the socioeconomic status ladder were much more anti-immigration than were those higher up. For example, when we compare persons of different education levels, race, occupational status, and income, we note the following:[27]

In Favor of Halting Immigration	Percent
Education	
Grade school	81
High school	71
College	44
Race	
Black	79
White	64
Occupational categories	
Not labor force	74
Manual workers	73
Clerical and sales	68
Professional and business	48
Income level	
0–$5,000	78
5,000–9,999	78
10,000–14,999	72
15,000–19,999	59
20,000–24,999	60
25,000+	52

Persons of lower socioeconomic status and of a minority racial category are more likely to be anti-immigration. Immigrants, in their view, compete with them for jobs, housing, benefits, and their children's place in institutions of higher learning. The U.S. labor movement, as will be shown in later chapters, was also a strong advocate of restrictionist legislation in the first half of the twentieth century. Persons of higher socioeconomic status are less threatened by immigrants, especially when most of the immigrants are laborers and persons lacking professional and technical skills and experience. Higher-status respondents are less likely to believe that immigrants will take away their jobs or their children's opportunities.

Between 1977 and 1990, six national polls asked "Should immigration be kept at its present level, increased, or decreased?" The percentage of respondents who favored increasing immigration levels ranged from 4 to 9 percent. Thus, comparing the public's responses to this question over a 45-year time span, the data in Table 3.1 show that only once, in 1953, did more than 10 percent favor increasing the number of immigrants permitted to

TABLE 3.1
Distribution of Responses about the Number of
Immigrants That Should Be Permitted to Enter
(in percent)

Choices	1946[a]	1953	1965	1977	1981	1982	1986	1988	1990[b]
More/increase	5	13	8	7	5	4	7	6	9
Same/present level	32	37	39	37	22	23	35	34	29
Fewer/decrease	37 [14][c]	39	33	42	65	66	49	53	48
No opinion/ don't know	12	11	20	14	8	7	9	7	14

[a]In 1946, the question was phrased: "Should we permit more persons from Europe to come to this country each year than we did before the war, should we keep the number about the same, or should we reduce the number?" In the subsequent polls the question was usually phrased as follows: "Should immigration be kept at its present level, increased, or decreased?"

[b]In 1990, the question was phrased: "Is it your impression that the current immigration laws allow too many immigrants, too few immigrants, or about the right number of immigrants into this country each year?"

[c]"None" was offered as a choice of response only in 1946, and 14 percent selected that choice.

Source: Roper Center, (Storrs: University of Connecticut Press, 1991).

enter this country and that, throughout this period, at least three times as many supported decreasing the number of people permitted to enter.

The data in Table 3.2, which cover a 42-year time span, show that following the end of World War II, the U.S. public distinguished between immigrants whose movements were motivated primarily by economic factors and refugees who had to leave their homelands because of political oppression.

In the 1950s and 1960s, the U.S. public responded more positively to the special circumstances of various ethnic communities who sought admission to the United States as a result of revolution in their homelands or other extraordinary chaotic or life-threatening events. However, in 1975, when the people seeking refugee status were Vietnamese rather than European, the direction shifted, and more opposed than favored their admittance. In 1979, when a new wave of Cubans sought refugee status, public opinion opposed their admission as well.

The biggest immigration issue confronting U.S. society since the 1980s is the illegal aliens who enter this country, mostly from Mexico. It is the biggest problem because the number of Mexican illegal aliens currently in the United States is estimated to be in the millions (anywhere from 2 million to 10 million) and there appears to

TABLE 3.2
**Distribution of Responses about the Number of Refugees the
United States Should Admit**
(in percent)

Choices	1938[a]	1939[b]	1946[c]	1947[d]	1953[e]
Allow to enter	5[aa] 18[ab]		10[ca] 43[cb]		47
Keep out	68[ac]	83	23[cc] 17[cd]	72	48
Don't know	9[ad]		7		5

	1956[f]	1957[g]	1965[h]	1975[i]	1975[j]
Allow to enter	59	60	64	36	37
Keep out	34	31	23	52	49
Don't know	7	9	13	12	14

	1978[k]	1979[l]	1980[m]
Allow to enter	32	34	26
Keep out	57	57	66
Don't know	11	9	8

Notes:
   [a]What is your attitude toward allowing German, Austrian, and other political refugees to come to the United States?
      [aa]Encourage.
      [ab]Allow them to come, but do not raise quotas.
      [ac]With conditions as they are, we should keep them out.
      [ad]Don't know.
   [b]If you were a member of the incoming Congress, would you vote "yes" or "no" on a bill to open the doors of the United States to a larger number of European refugees than are now admitted under our immigration quota?
   [c]There are still a lot of refugees or displaced persons in European camps who cannot go back to the homes they had before the war. Which of these four statements comes closest to what you think this country should do about these refugees?
      [ca]We should admit all of these refugees who are well and strong to the United States, no matter what other countries do.
      [cb]We should take only our share of these refugees and insist that other countries do the same.
      [cc]There are still too many here now, and we should not admit any more at all, but we should help to get them settled elsewhere.
      [cd]They are a problem for the European countries to worry about, and we should let those countries handle the problem.
   [d]Would you vote "yes" or "no" on a bill in Congress to let 100,000 selected European refugees come to this country in each of the next four years in addition to the 150,000 immigrants now permitted to enter every year under our present quota?
   [e]Do you favor a law that President Eisenhower asked the Congress to pass that would admit 240,000 refugees to enter the United States over a two-year period?

TABLE 3.2, continued

---

[f]Do you feel the United States is letting in too many refugees from Hungary, about the right number, or not enough?

[g]There are an estimated 15 million refugees in different parts of the world. These people have been forced to leave their home countries or have fled for various reasons. Are you in favor of or against allowing any of those refugees to come to the United States to make their new home?

[h]Do you think the United States' immigration policy should or should not have provisions for admitting people who escape from communism?

[i]If these South Vietnamese are evacuated, should they be permitted to live in the United States or not?

[j]Do you favor or oppose 130,000 Vietnamese refugees coming to live in the United States?

[k]Thinking now about the Indochinese refugees, the so-called boat people, would you favor or oppose the United States relaxing its immigration policies so that many of these people could come to live in the United States?

[l]Should the U.S. government permit these Cubans to come and live in the United States?

[m]Some people say that the U.S. government should permit persons who leave other countries because of political oppression to come and live in the United States. Others say that the federal government should halt all immigration until the national unemployment rate falls below 5 percent. Which point of view comes closer to the way you feel — that political refugees should be permitted to immigrate to the United States or that immigration should be halted until the unemployment rate in the United States drops?

Source: Roper Center (Storrs: University of Connecticut Press, 1981).

be no decline in the number who continue to come. The Mexicans far outnumber all other categories of illegal immigrants who enter the United States each year.

Illegals are the biggest problem in another sense. They are thought by many Americans to displace native workers in low-skilled jobs, to lower the standard of living of native workers, and to contribute to the cultivation and expansion of a culture of poverty among the native lower classes in U.S. society. When Leonard Chapman was commissioner of the Immigration and Naturalization Service in 1975, he claimed that removal of illegals would create at least 1 million jobs for citizens of the United States. Secretary of Labor Raymond Marshall told the *Los Angeles Times* in December 1979 that unemployment could be decreased from 6 percent to 4 percent if half the jobs held by illegals were taken by natives.

When the U.S. public was asked in October 1977: "It has been proposed that illegal aliens who have been in the United States for seven years be allowed to remain in the United States. Do you favor or oppose this proposal?" the majority opposed the proposal (favor, 39 percent; oppose, 52 percent; no opinion, 9 percent).[28] In 1981, one of the recommendations of the Select Commission on Immigration and

Refugee Policy was that "a program to legalize undocumented/illegal aliens now in the United States be adopted." The commission recommended that

> Eligibility be limited to undocumented migrants who illegally entered the United States or had an illegal status prior to January 1, 1980, and who by the date of enactment of legislation, have continuously resided in the United States for a minimum period of time to be set by Congress.[29]

The commission also recommended the passage of legislation making it illegal for employers to hire undocumented workers.

When asked, "Do you think it should or should not be against the law to employ a person who has come into the United States without proper papers?" between 71 and 79 percent of those polled between 1977 and 1990 favored banning employment of undocumented immigrants.[30] Also, when asked between 1977 and 1985 whether "illegal aliens who have been in the United States for several years should be allowed to remain in the U.S."[31] between 61 and 65 percent opposed granting amnesty. Social class, race, or age did not noticeably differentiate the respondents' opinions.

Another controversial proposal that the commission considered but did not recommend was a requirement that everyone carry an identification card. Questions about identification cards appeared on two national polls during World War II, and at that time 72 and 69 percent favored the identification card.[32] In March 1977 and again in October, the following question was asked: "Do you believe everyone in the United States should be required to carry an identification card, containing among other things, his picture and fingerprints?"[33] Responses shifted from 45 percent "yes" in March to 65 percent "yes" in October.[34] Each time, only 5 percent had no opinion. Both times, nonwhites, as compared with whites, were more likely to favor the measure.

	Percent in Favor	
Race	March	October
White	42	63
Nonwhite	62	74

Grade-school graduates, as compared with college-educated respondents, were also likely to favor the proposal.

	Percent in Favor	
Education	March	October
Grade school	62	77
High school	49	70
College	27	47

The same question was asked in 1980, 1983, 1984, and 1989, with basically the same results: 62, 63, 62, and 62 percent of the respondents, respectively, favored identification cards.[35]

A major provision of the 1986 Immigration Reform and Control Act was the establishment of sanctions against employers who knowingly hire illegal aliens, including fines of $1,000 per alien for a first violation, $2,000 per alien for a second violation, and criminal penalties if the attorney general finds a "pattern or practice" of violations. Based on the poll data reported in this chapter, employer sanctions have widespread public support.

The most consistent theme that emerges from all of the public opinion surveys is the essentially negative attitudes held by a majority of the U.S. public toward persons wishing to come to the United States. Whether the polls were conducted during the 1930s, a period of severe economic depression, or during the 1960s, a time of economic growth and prosperity, public support for increasing the number of immigrants permitted to settle in the United States has remained low. Nevertheless, when the same public is asked whether immigrants have been "a good or a bad" thing for this country, a very interesting pattern emerges. The following question appeared on a national poll in 1982:[36]

Since the beginning of our country, people of many different religions, races, and nationalities have come here and settled. Here is a list of some different groups. Would you read down that list and, thinking both of what they have contributed to this country and have gotten from this country, for each one tell me whether you think, on balance, they have been a good thing or a bad thing for this country?

| | *Percent** | | |
	Good	Bad	Difference
English	66	6	60
Irish	62	7	55
Jews	59	9	50
Germans	57	11	46
Italians	56	10	46
Poles	53	12	41
Japanese	47	18	29
Black	46	16	30
Chinese	44	19	25
Mexicans	25	34	-9
Koreans	24	30	-6
Vietnamese	20	38	-18
Puerto Ricans	17	43	-26
Haitians	10	39	-29
Cubans	9	59	-50

*The two categories not shown are "mixed feelings" and "don't know."

The responses show that immigrant groups who have been in the United States longer tend to receive more positive evaluations than do recent immigrant communities, even if the earlier ones had been feared, opposed, and disliked at the time of their arrival. Note, for example, that the Chinese and Japanese, whom we once passed special legislation to exclude, received more positive than negative ratings, as did Jews, Italians, and Poles, against whom the quota acts of the 1920s were largely directed. However, all of the more recent immigrants, from the Mexicans on down, are more likely to be viewed as bad, rather than good, for this country. The more recent the arrival, the higher is the percentage of respondents who rate them as bad for the United States.

In the 1990 Roper poll (48 percent of the respondents believed the United States was admitting too many immigrants), when asked to name specific countries from which too many immigrants were coming, the list of countries was ordered as follows:[37]

Country from Which We're Accepting Too Many Immigrants	Percent
Mexico	33
Cuba	16
Orient (nonspecific)	14
Japan	10
Vietnam	9
South America (nonspecific)	8
China	7
Latin America (nonspecific)	5
Korea	5

There is quite a bit of overlap between the countries that appear on the bottom half of the "good and bad for this country" list and the countries most frequently cited in the 1990 survey.

Anticipated immigrants and the prospect of higher immigration levels is not, and has never been, a popular issue with the U.S. public.

NOTES

1. Rita J. Simon, *Public Opinion in America: 1936–1970* (Chicago: Rand McNally, 1974), p. 7.

2. Ibid.

3. Ibid., p. 123.

4. Ibid., p. 125.

5. Fortune (FOR), *The Roper Center* (Storrs: The University of Connecticut, May 1938).

6. Simon, *Public Opinion in America: 1936–1970*, p. 95.

7. By 1938, the Nuremberg laws had been in effect three years. These laws deprived German Jews of their citizenship and made it almost impossible for them to earn a living in Germany except in the lowest occupations and then with difficulty. See Simon, *Public Opinion*.

8. Ibid., p. 96.

9. American Institute of Public Opinion (AIPO), *Roper Center*, January 1946.

10. AIPO, *Roper Center*, August 1946.

11. Simon, *Public Opinion*, p. 99.

12. FOR, *Roper Center*, November 1947.

13. Ibid.

14. National Opinion Research Center (NORC), *Roper Center*, May 1953.

15. NORC, *Roper Center*, April 1955.

16. AIPO, *Roper Center*, November 1956.

17. NORC, *Roper Center*, December 1956.

18. AIPO, *Roper Center*, September 1957.

19. FOR, *Roper Center*, April 1959.

20. John Crewdson, *The Tarnished Door* (New York: Times Books, 1983), pp. 95–96.

21. AIPO, *Gallup Opinion Index*, August 1965, Report No. 3.

22. AIPO, *Roper Center*, April 1975.

23. Louis Harris, *Roper Center*, July 1957.

24. AIPO, *The Champaign-Urbana News Gazette* (Champaign-Urbana, Illinois), August 26, 1979, p. 9.

25. AIPO, *Public Opinion*, June/July 1983, p. 50.

26. AIPO, *Roper Center*, May 1980.

27. Ibid.

28. AIPO, *Roper Center*, September/October 1977.

29. *U.S. Immigration Policy and the National Interest: The Final Report and Recommendations of the Select Commission on Immigration and Refugee Policy*, (Washington, D.C.: U.S. Government Printing Office, March 1981), p. 76.

30. AIPO, *Roper Center*, March 1977.

31. AIPO, *Roper Center*, October 1985.

32. AIPO, *Gallup Opinion Index*, 1944.

33. AIPO, *Roper Center*, October 1977.

34. The 20-percent spread might be explained by the wording of the question. In October the identification card was compared with a Social Security card, and in March it was described as an identity card that contained a picture and fingerprints.

35. AIPO, *Roper Center*, 1980, 1983, 1984, 1989.

36. AIPO, *Roper Center*, 1982.

37. AIPO, *Roper Center*, 1990.

II

THE MEDIA SURVEYED

This section is the heart of the book. It describes how the leading magazines in the country covered and interpreted immigration policies, beliefs, and attitudes about the impact of immigrants on the U.S. economy and its social fabric from 1880 to 1990. It also reports the results of a sample of *New York Times* editorials from 1880 to 1980, plus a full analysis of all the pieces that appeared on the editorial page of the *New York Times* between 1980 and 1990.

The magazines included are *North American Review, Saturday Evening Post, Literary Digest, Harper's, Scribner's, Atlantic Monthly, The Nation, Christian Century, Commentary, Commonweal, Reader's Digest, Time, Life, Newsweek,* and *U.S. News and World Report.* Not all of them were published during the entire 110-year time span; some were founded earlier and did not survive past World War II, and others began publishing later and continued to the present.

This section also contains a summary of the media coverage for the 110-year time span. Appendix A provides a profile of each of the magazines included in the study. The date of its founding, the circulation size, the characteristics of its readers and an assessment of its influence are some of the information contained in this appendix. Appendix B provides a brief account of the current array of anti-immigrant movements in the country and discusses the bases of their opposition.

4

North American Review

The *North American Review* and the *Saturday Evening Post* are the two oldest magazines in this survey. The *North American Review* began publishing in 1815, and articles about immigrants appeared as early as 1820. Before the Civil War, it ran several long pieces on the characteristics of the Irish and German communities in the United States. At the beginning of the 110-year span surveyed, the *North American Review*'s circulation was smaller than that of the *Saturday Evening Post* or *Atlantic Monthly*. At 7,500, it rivaled *The Nation*, which claimed a circulation of 8,000. It grew considerably over the next four decades until its demise in 1940. It was most influential in the last decade of the nineteenth and the first three decades of the twentieth centuries.

Between 1880 and 1890 the *North American Review* published three articles concerning immigration. Each article contained statistics describing the immigrants' countries of origin, their occupational skills, and their age and sex distributions. In the first of two pieces by Edward Self, the author estimated the monetary gain the United States accrued from immigration in 1881. Self put the figure at $5.72 million by assuming that each immigrant had "in his brain and muscle a power equal to a capital of $51,000."[1] Additionally, he speculated on how the U.S. population would have suffered without immigrants, and concluded,

> In ninety years, a feeble people of 3,900,000 occupying the country adjacent to the sea has been transformed into one of the greatest nations of the world, having a population of 50,000,000 spanning a continent, and possessing untold wealth and boundless resources.[2]

In his second piece, published in January 1884, Self focused on "The Evils Incident to Immigration."[3] Although he continued to portray immigration as a positive contribution, he also called attention to negative repercussions. The evils, he explained, could be attributed to the fact that some of the immigration groups included a high percentage of untrained laborers and servants who came as individuals rather than in family units. The Chinese offered noticeable examples of both. Immigrants, in the author's view, also contributed disproportionately to the criminal, pauper, and insane population. By the end of the second article, Self noted more negative than positive features about the immigrants' contributions and warned of their future impact.

In the third article of the decade, entitled "A Menacing Eruption," T. V. Powderly advocated restrictions on immigration because "the population that is coming today is semi-barbarous. They are willing and used to living in filthy crowded conditions." Of the immigrants who came prior to 1860, Powderly claimed "we owe them our greatness as a nation; they gave us brain, bone, and muscle . . . they gave us laborers, mechanics and states-men; they were healthy and good."[4] In conclusion, Powderly urged restricting immigration to those who were literate, had a means of support, and did not have a criminal background or history of insanity.

Beginning in the 1890s and continuing for the next three decades, the *North American Review* maintained an ongoing debate about the pros and cons of immigration. Until the 1920s, its coverage was balanced. After that it tilted strongly toward a restrictive immigration position, a view it retained until its demise. The first two pieces in 1890 were written by Henry Cabot Lodge, then a member of the House of Representatives. Lodge was a forceful opponent of immigration and an ardent defender of isolationism. In his first piece, Lodge included many statistics and tables that described the flow of immigrants from the mid-1870s to the 1890s. He reported that 6,418,633 immigrants had entered the country, and that figure, he said, did not include the Mexican and Canadian immigration over the previous 16 years.[5] Lodge pointed out that that figure was equal to 10 percent of the entire population of the country. He argued that immigration was increasing over time and that it was making its greatest relative increase from races "most alien to the body of the American people and from the lowest and most illiterate classes among those races." Conditions in the United States had changed, he claimed. For example, there no longer were endless tracts of fertile land to be settled.

We have now a large population, the national increase of which is quite sufficient to take up our unoccupied lands and develop our resources with due rapidity. . . . Our labor market . . . is over-stocked in many places and that means a tendency toward a decline in wages.[6]

Lodge concluded with a plea for imposing literacy requirements on prospective immigrants, a position for which he was to argue eloquently many years on the floor of the House and the Senate.

His second piece, "Lynch Law and Unrestricted Immigration," was more colorful and more strident in tone than the earlier one. Prompted by a lynching in New Orleans of 11 Italians who had been charged with the murder of the chief of police, Lodge deplored the action but sympathized with the sentiments of the citizens of New Orleans. The lynch mob was convinced that a gross miscarriage of justice had been committed, that these defendants were members of the Mafia, and that the trial that resulted in their acquittal had been rigged. Lodge used the incident in New Orleans as the occasion to assess the quality of immigrants who were coming to the United States during this period. He was concerned particularly about the Italians, because he believed many of them stayed only to earn money and then took their savings and returned to Italy. Lodge called them mere "birds of passage" who had no interest or stake in the United States. He warned,

> More important to a country than wealth and population is the quality of the people. Far more valuable than sudden wealth is the maintenance of good wages among American working men and the exclusion of an unlimited supply of low-class labor with which they cannot compete.[8]

Finally, Lodge came up with a list of "good" and "bad" immigrants. He categorized Germans, Scandinavians, French, Belgian, and Dutch as "good" and Poles, Bohemians, Hungarians, Russians, and Italians as "bad."

Another article, titled "Our National Dumping Ground," by John Weber, U.S. commissioner of immigration, and Charles Stewart Smith, president of the New York Chamber of Commerce, was a debate in which the commissioner supported immigrants and Smith denounced them. The latter's opposition stemmed from his belief that immigrants were poor and illiterate and breeders of crime, mental illness, and other social problems. Weber argued that the character and social quality of the people who were coming in the 1880s and 1890s were substantially the same as those of immigrants who came earlier and had so materially aided the development of our national resources. Weber assumed that those who were coming today would continue to add to the national wealth.[9]

Between 1892 and 1898, the *North American Review* published three articles on Chinese immigration: "The Chinese Question Again" by Congressman John Russell Young, "Should the Chinese Be Excluded?" by Colonel Ralph G. Ingersoll and Representative Thomas Geary of California, and "Farce of the Chinese Exclusion

Law" by Thomas Scharf, former U.S. Chinese inspector at the port of New York.[10]

The first piece criticized the congressional debate that preceded passage of the Chinese Exclusion Act on grounds that the 15-minute length of the debate was too short and that debaters were ill-informed and prejudiced. The author opposed the bill, saying that it performed an injustice to the Chinese people and that it was harmful to U.S. interests in the Far East.[11]

"Should the Chinese Be Excluded?" presented an exchange between Ingersoll and Geary in which the former argued that the Chinese are one more immigrant group toward whom the U.S.-born feel superior. "Their attitudes to the Chinese are no different than they were toward the Irish, the Germans and the Italians, all of whom we hated." The Chinese laborers, Ingersoll wrote, are inoffensive, peaceable, law abiding, industrious, patient, and stoical. "There is plenty of room in the country for 500,000,000 people — let the Chinese in."[12]

Geary, a representative from California who was one of the congressional leaders in favor of the Chinese Exclusion Act, claimed that "the Chinese are different from all other immigrant groups we have admitted." Geary said, "they are as enslaved by their masters [heads of secret organizations] as were the negroes in the South." He also claimed that even though there had been an exclusion act on the books since 1882, the Chinese continued to immigrate illegally with the support of the Chinese government.

Inspector Sharf agreed with Geary. He added that it was the will of the U.S. people to exclude the Chinese, as evidenced by the laws that were enacted in 1882, 1884, 1888, 1892, 1893, and 1894. In Sharf's view the laws still fell short. He wrote "Laws deemed apparently faultless have proven but legislative makeshift. They do not meet the evil, but rather aggravate it by offering opportunities for their evasion through perjury, chicanery, and fraud."[13]

The other nationality that received special attention in this decade was the Italians. J. H. Senner, then commissioner of immigration, believed immigrants from Italy were receiving negative press and responded by attempting to present the facts as he perceived them.

Italian immigrants, even in the first generation, succumb sooner or later, like those of the European nationalities, to the irresistible influence of freedom and prosperity; while in the second generation as a rule, and in the third invariably, they become thoroughly Americanized.

The common opinion as to the inability of Italian immigrants to assimilate is, I am frank to state, not shared by me. It must be admitted that Italians who come over in mature years, without education, even in their own language and during their sojourn in the United States move almost exclusively among their countrymen, find it exceedingly difficult to acquire even the rudiment of the national language; but such is the common experience with most other non-English speaking immigrants as well. On the other hand, we find that an Italian who has come here younger in years, or who has received a good education, becomes speedily a thorough American, even if his occupation brings him into contact mostly with his countrymen.[14]

Prescott Hall, secretary of the Immigration Restriction League, disagreed. In a comment that appeared in the August 1896 issue, Hall, like Lodge, claimed that most of the Italians who came were "birds of passage" and that they would come for a time and live under degraded conditions at a low wage and soon carry their savings back to Italy. "When they use them up, they come again," he charged, adding, "they live in a way in which no American, German or Irishman would live for a day."[15]

From January 1893 through October 1897, the *North American Review* carried five pieces that asked "Should Immigration Be Suspended?" Two authors said yes, three said no. Senator William Chandler, Republican from New Hampshire, whose piece appeared in January 1893, urged the United States to take advantage of what he perceived as an unexpected opportunity. The cholera epidemic of 1892 had brought almost all immigration to a halt, and Chandler urged the United States to take advantage of that situation by indefinitely prolonging the cessation. Chandler believed that the United States could not safely and should not undertake the assimilation of the "ignorant and debased human beings" he said were coming to the United States in such high numbers.[16]

Senator Henry Hansbrough of North Dakota disagreed. His views, which appeared in the next issue, were that the immigrant

Is a necessary part of the human machinery that causes the commercial and financial world to revolve in its daily orbit. Without the immigrant we would not have developed as a nation — they built our railroads and opened our mines. Now his children are teachers in the public schools and practicing the skilled professions in the cities and villages. His grand-children are foremost among scientists and rank high as authors and statesmen.[17]

Hansbrough believed there was room in the United States for 500 million people. He quoted Frederick Knapp, former New York state commissioner of immigration, who had estimated the economic value of each immigrant at $1,125. Hansbrough argued against any suspension of immigration to the United States.

In May 1897, Simon Croswell asked "Should Immigration Be Restricted?" He concluded that it should not because "we have plenty of room to take in many, many people and because most immigrants are good material out of which to make American citizens," citizens willing to learn how to live in a free, democratic society.[18]

Prescott Hall answered for the opposition (August 1897). He framed it as a choice that he (and the Immigration Restriction League) saw as between having the United States peopled by British, German, and Scandinavian stock who historically had been free, energetic, and progressive and by Slavs, Latins, and Asiatic races, who he said had been historically downtrodden, atavistic, and stagnant. As a basic minimum for restricting immigration, he urged passage of a literacy test. This, he explained, would exclude the dangerous and unassimilable element and would preclude fewer desirable immigrants than any other test.[19]

Of 11 articles on immigrants published in the *North American Review* between 1900 and 1910, 9 declared that immigrants were a menace because they were anarchists and radicals of other sorts;[20] that they were carriers of favus (a contagious skin disease especially of the scalp) and trachoma;[21] and that since they were sources of cheap labor, they were a threat to the U.S. worker.[22] According to the *North American Review*, immigrants and their children were burglars, pickpockets, and thieves of all sorts;[23] they were illiterate;[24] and they lacked self respect, intelligence, and skills.[25] They were also criminals.[26]

Among that litany appeared an article by Thomas James, a former postmaster general, who reminded readers that prior to the time when Americans were anti-Japanese and anti-Chinese, they had been anti-Irish and anti-German. He said that for reasons of self-interest, namely, U.S. trade with China and Japan, the United States should reconsider its anti-Orient policies.[27] Oscar Strauss, U.S. secretary of commerce, shared James' view and suggested that laws be shaped to prevent entrance of only skilled and unskilled Chinese laborers into the United States and to permit other Chinese to come. That, Strauss asserted, would allow us to maintain "our integrity."[28]

A dollars-and-cents analysis of the immigration issue was offered in an article by Charles Speare titled "What America Pays Europe for Immigrant Labor." Speare argued,

Assume that of the million and a quarter immigrants who come to America each year, 65 percent are able to work. That figure increases the potential value of American labor by over a billion dollars annually. Against that amount, is the loss of about $250,000,000 in money remittances by the entire 15,000,000 foreign born residents in the United States. The

United States is left with a 4:1 credit ratio. Immigration viewed this way is clearly a positive force for the United States. It also, however, does not cause great harm to the country from which the immigrants have come.[29]

A piece by William Rossiter, chief clerk of the U.S. census office, "A Common Sense View of the Immigration Problem," pitted the restrictionist views of Congressman Gardner of Massachusetts against the antirestrictionist views of Congressman Bennett of New York. From Gardner he distilled the observations that immigrants (half of whom are Slavs and 25 percent are Mediterranean types) were poor human material who lacked self-respect and intelligence and the great majority of whom were unskilled and a menace to U.S. institutions. From Bennett he took the views that immigrants were intensely earnest, frugal, and industrious. He presented Bennett's claim that the United States always needed the immigrant "to aid us in amassing wealth and we shall need him in the future." Rather than being imperiled by immigrants, Bennett's view was that Americans were in debt to them.[30]

For police commission of New York Theodore Bingham, crime and immigrants went hand in hand. Beginning with the assertion that 85 percent of the population of New York City was either foreign born or of foreign parentage, he noted that it was only a logical conclusion that "something like 85 out of one hundred of our criminals should be found to be of exotic origin."[31] The remainder of the article was an anthology of the criminal tastes and propensities of different ethnic groups. For example, Bingham wrote of the Russians, "they generally commit crimes against property; pocket-picking is the one to which they seem to take most naturally." The Italians, however, were considered the most dangerous of all the nationalities and the greatest menace to law and order. "It is impossible," Bingham claimed, "to exaggerate the enormity of the offenses committed by these malefactors: murder, arson, kidnapping, bomb throwing, black mail, robbery." He charged the French and Belgians with running a white slavery racket. The Chinese and Armenians, he said, developed expertise in other criminal specialties.[32]

Five of the 15 articles and editorials about immigrants that appeared in the *North American Review* between 1910 and 1920 praised them and saw them as a positive contribution to the United States; 10 portrayed them negatively and claimed that they were detrimental to the United States. The *North American Review* ran an editorial claiming that one of the positive by-products of the war was that it brought a halt to immigration. According to the editor, "it is indisputable that immigrants from the North Western countries are decidedly preferable to those from the South Eastern. Their morals are better, their average of literacy and of general intelligence are far higher, their physical condition is better and their civic usefulness is superior."[33] Another editorial commented, "illiteracy is not the major reason why the United States should restrict immigration. Criminal and economic worthlessness are better grounds."[34]

The war raised suspicions about the loyalty of the foreign born, especially those who were still aliens. Two editorials warned Americans to be aware of alien immigrants and ethnic organizations whose loyalty remained with the motherland or fatherland and who would work against the interests of the United States. They advocated doing away with all teaching of foreign languages in the public schools, and one said, "Immigrants should conform to American manners, customs and principles and become in heart and soul Americans."[35]

The anti-immigrant articles harped on four major issues: the biological and social inferiority of the new immigrants, their negative economic impact on the United States, their lack of loyalty or their divided allegiance to their new country, and their unwillingness or inability to assimilate U.S. traditions and values.

Robert De C. Ward, in his article "National Eugenics in Relation to Immigration," focused on the first: "Immigrants from most of the world except Britain and Northern Europe are inferior. They threaten our vitality and our national intelligence."[36]

Economist W. Jett Lauck had two pieces, "The Real Significance of Recent Immigration" (February 1912) and "The Lesson from Lawrence" (May 1912) that emphasized immigration's negative economic impact but also considered immigrants' divided loyalties and inability to assimilate. Lauck asserted that the new immigrants, unlike those who came in earlier times, were not motivated by a desire for religious and political freedom, nor were they coming with the expectation of establishing a home in their new country. Lauck claimed that most of them hoped to be able, after a comparatively short period of labor in the United States, to accumulate enough money to return to their native land, raise a mortgage, and buy a small piece of land or a business. Lauck argued that most did not have any interest in acquiring U.S. citizenship, that immigrants lowered the average wage and the conditions of employment (especially in mining and manufacturing) because of their willingness to live under conditions that were unacceptable to native workers, and that immigrants had weakened and demoralized the labor organizations that were developing in some industries. In mining, for example, Lauck reported that employers had a conscious policy of "mixing races" in certain departments to decrease the opportunities for unified action. No one race, he wrote, "is permitted to secure a controlling number in the operation force of a single mine because of the fear that a common language would enable them to be readily organized."[37]

A piece entitled "Our National Fences" focused on the immigrants' unwillingness or inability to assimilate in "blood, traditions, sympathies and ideals." It also asserted that many of these "new immigrants" may have appeared normal but "are carrying the seed of multiple numbers of defective children who will lead degenerate, criminal lives, become public charges and place a great social and economic strain on the United States."[38]

"Illiteracy and Democracy" attacked the new immigrants for their illiteracy. The author, Winthrop Talbot, claimed that although every other class of illiterates had declined, the foreign born had not. Illiteracy, he argued, built a barrier against democracy.[39]

Frances Kellor contributed two pieces to the *North American Review* that urged the federal government to establish resettlement programs for the immigrants and, especially, for their children in order to help them learn English and become more informed about medical and social services and housing as soon as they got off the boat.[40] Virginia Remnitz's article "The Story of Senate Bill 5464" celebrated the passage of an act that would appropriate $12 million for a new federal program aimed at eradicating illiteracy among the native and foreign born throughout the United States.[41]

Two pieces, "American Ideals and Race Mixture" and "The Crux of the Immigration Question," which appeared in 1912 and 1914, provided an antidote to the xenophobia that pervaded many of the articles in the *North American Review* in this decade. The first piece, by Perry Grant, opened with the observation that "the most impressive sight to be seen in America is the stream of immigrants coming off ships at Ellis Island."[42] Grant labeled apprehension of harm to U.S ideals because of race mixture as prejudice and mocked beliefs in Teutonic superiority and Latin degeneracy. Quoting from famous geneticists and anthropologists, he belittled notions of biological inferiority and asserted that "the great problem for us in dealing with the immigrants is not that of their nature but that of their nurture." He urged leaders to reconstruct their ideas about U.S. democracy and, in doing so, to welcome the rugged strength of the peasant or the "subtle thought of the man of the Ghetto."[43]

In "The Crux of the Immigration Question," Piatt Andrew showed how immigration to the United States had been restricted from the earliest decade of the English settlement in Massachusetts. Quakers, Baptists, Episcopalians, and Catholics were banished on grounds that they would impair U.S. standards. "Immigrants who came earlier and their descendants have always tried to keep this country for those who were already here and for their kinfolk."[44] Each generation also believed that the country was rapidly filling up and that there was no room for any more newcomers, he observed. Andrew provided congressmen's quotes from as far back as 1797 that urged restriction of immigrants with the same stridency as was heard in the 1900s. He reviewed the history and policies of the Know Nothing movement and the fear and antipathy with which the Irish and German immigrants were greeted. In considering the new immigrants, he asked,

Are the new immigrants less sound of body and mind than those of earlier generations? Do they more frequently evince criminal proclivities, are they more apt to become a charge upon the state? Is their standard of living lower? Are they less capable of becoming loyal, worthy American citizens?[45]

For his answers, Andrew relied heavily on the reports prepared by Professors Jenks and Lauck for the immigration commission. He concluded that to all of the questions, the data available answered "no." On the matter of sheer numbers, that is, even if we were to assume that these "new immigrants are not inferior to the old, do we have room for all those who want to come?" Andrew claimed, "If the present population of the whole of the United States were located in the state of Texas alone, there would still be two-thirds as many inhabitants per square mile in that state as there are in England today."[46] Our net immigration, he reported, "amounted to little more than one-half of one percent of our present population."

Andrew concluded with an appeal for more, rather than fewer, immigrants on the grounds that they were needed to develop the almost boundless resources of the United States. The Andrew piece stands out as being the most proimmigrant article that the *North American Review* published during its entire career.

Anti-immigrant sentiments peaked in the 1920s. The articles in the *North American Review* during that decade espoused the most extreme anti-immigrant sentiments that the magazine had ever published. The articles shared opinions and sentiments similar to those in the *Saturday Evening Post* and some of the earlier articles in the *Atlantic Monthly*. The opinions ranged from advocating a ban on all immigration to warnings about the dangers to the economy, to the social and cultural institutions, and to the soul of America "if the United States allowed any more of the rabble from Southern and Eastern Europe to enter."[47] In the first of eight pieces he published between 1920 and 1929, Prescott Hall warned that unless the United States did something about it, "the number likely to come in the next few years will be limited only by the capacity of the steamships to bring them." Going back to the beginning of our nation, Hall claimed that even in the days of sparse settlements, "Washington, Adams, Jefferson and many others were strong in their demand for immigration restriction." Hall reminded readers that before the Civil War, the population was almost entirely Nordic "and our political and social institutions were developed along the lines of the Nordic spirit." After warning of dangers to the United States' racial stock that would result if the Alpines, Mediterraneans, Semitics, and Asians were to continue to pour into the country, he concluded that the best plan for simultaneously shrinking the total number of immigrants and favoring Nordic races would be to base the plan on the alien's capacity for assimilation. He concluded,

> If the United States is to continue to stand for that which it has always represented, not only within its borders but to the world at large, if it is to be protected from that preponderance of those who are foreigners, not only in name but in character, which as Le Bon says destroys a nation's soul, some such legislation should be speedily enacted.[48]

"Throwing Away Our Birthright" by William Roscoe Thayer contained similar sentiments. "Numbers do not make a nation strong. Only the character of its people can make it strong," he wrote. Thayer charged that the governments of certain southern and eastern European nations were working in collusion with the steamship companies to send the worst elements in their populations to the United States.[49]

Drawing upon data from mental tests given by the army during World War I, Dr. Arthur Sweeny argued that immigrants from southern and eastern Europe were neither educable nor assimilable. "They are morons and imbeciles," he asserted. Unlike Thayer and Hall, Sweeny believed that the United States needed more immigrants to cultivate its fields and to harness its resources but that it needed honest, intelligent, hard working, thrifty men; as he summarized, "All of the qualities that are lacking in the people we have permitted to come from Southern and Eastern Europe." In Sweeny's words, "we have no place in this country for the man with the hoe; stained with the earth he digs, and guided by a mind scarcely superior to the ox, whose brother he is."[50]

In "Selecting Citizens," Cornelia James Cannon wrote of the current immigrants,

> They come in far greater numbers, vermin infested, alien in languages and in spirit, with racial imprints which can be neither burned out nor bred out, packs on their backs, leading little children by the hand. And like the hordes of old, they are destined to conquer us in the end, unless by some miracle of human controversy we conquer them first. . . . So far as we can judge the Tartar is a race which has always been barbarian. It has been a virile and predatory race, but has never developed a civilization worthy of the name. The infusion of its blood has doubtless hampered and retarded the development of the

Balkans. The Mexican, the South Sea Islander, the African Negro belongs to a similar category. Are we not justified in exercising discrimination before adding such strains to our racial blood?[51]

She concluded by allying herself with Lincoln in the following manner:

Those who deny freedom to others, deserve it not for themselves and under a just God cannot long retain it. But as we keep out certain plants and animals lest they bring in physical disease, we are equally justified in excluding those who may bring in social diseases. Our civilization is complicated enough and full enough of obscure pitfalls of misunderstanding to make us wary about introducing any more unassimilable elements than we can help.[52]

In any anthology of "racist thought," Madison Grant is likely to appear as a leading proponent of the Aryans. In his article "The Racial Transformation of America," Grant reprimanded the United States for making the same mistake twice.

We should have learned from our experiences with the Negro problem that you cannot expect inferior people to make good citizens. The immigrants from Southern and Eastern Europe are far below the average intelligence of the Nordics (in the United States). If we continue to let these people come in the numbers that they have been, the American people will be mongrelized by these alien hordes and the average intelligence of the country will be steadily reduced by newcomers.[53]

He claimed that the United States would contain substantially the same population if no immigrants had come during the previous hundred years and that Americans would have learned not to despise manual labor as they do. He urged the United States to take action now before it was too late, saying "Restrict immigration and apply the principles of race eugenics to check the evils of the Melting Pot."[54]

An anti-immigration author who wrote regularly for the *Saturday Evening Post*, economics professor Ray Garis, had a piece in the September 1924 issue of the *North American Review* that claimed that U.S. leaders form the Puritans in the Massachusetts Bay colony to Benjamin Franklin, George Washington, and Thomas Jefferson all warned against the evils of excessive immigration. He recounted the anti-Catholic riots in New York City and Boston in the 1830s, the Know Nothing movement, and the actions taken by various states

(New York, California, Massachusetts, and others) to restrict immigration. Of the difference between the "old" and the "new" immigrants, he wrote,

> According to every test made in recent years and from a practical study of the problem, it is evident beyond doubt that the immigrants from Northern and Western Europe are far superior to the ones from Southern and Eastern Europe. The vital thing is to preserve the American race — build it up with Nordic stock: intelligent, literate, easily assimilated, appreciating and able to carry on our American institutions.[55]

Referring to the recently enacted Quota Act, he asserted, "the percentage law based on the census of 1890 will in time automatically bring about such a result."[56]

"Perils of the Mexican Invasion" by professor of zoology S. J. Holmes, published in March 1919, warned of the dangers to this country from the south. In Holmes' view, "The United States seems fated never to be free from trouble attendant on race and immigration. First it was the Negroes, then it was the Chinese and Japanese, now it is the Mexicans. Soon it will be the Filipinos." He accused the Mexicans of a multitude of evils. According to the professor, they bred like flies, they had high rates of tuberculosis and syphilis, they were hopelessly ignorant, they frequently got into difficulties, and they were, and would remain, paupers. He believed that "of all the foreign stocks represented in any considerable numbers in our population, the Mexicans appear to be the least assimilable." Holmes urged legislators to learn some elementary principles of population and to read the works of Malthus on the subject of population.[57]

In the 1930s, the *North American Review* carried only two pieces on immigration. One, "Alien vs. Free Born," described how the United States used deportation of aliens as one means of controlling immigration. Its other piece, by economist Bernhard Ostrolenk, "Immigration and Unemployment," claimed that

> The fundamental fallacy of Malthusians is that they assume that the number of jobs is fixed or decreasing, and hence every additional worker becomes a competitor for the available job. . . . This is the theory of immigration restrictionism. The facts of course support no such arithmetic assumption. The number of jobs is not fixed by some occult power but increases with industrial activity. But one important factor in increased industrial activity is population growth. . . . The period of greatest immigration is the 120 year period from 1800 to 1910 when the country admitted 12,500,000 immigrants. But that

period instead of being a period of unemployment also saw an increase in the number of gainfully employed by 15,000,000 from 23,300,000 to 38,200,000. . . . Not only is it fallacious to attribute unemployment to immigration, but the corollary that restriction of immigration brings high wages is equally misleading. High wages in large measure are the consequences of efficient production rather than scarcity of labor or high standards of living. . . . The immigrant comes here to improve his economic status. For a short period he may be exploited, but immigrants are among the most loyal supporters of all movements to better labor conditions. . . . For every immigrant that comes, many jobs would be created.[58]

The Ostrolenk article provides a sharp contrast to all of the other articles on immigration published in the *North American Review* during the 1920s. It was also the last article that the *North American Review* published on the subject of immigration.

NOTES

1. *North American Review*, Vol. 134 (April 1882), p. 351.
2. Ibid., Vol. 134 (April 1882), p. 366.
3. Ibid., Vol. 138 (January 1884), p. 79.
4. Ibid., Vol. 147 (1888), pp. 165–66.
5. Ibid., Vol. 151 (January 1891), p. 424.
6. Ibid., Vol. 152 (January 1891), p. 34.
7. Ibid., Vol. 151 (February 1891), p. 620.
8. Ibid., Vol. 152 (May 1891), p. 611.
9. Ibid., Vol. 154 (April 1892), p. 704.
10. Ibid., Vol. 152 (August 1892), p. 149; Vol. 162 (July 1893), p. 52; Vol. 166 (January 1898), p. 85.
11. Ibid., Vol. 154 (August 1892), p. 149.
12. Ibid., Vol. 157 (July 1893), p. 56.
13. Ibid., Vol. 166 (January 1898), p. 97.
14. Ibid., Vol. 162 (June 1896), p. 655.
15. Ibid., Vol. 163 (August 1896), p. 283.
16. Ibid., Vol. 156 (January 1893), p. 119.
17. Ibid., Vol. 156 (February 1893), pp. 223–24.
18. Ibid., Vol. 164 (May 1897), p. 525.
19. Ibid., Vol. 165 (October 1897), p. 623.
20. Ibid., Vol. 173 (October 1901), p. 111.
21. Ibid., Vol. 175 (July 1902), p. 430.
22. Ibid., Vol. 179 (August 1904), p. 518.
23. Ibid., Vol. 179 (November 1904), p. 648.
24. Ibid., Vol. 183 (December 1906), p. 702.
25. Ibid., Vol. 188 (September 1908), p. 510.
26. Ibid., p. 543.
27. Ibid., Vol. 184 (February 1907), p. 209.
28. Ibid., Vol. 164 (May 1897), p. 536.
29. Ibid., Vol. 187 (July 1908), p. 115.

30. Ibid., Vol. 188 (September 1908), p. 349.
31. Ibid., p. 389.
32. Ibid.
33. Ibid., Vol. 201 (May 1915), p. 669.
34. Ibid., Vol. 201 (March 1915), p. 350.
35. Ibid., Vol. 206 (October 1917), p. 520.
36. Ibid., Vol. 192 (July 1910), p. 321.
37. Ibid., Vol. 195 (February 1912), p. 208.
38. Ibid., Vol. 199 (March 1914), p. 387.
39. Ibid., Vol. 202 (December 1915), p. 692.
40. Ibid., Vol. 209 (February 1919), p. 247. Kellor's recommendations seem to be similar to the federal and state programs that were adopted in the late 1970s and early 1980s for the absorption and adjustment of Vietnamese, Cuban, and Soviet Jewish refugees to the United States.
41. Ibid., Vol. 210 (August 1919), p. 627.
42. Ibid., Vol. 195 (April 1912), p. 513.
43. Ibid., p. 522.
44. Ibid., Vol. 199 (June 1914), p. 866.
45. Ibid., p. 869.
46. Ibid., p. 874.
47. Ibid., Vol. 213 (May 1921), p. 632.
48. Ibid., p. 607.
49. Ibid., Vol. 215 (February 1922), p. 343.
50. Ibid., Vol. 215 (May 1922), p. 611.
51. Ibid., Vol. 218 (September 1923), pp. 330–31.
52. Ibid., p. 333.
53. Ibid., Vol. 219 (March 1924), p. 417.
54. Ibid., p. 352.
55. Ibid., Vol. 220 (September 1924), pp. 75–76.
56. Ibid., p. 612.
57. Ibid., Vol. 229 (March 1929), p. 372.
58. Ibid., Vol. 240 (March 1935), pp. 212–17.

5

Saturday Evening Post

The *Saturday Evening Post*, founded in the 1820s, did not carry any articles on immigration between 1880 and 1899. The first of two articles in 1899 focused on the number of foreign born in the United States and raised questions about whether the foreign-born population was growing at a faster rate than the native population.[1] The second piece also asked, "Is the American stock maintaining its vigor, or are small native families bringing this race to the condition of the French?"[2]

Between 1900 and 1909, the *Saturday Evening Post* published 28 pieces on immigration. The first 18 of those pieces, which appeared between 1900 and 1907, were positive and favored more immigration to the United States. For example, in an article entitled "Attraction of Prosperity," the magazine reported,

> Last year the immigrant brought to the United States more than $7,000,000. Seven million dollars represents a very small part of the value of the newcomers. Each citizen is worth on the average from $1,000 to $1,200 so that the money value of our new settlers last year, outside of the cash they brought, is at the very least several hundred million dollars.[3]

In 1901 and 1902, the magazine carried articles extolling the virtues of German and Irish immigrants, reporting that they accepted hard work with an enthusiasm that was "infectious and that helped to set the pace for the whole population."[4]

On December 12, 1901, the *Saturday Evening Post* editors commented that "for all practical purposes our native children of foreign parents are just as good Americans as those who can trace their ancestry back to the Pilgrim fathers and the same thing can be said of at least half of the population of foreign birth." It also reported favorably on the record-breaking number of immigrants who were arriving during the current decade.

We have been a composite people from the beginning. The 13 colonies were settled by English, Scotch, Irish, Dutch, Swedes, Germans, French and Negroes. Before the Revolution all these except the Negroes had been welded into one homogeneous people — common language and common political ideals. We are receiving a good many Italians, Poles, Hungarians and Russian Jews at present, but it will be many years before their numbers compare with those of the Irish and German who have already successfully assimilated. And by that time no doubt the stream will slacken, as the former seems to have done. Meanwhile the race that has produced Marconi will still further enrich a stock which the mixture of blood has made already the richest in the world.[5]

In February 1904, the *Saturday Evening Post* complained that the United States was not getting enough immigrants. Its editors wrote "some of the most conspicuous advocates of restraining immigration are also conspicuous examples of that type of supercilious ignorant man of education, which is such a deplorable factor in our public life today."[6] The same theme was emphasized in *Saturday Evening Post* stories on May 7 and December 10, 1904. They expressed concern over the decline in the number of immigrants who were coming and the notion of the "immigrant bogey man" was attacked. The *Saturday Evening Post* sought to allay fears readers might have had about U.S. civilization being overwhelmed by "barbarian hordes."

There were no pieces on immigration in the *Saturday Evening Post* in 1905, but four stories appeared in 1906. Two were collective profiles, one describing life on New York's lower east side among the Jewish immigrants who had settled there, the other extolling the virtues of Chinese cooks. In August and September 1906 there were two articles urging more immigration. The September piece quoted the *Wall Street Journal* as follows: "A million healthy immigrants, quite uneducated, are capable of adding and probably would add a hundred million dollars a year to the wealth of the country."[7]

It was in 1907 that the *Saturday Evening Post* carried its first anti-immigration piece. "Undesirable Citizens" was an interview with Frank P. Sargent, commissioner general of immigration, who warned of the negative characteristics of the new immigrants. Sargent was quoted as saying:

Unfortunately, during the last few years there has been a marked change for the worse in the character of the immigrants into the United States. Until recently this inflow was composed mainly of English, Irish, Scott, Scandinavians and Germans — people whose race characteristics and ideals in the main agree with our own and whom, therefore, we could assimilate racially and politically. But at present two-thirds are from Southern and Eastern Europe.[8]

Sargent also warned that the present-day immigrants carried with them dangerous diseases, such as trachoma, and dangerous political ideas.

The other two pieces in 1907, three that appeared in 1908, and one in 1909 encouraged more immigration. The Japanese and the Jews were each singled out for favorable attention. In its last article of the decade, the *Saturday Evening Post* noted that 20 million immigrants had come to the United States since the Civil War and that even though less than 25 percent could speak English at the time of their arrival and although "we [still] speak a good many languages, politically we all seem to be saying pretty much the same thing."[9]

The second decade of the twentieth century, however, marked a shift in the magazine's position on immigration, from advocate to opponent. Of the 43 articles that appeared during this decade, most of them, beginning in 1913, were anti-immigrant and prorestrictions. In 1910 the *Saturday Evening Post* was still favorably disposed to immigrants, but during 1911 and 1912, that tone began to change. For example, in January 1911, the *Saturday Evening Post* reported 9 million foreigners had arrived in the past ten years and commented "that is not trivial."[10] The writer expressed fear that the immigrants would be exploited and that exploitation would be harmful to society as a whole.

In September of the same year, the *Saturday Evening Post* published two articles on the Chinese, one describing the low wages paid to Japanese and Chinese laborers in Hawaii for skilled work and the other declaring, "From no other alien worker of the soil can the native American farmer learn more than from the 'despised' and 'excluded' Chinese."[11]

A mixture of mainly proimmigration and some anti-immigration articles appeared in 1912. For example, in commenting about what good farmers the Italians, Japanese, Chinese, and other immigrants were, the magazine also noted the decline in number of such immigrants who arrived in 1911 and the increasing percentage of illiterate immigrants. Later that year, it advocated the adoption of literacy tests as a requirement for admission to the United States.

Of the seven stories about immigration that appeared in the *Saturday Evening Post* in 1913, all but one recommended introducing restrictions based on literacy or health. The following excerpt captures the magazine's new position:

We think, on the whole, the great immigration of recent years has been good for the immigrant and the country. The only practical question is whether we have now reached the point where it would be better for the country to exercise some choice — to select, so far as possible, those immigrants who are most likely to be profitable. A literacy test would be the best instrument for making the appropriate selections.[12]

From 1914 through 1916, when Europe was at war and before the United States entered the war, the *Saturday Evening Post* carried eight articles on immigration, three of which examined the impact of the war on immigration. In October 1914 it commented that as a result of the war the United States was likely to gain more immigrants from "advanced nations of Western Europe,"[13] but in 1915 and 1916 it observed that the war had made a severe dent in the number of immigrants seeking entry to the United States. The magazine said in a May 1916 article, "For a dozen years before 1914 we drew an average of nearly a million immigrants annually. We cannot expand industrially without a continually expanding supply of labor."[14]

The other main theme of this period continued to be the need for restrictions and the advantages of the literacy test. The *Saturday Evening Post* argued that "the people want a literacy requirement as witnessed by the fact that three Congresses passed such a test; only to have them vetoed by three Presidents."[15] Its editors wrote in June 1916, "Practically, the whole question is 'Do we want any real restrictions upon immigration or a wide open white door?'" The magazine answered its own question, "Ten million immigrants in 10 years is too large an order for any national digestive apparatus."[16]

In 1917 the *Saturday Evening Post* reminded its readers:

To say that we will admit only those who on the whole are most likely to make desirable additions to the population is still a sound principle. It overthrows theory that we are morally bound to hold an open door for whomever seeks residence here — a theory which, in fact, we have never practiced, for we have always put restrictions upon immigration.[17]

In 1918 the *Saturday Evening Post* made the transition from initially a proimmigrant position to a neutral stance and, finally, to an anti-immigrant, antiforeigner position. With the pen of popular history-fiction writer Kenneth Roberts, author of *Northwest Passage*, the anti-immigration theme reached fever pitch. Seven pieces in 1918 described the foreigner as a subversive, a troublemaker, and an agitator. Anti-German and anti-Bolshevik feelings were running high in the United States, and the foreign born, especially those from Germany and the newly formed Soviet Union, were natural targets. The author of a piece titled "Scum of the Melting Pot" wrote,

We had a happy go lucky, don't care theory that nobody need worry about what the unassimilated foreigner did, as though that everything would come and transform the lazy, the weak, the vicious into hard workers, honest, desirable American citizens. We have considered the rights of every nationality in the world except our own. The immigrant who comes to America to become an American and who works at that job should be welcome; but of late years, too many of another kind have settled here. It has been the refuge of the oppressed, but it has also been the haven of a lot of rascals who have abused our hospitality and besmirched our institutions; not only from the soap box but from the forum.[18]

The next five articles on immigration, which appeared later in 1918, characterized the foreigner as a troublemaker and as the carrier of a dangerous foreign culture. In November, the *Saturday Evening Post* carried a story that portrayed foreign-born soldiers as having performed admirably under fire. The article concluded: "they have proven their loyalty to their new country."[19] That theme died quickly, however.

Playing on Lincoln's theme that the United States could not exist half-slave, half-free, the *Saturday Evening Post* warned: "We shall not be able to exist 'half-foreign, half-American.'"[20] It advocated expelling Bolshevik agitators along with Germans.

The 1920s marked the summit in the *Saturday Evening Post*'s attack on immigrants and in its efforts to halt all immigration to the United States. Kenneth Roberts became the magazine's leading authority on the evils and dangers of immigrants, especially the "new" immigrants. Of 44 articles (plus 9 editorials) about immigration that appeared during that decade, 10 were written by Roberts. In the first of them, Roberts contrasted the "old" immigrant with the "new" in the following manner:

The old immigrants came from England, Ireland, Scotland, Wales, Denmark, France, Germany, Holland, Norway and Switzerland. They came to the United States with the idea of remaining permanently and a large proportion of them took up land and became farmers. . . . The common view of the melting pot in which the people of the world were fused together into one people was justified.

The new immigration is made up of people from Eastern and Southern Europe. . . . They come, to a great extent, with the intention of making as much money as they can in as short a time as they can and going back home to settle down when they have a sufficient quantity of money. More than a third of them cannot read and write; generally speaking they have been very difficult to assimilate. . . . They have been hot beds of dissent, unrest, sedition and anarchy. If the United States is the melting pot, something is wrong with the heating system, for an inconveniently large portion of the new immigration floats around in unsightly indigestible lumps. Of recent years, the contents of the melting pot have stood badly in need of straining in order that the refuse might be removed and deposited in the customary receptacle for such things.[21]

More of Roberts' pieces appeared in June, August, and November 1920. In these he extolled the virtues of the Irish and German immigrants and maligned the Italians, Poles, Czechs, and Hebrews. Of the Italians, he wrote, "They want the money and that's all."[22] He advocated sending immigrants to training camps to teach them how to assimilate. He also argued that they should be "properly distributed" over the country instead of being allowed "to throw themselves into the foul, congested anarchy-breeding, anti-American slums, that reproduce faithfully the European conditions they have just left and in which they sink naturally."[23]

The following year, Kenneth Roberts declared that businessmen who hitherto had advocated unrestricted immigration were now frightened by the changes they saw occurring in the United States as a result of the immigrant. "The complete cessation of immigration," Roberts urged, "is a matter of life and death."[24] Roberts also warned of the dangers of phony passports, claiming that there were indications of the existence of a Bolshevik organization whose sole purpose was the railroading of Bolshevik propagandists to the United States by means of false passports and visas.

Another story in 1921 on immigrants was called "European Homes and American Farmers." The author disputed a piece in the *Herald Tribune* that claimed that the U.S. farmer was dependent on immigrant labor. Instead, the *Saturday Evening Post*'s writer claimed that the U.S. farmer did not want to hire the southern European immigrant because although he may have had a farm in his home country, he was a "hoe man" who lacked knowledge about machinery and food products, and he would not gain such knowledge for generations.

Of the two pieces on immigration that appeared in 1922, one was an editorial that bemoaned the low quality of people who were arriving from Europe. "Europe has much to teach us but she has also been sending us the wrong teachers. From them, we have been learning the worst and not the best of Europe's manner, methods, morals and beliefs."[25] The other piece was a long article by Kenneth Roberts cheering the passage of the 1921 Quota Act (referred to as the 3 percent law) and extolling the virtues of the Nordic race. "Race purity is the prime essential for the well-being of our children and the continued existence of the America of Washington and Franklin and Lincoln and Emerson and Lowell and Roosevelt," wrote Roberts.[26]

In 1923, the *Saturday Evening Post* printed 13 pieces on immigration, the most articles on that subject it would ever carry in a single year. In its February 24 editorial, the *Saturday Evening Post* warned that "without the addition of additional immigrants, the population of the United States in the year 2000 would be at least 200 million." It went on to ask, "If we anticipate such an enormous figure, why should millions of Southeastern Europeans be admitted? Why drag in the dullest and dumbest people in Europe in order that the United States may raise more farm products and manufacture more goods than the world can produce?"[27]

In the April issue, Kenneth Roberts cited experts to make his anti-immigration argument. Roberts quoted Dr. Harry Laughlen, a biologist and "eugenics expert" at the Carnegie Institution, as follows: "Immigration, besides being a very important economic and social problem, is essentially a fundamentally racial and biological problem." He reported Laughlen's account of how poorly the immigrants fared on the intelligence tests. Roberts concluded, "If America doesn't keep out the queer alien mongrelized people of Southern and Eastern Europe, her crop of citizens will eventually be dwarfed and mongrelized in turn."[28]

The other pieces all carried a similar message, that is, that the new immigrants from southern and eastern Europe were the dregs of the earth and they would erode, destroy, and mongrelize U.S. society. Isaac Marcosson compared the care that the United States gave to the importing of domestic animals, for example, insisting on pedigree, and declared, "We should have the same high standards for humans."[29] Several authors warned against the Bolsheviks and criminals who were coming in, while others described the high rates of insanity among Italians and Jews.

Secretary of Labor James J. Davis published two articles in the *Saturday Evening Post* in December 1923. The first reported the same army intelligence test data that Roberts had cited earlier in the year, and the other reported that "there are more foreign-born in our jails, penitentiaries, insane asylums, homes for the feeble-minded, deaf, dumb and blind in proportion to the foreign-born population than there are of native-born stock." He warned of the danger of illegal aliens, characterizing them as the dregs of humanity, and suggested a registration system for all aliens, making the analogy, "No man whose life is open and above board would object to enrolling himself as a prospective good citizen any more than an American today objects to enrolling himself as a voter."[30]

In an article titled "Immigrant of Tomorrow," Marcus Eli Ravage offered the following definition of a desirable immigrant: "A person who can with the least expenditure of time and trouble be made into an American." Ravage continued,

> Given two individuals of equal intelligence, energy, and of power of adaptation, one from Eastern Europe and the other from Western Europe, there cannot be a moment's doubt as to which one will be the first to fit into the American scheme of things: the person from Western Europe.

The author acknowledged that he himself was of eastern European background and observed, "I had five centuries to travel before I could stand shoulder to shoulder with my peers from the west. I was like a man from another planet."[31]

Kenneth Roberts started off 1924 with a piece titled "Slow Poison," the "poison" being the new immigrants who were permitted to enter the United States. Roberts claimed,

> Because of the persistence of a few noisy propagandists for racial minorities in the United States, because of the timidity of vote hunting politicians and because of gross misinformation disseminated by sentimental uplifters, there has sprung up in America the conviction that lawmakers, public speakers and people who wish to preserve a reputation for fair mindedness must not openly say that certain races of people are less desirable material for future citizens of America than certain other races.[32]

Roberts cited the northern Italians as an example of a more desirable race and southern Italians as a less desirable race. He also theorized that the decline of ancient Rome was due to too many people of foreign stock in the city; thus, the United States must beware to avoid the fate of Rome.

His next article, in the February 23, 1924, issue, also emphasized racial superiority and inferiority. This time he distinguished between eastern and western Europeans. The latter, he asserted, were more desirable because they had a higher mental ability and learned English and became citizens more rapidly than the former.

Of the seven articles and one editorial that appeared on immigration in 1924, two were written by Henry Curran, then U.S. commissioner of immigration at the port of New York. Both pieces were strongly anti-immigrant, in much the same vein as the pieces by Roberts. For example, Curran wrote in the April 26 issue,

> The more I see coming in, the stronger is my wish that few would go by — a smaller quantity and a better quality — or with certain exceptions — none at all. We have reached the

saturation. They are making slums of our cities. We used to get farm hands, artisans and mechanics. Now we are getting peddlers. Immigrants are dirty, they have bugs.[33]

His piece on November 15 entitled "Fewer and Better" carried the same message. He strongly endorsed passage of the 1924 Quota Act.

A *Saturday Evening Post* editorial in June applauded the success of the new immigration law (Quota Act of 1924) and called it "Our Second Declaration of Independence," saying it reaffirmed our right to determine whom we shall let into the United States and whom we shall turn away. "Good blood attracts good blood," the editorial writer alleged.[34]

An article titled, "Lo, the Native America," which appeared in the August 9 issue, made the strongest arguments against immigrants, for reasons similar to those expressed previously in the *Saturday Evening Post*. The author, Garet Garrett, described the United States of 1915 or 1920 as unrecognizable from the nation it was in 1880. Garrett argued,

American institutions represented the needs and expressed the genius of a Nordic people. Any other race of people in the same circumstances would have been bound to create different institutions, and it is very possible that a motley of races such as now exist in the country, under the same physical and economic conditions would have been unable to create enduring institutions of any kind.[35]

The article contained quotations from Madison Grant, a leader in the movement for racial purity, Francis Walker, U.S. commissioner of immigration and a leading opponent of the "new immigrants," and Prescott Hall, economist and author of *Immigration and Its Effects on the United States*. Relying largely on the comments of these three, Garrett argued, "The country owes neither the growth of its population nor the development of its material resources to immigration. Everything that has been accomplished might otherwise have been done by the natural increase of the native American stock.[36] Comparing the old and new immigrants, he described the former as people of "courage, will and imagination," and the latter as people whom the steamship companies "simply picked up and moved." They were lame, tractable, uncomplaining, ideal automatons for machine processes, he attested.

Illegal immigration, mostly involving Chinese who were smuggled in from Canada and West Coast ports, was the theme of three of the seven pieces on immigration that the *Saturday Evening Post* carried in 1925.

An editorial in September, titled "Put the Bars up Higher," attacked the work of Harvard economist Robert De C. Ward, who had recommended revisions of the 1924 Quota Act such that the number of immigrants each year would be regulated by the economic requirements of the country, allowing maintenance of a flexible labor supply. The *Saturday Evening Post*'s editorial argued for putting the bars higher because "we have reached our saturation point." It also reminded its readers that "the thought of millions of people has been warped and twisted into evil shape by the leadership of many of these aliens who have not become Americanized in thought and act."[37]

The first of a series of pieces by economist Ray Garis appeared in October and advocated annual registration of aliens and passage of legislation that would allow the United States to deport aliens who were in the country after five years and who were politically or otherwise undesirable. He too referred to the Quota Act of 1924 as the second Declaration of Independence of the United States.

From 1927 until the end of the decade, there was a decline in the number of articles and editorials on immigration published in the *Saturday Evening Post*. Of three in 1927, one adopted a positive tone toward Italians. A piece titled "Laborers, East and West," described Italian immigrants as "American capitalists who start out as laborers and through hard work became entrepreneurs, running, for example, their own business."[38]

An editorial in October reiterated the *Saturday Evening Post*'s familiar theme — the Quota Act of 1924 was a step in the right direction, but it did not solve "the immigration troubles." As an illustration, the magazine cited the presence of 3 million illegal aliens in the country.[39] Later in the month, an article reported that between the passage of the 1921 Quota Act and 1927, a total of 2,008,287 immigrants arrived.

"Protecting American Laborers" was the theme of two editorials in 1928. In one, the *Saturday Evening Post* quoted remarks made by Samuel Gompers in 1923, when, as head of the American Federation of Labor (AFL), he said, "AFL will use every influence in its power to prevent immigration legislation that will be inimical to the people of our country. It is not only the wage earners who are injured by the hordes of immigrants coming into the country, but the businessman and merchant, too."[40]

In 1929, Kenneth Roberts returned to the pages of the *Saturday Evening Post* in an article entitled "The Existence of an Emergency." Roberts argued that the United States had been confronted with an immigration emergency for years,

> But the situation gets continually worse. Instead of being a great melting pot which it was prior to 1880 because of the similarity of the early Nordic immigrant, America has largely become the dumping ground for the world's human riffraff, who couldn't make a living in their own countries.[41]

Roy Garis attempted to connect the increase in the U.S. crime rate with the "mass of degraded, lawless, and mentally defective aliens who have gained admission or who have come in illegally." He asked, "Is not the enormous expense of maintaining asylums, institutions, hospitals, prisons, penitentiaries and the like due in considerable measure to the foreign born, socially inadequate aliens?" He concluded with this quote from Senator Reed of Pennsylvania (coauthor of the 1924 Quota Act): "What I want is to end the discrimination against the American-born and against the nations of Northwest Europe."[42]

The last article of the decade was consistent with the general attitude of restricting, limiting, and barring "the new immigrants."

The laws plainly stipulated the descendant of slave immigrants should not be considered as inhabiting the United States in computing the national origins quotas. The white scheme was devised in an attempt to proportion European immigrants in accordance with the ethnic strains of the founders of the American Republic and the source of language, literature and lore which characterize the history of the American people. If British immigrants do not come, there is no ground for allotting the British quota to some other people. The law was intended to restrict as well as select immigrants.[43]

The 1930s was the first decade in U.S. history when more people departed from than immigrated to the United States. The *Saturday Evening Post* in the 1930s and subsequent decades carried fewer and fewer pieces about immigrants or immigration policy. In the 1930s it carried 13 articles and 24 editorials. Twelve of these pieces appeared in 1930, eight of which were editorials urging more restrictions, warning about the danger of Mexican migrants, and recommending greater controls over aliens already in the country.

In "The Mexican Invasion," Roy Garis claimed that Mexican immigrants "are making a reconquest of the Southwest; more certainly than America made their conquest in 1845, 1848 and 1853." The Mexicans, according to Garis, are "men of few wants, apathetic, without ambition, not concerned with the future." He wrote, "We can search in vain throughout the countries of Europe for biological, economic and social conditions fraught with a fraction of the danger inherent in the immigration of peons to the United States."[44]

The *Saturday Evening Post* also carried an editorial in the same issue warning the United States against allowing "the land to be inundated by hordes of newcomers who compete with our own people in a labor market already glutted." It urged Congress to appropriate funds that would provide the resources for greater surveillance of illegal immigrants.

Isaac Marcosson returned to the theme of the "Alien and the Unemployed in the United States" and reported that the illegal workers were "clogging the industrial process" and were a constant peril to employment of U.S. workers.[45]

For the rest of the year, the *Saturday Evening Post* ran four editorials that made claims such as the following: "organized crimes are the work of the offspring of that type of immigrant which the majority of the people of this country decided some years ago to reduce to a minimum."[46] The publication recommended reduction of immigration from all countries by 50 percent and asserted that "from the point of view of unemployment and absorbing undesirables or even criminal elements, there is a need for further restriction."[47] It endorsed the recently published reports of the American Eugenics Society, which urged extending the quota system to the Western Hemisphere, registering resident aliens, and introducing overseas medical inspection of intended immigrants. One editorial referred to the report as representing "enlightened current thought about our immigration problem."[48] In its last editorial of the year, the *Saturday Evening Post* urged the adoption of a plan introduced by Senator Reed that would close the United States to all immigration for at least two years.[49]

Between 1930 and 1935, the *Saturday Evening Post* ran 11 editorials on immigration but no articles. It urged greater vigilance in detecting and barring illegals and stricter quotas. It noted that in fiscal year 1931, immigration fell below 100,000 and commented that this was "excellent, but suspension of all immigration would be better."[50]

The sole editorial on immigration in 1933 bemoaned the changed character, as of the 1880s, of the immigrants who were coming to the United States. It characterized the "hordes from Southern and Eastern Europe" as an "unassimilable bloodstain" who had abused their own found liberties. "As a people, we foolishly thought we could Americanize them by dressing them in American clothes."[51]

The same theme was picked up in the first of the magazine's six editorials on the topic of immigration in 1934. In "Who Made America?" the editors described two types of immigrants as first, the sturdy yeoman of the seventeenth century, who they said came to find religious liberty, and second, those from southern and eastern Europe, who started coming in 1880.[52] The next editorial rhetorically queried, "Do you want more unemployed? Even if you are not impressed by racial values, you must recognize the need to do something because of our 12 million unemployed."[53] Another 1934 editorial, titled "Do You Want More Mouths to Feed?" mentioned refugees from Germany for the first time. It denounced a resolution proposed in Massachusetts calling for the president to increase existing immigration quotas in order to enable persecuted people in

Germany to enter the United States; the grounds for the denunciation were that "we need to look after ourselves first."[54]

A connection was drawn linking the kidnapping of the Lindbergh
baby and immigration. The *Saturday Evening Post*, in 1935, pointed to
Bruno Hauptman, the person charged with and convicted of
kidnapping and murdering the baby, and warned that Hauptman
had entered the country illegally and that there were thousands,
maybe millions, more like him. Illegal aliens must be deported, it
insisted.[55]

The other articles and editorials in 1935 called for the deporting of
aliens, the reduction of existing quotas by 60 percent, and the extension of quota restrictions to the Western Hemisphere.[56]

Four articles in 1936 and two editorials in 1937 connected the
depression and, specifically, unemployment to the immigration issue
by claiming that the United States was becoming overpopulated. The
Communists had dumped their surplus labor on the United States,
aliens were employed while U.S. workers were receiving welfare,
and there were too few jobs to go around.[57]

The *Saturday Evening Post* carried nothing on immigration in
1938. In 1939, it had one editorial that claimed, "America cannot be
properly understood by anyone not born of her soul."[58]

Once World War II began, immigration as a fact and as an issue
dropped sharply. Between 1940 and 1980, the *Saturday Evening Post*
carried 25 stories about immigration: 10 in the 1940s, 12 in the 1950s,
2 in the 1960s, and 1 in the 1970s. Of the ten that appeared in the
1940s, three were written before and during the U.S. involvement in
World War II; these mainly expressed concern about the alien as a
threat to internal security. On August 31, 1940, the *Saturday Evening
Post* warned of a large number of foreign agents among the alien
population in the United States, especially among the Germans,
Italians, and Japanese. Writing in 1942, former presidential
candidate Wendal Wilkie warned of the dangers of "over zealousness
in protecting ourselves from the enemies within." He observed, "Now
more than ever we must keep in the forefront of our minds the fact
that whenever we take away the liberties of those we hate, we are
opening the way to loss of liberty for those we love."[59]

An editorial in 1943 called for the end of Chinese exclusion, in
part because the Japanese used it in their propaganda effort in
China. The editorial pointed out: "The Chinese quota would work out
to be about 107 a year. Small as the number is, however, it would have
a great moral effect on the Chinese. It isn't the inability to get into
America that annoys them, but the insult implied in total
exclusion."[60]

The last seven pieces appeared after the war's close. The first,
titled, "Should We Open Our Doors to Immigrants?" reviewed U.S.
immigration policies and noted that, during the war years, less than

10 percent of the annual quota arrived and that about 250,000 refugees were admitted over a spread of 12 years. The author concluded, "Everyone seems to agree that America should not return to the unrestricted wide-open door policy which prevailed from colonial times until 1924."[61]

Beginning on October 2, 1948, and extending for six weeks through November 13, the *Saturday Evening Post* ran a series titled "How Our People Live." The people described were Mexican-Americans, Norwegian-Americans, Chinese-Americans, German-Americans, Italian-Americans, and Jewish-Americans. The avowed purpose of the series was to point out to the United States "that it is important for diverse religious and racial groups to learn to live with one another in tolerance and harmony." The magazine claimed that this "happy state" can be achieved only through better understanding.[62]

The 1950s marked the passage of a major immigration bill, the McCarran-Walter Act, in 1952. Most of the *Saturday Evening Post*'s 12 pieces on immigration in the 1950s focused directly or indirectly on that bill and on the debate that surrounded its passage.

Support for the bill appeared for the first time in an editorial in February 1953 that urged continuance of the national origins system, with the claim that it "represents pretty well the views of the average American on how new arrivals should be distributed among the various emigrating nations."[63] The same editorial denounced recommendations by the Truman Commission that immigration be determined less by the needs and capacities of this country than by the desires of other peoples to come here. "We cannot," the *Saturday Evening Post* said, "substantially relieve overpopulation and admit 150,000 people a year to the United States. Much as we might wish to do so for humanitarian reasons, we cannot destroy our immigration standards to take care of people who are surplus elsewhere."

Two editorials in 1954 attacked "liberal columnists and members of Congress" who were pushing for faster action on admitting refugees and visiting scientists. The magazine claimed that the worthy reason for careful screening was to keep out potential subversives.[64] George Washington's philosophies were cited in defense of the McCarran-Walter Act, when the *Saturday Evening Post* reminded its readers that Washington said the country to which immigrants elect to flee should have an equal right to decide which to admit.

Its one editorial on immigration in 1957 defended national origins as the basis for immigration policy by noting, "Its [the Quota Act's] aim was to see to it that new arrivals would not upset the balance among racial and national groups which now exist. It was a good aim then, and it is a good aim now."[65]

The *Saturday Evening Post* took on critics of U.S. immigration requirements in a long editorial on January 4, 1958. It started out by asking, "What is the basic criticism of the current regulation?" It answered, "That more immigrants should be admitted." The editorial recounted the following facts:

The largest number of immigrants to enter this country in 30 years came in fiscal year 1957 and only a few less in 1956 — a total of 647,000. Since the end of World War II, 2,600,000 immigrants have been admitted. Since the much denounced 1924 Quota Act passed, some 5,500,000 have been admitted.[66]

and concluded with the following warning:

Today there are 70,000,000 more people in the United States than when numerical quotas first went into effect. If the present birth rate in the United States continues and the present scale of immigration continues, we may have nearly 40,000,000 additional population in only 12 or 13 years from now. To open wide the flood gates of immigration could well depress our standards of living to a dangerous level without making more than a dent on the world problem of overpopulation. Is it wrong for us to consider first the interest and welfare of the American people?[67]

In October 1959 the *Saturday Evening Post* used the same stridency to maintain, "What too many Americans fail to realize is that the restrictions in the immigration laws constitute the first line of defense in keeping out of the country subversive, criminal and other utterly unfit elements."[68]

Then, suddenly, and with no reference to its own history on the topic, the *Saturday Evening Post* carried an editorial in the early part of the 1960s that claimed, "We are all immigrants, except for the American Indian."[69] The editorial favored changing the immigration law because, it said, the 1924 quota system was discriminatory. It pointed out that, "U.S. citizens with close relatives in Southern European countries must wait many months before their relatives can join them, while tens of thousands of quota allotments for Northern European countries go unused." It urged changes in the law, such that close relatives of U.S. citizens should be taken out of the quota system and that a new formula should be worked out based on need rather than on prejudice in favor of northern European values.

The second and last of its pieces on immigration in the 1960s appeared on October 3, 1964, in the form of excerpts from a book by John F. Kennedy that he had been working on before his assassination. The *Saturday Evening Post* quoted Kennedy as having written: "Immigration policy should be generous; it should be flexible. With such a policy we can turn to the world and to our own past with clean hands and a clear conscience."[70] It quoted Kennedy's recommendations that the national origin system be replaced by a formula that took into account the skills of the immigrant and their relationship to our needs and the family relationship between immigrants and persons already here, and that registration be prioritized on the basis of ability and national welfare. The *Saturday Evening Post* concluded,

> The bosom of America is open to receive not only the opulent and respectable stranger, but the oppressed and persecuted of all nations and religions; whom we shall welcome to a participation in all our rights and privileges, if by decency and propriety of conduct they appear to merit the enjoyment of those rights.

The *Saturday Evening Post* folded in 1969. It reappeared as a monthly in 1971. In September 1977 it carried an editorial that compared illegal Mexican immigrants to blacks in South Africa. "Both groups," the editorial pointed out "do the 'stoop labor' for the rest of the society." Illegal Mexicans, the magazine claimed, have become a "servant class, doing the work which American citizens with their lavish welfare system will no longer stoop to do." The editorial estimated that there were 15 million illegal Mexicans in the country. It argued that both illegal Mexican immigrants and blacks in South Africa were deprived of their political rights and called upon both countries to solve the problem.[71]

The *Saturday Evening Post* did not carry any articles on immigration in the 1980s.

NOTES

1. *Saturday Evening Post*, March 10, 1899.
2. Ibid., September 6, 1899.
3. Ibid., February 2, 1901.
4. Ibid., August 28, 1902.
5. Ibid., December 12, 1901.
6. Ibid., February 6, 1904.
7. Ibid., September 8, 1906.
8. Ibid., August 24, 1907.
9. Ibid., December 29, 1909.
10. Ibid., January 28, 1911.
11. Ibid., September 16, 1911.
12. Ibid., March 8, 1913.
13. Ibid., October 17, 1914.
14. Ibid., May 20, 1916.
15. Ibid., March 6, 1915.
16. Ibid., June 24, 1916.
17. Ibid., March 17, 1917.

18. Ibid., May 4, 1918.
19. Ibid., November 2, 1918.
20. Ibid., February 22, 1919.
21. Ibid., February 14, 1920.
22. Ibid., August 21, 1920.
23. Ibid., November 6, 1920.
24. Ibid., February 12, 1921; May 7, 1921.
25. Ibid., March 4, 1922.
26. Ibid., January 28, 1922.
27. Ibid., February 24, 1923.
28. Ibid., April 28, 1923.
29. Ibid., May 5, 1923.
30. Ibid., December 8, 1923.
31. Ibid.
32. Ibid., February 2, 1924.
33. Ibid., April 26, 1924.
34. Ibid., June 14, 1924.
35. Ibid., August 9, 1924.
36. Ibid.
37. Ibid., September 26, 1925.
38. Ibid., February 12, 1927.
39. Ibid., October 22, 1927.
40. Ibid., November 3, 1928.
41. Ibid., April 30, 1929.
42. Ibid., January 5, 1929.
43. Ibid., November 16, 1929.
44. Ibid., April 19, 1930.
45. Ibid., June 24, 1930.
46. Ibid., August 9, 1930.
47. Ibid., September 6, 1930.
48. Ibid., September 20, 1930.
49. Ibid., December 27, 1930.
50. Ibid., December 10, 1932.
51. Ibid., February 10, 1933.
52. Ibid., September 8, 1934.
53. Ibid., April 21, 1934.
54. Ibid., May 19, 1934.
55. Ibid., April 6, 1935.
56. Ibid., August 12, 1935.
57. Ibid., March 14, 1936.
58. Ibid., May 6, 1939.
59. Ibid., June 27, 1942.
60. Ibid., October 23, 1943.
61. Ibid., February 6, 1947.
62. Ibid., November 13, 1948.
63. Ibid., February 10, 1953.
64. Ibid., July 27, 1954.
65. Ibid., November 9, 1957.
66. Ibid., January 4, 1958.
67. Ibid.
68. Ibid., October 10, 1959.
69. Ibid., February 15, 1964.
70. Ibid., October 3, 1964.
71. Ibid., September 1977.

6

Literary Digest

Unlike the other magazines included in this survey (except for the *Reader's Digest*, which was founded in 1922), the *Literary Digest*'s articles on immigrants are largely a collection of opinions and news stories culled from newspapers, magazines, and books that were published in different areas of the country. Thus, by itself, the *Literary Digest* represents a survey of opinion, news, stories, and debate on the issues surrounding immigrants and immigration. The survey begins with the *Literary Digest*'s inauguration in 1890 and continues until its demise in 1937. In its first decade, the *Literary Digest* carried 71 pieces on immigration. Although that decade turned out to be the high point in the magazine's coverage of immigration, it continued to provide space for a great many articles in subsequent years: 39 between 1900 and 1909; 43 between 1910 and 1919; 69 from 1920 to 1929; and 17 from 1930 through 1937.

The theme of its first piece has a contemporary ring to it. In a review of a book by Richmond Mayo Smith, professor of political economy and social science at Columbia University, the reviewer comments, "constant immigration to a certain extent tends to displace American labor, thus to lower wages and standards of living."[1] Although social effects may be more difficult to determine, Smith was also alleged to have argued that the foreign born have a higher rate of defectives, delinquents, and illiterates in their population. He defended the exclusion of Chinese immigrants on the ground that they would never assimilate with U.S. civilization and would always remain an alien element.

The six pieces about immigrants that the *Literary Digest* carried during the rest of the year contained many of the same themes, including the need to restrict immigration in order to protect the country's economic and social well-being and to prevent the importation of diseased, degenerate, and subversive types. For example, in a piece excerpted from the *Arena*, the author warned that immigrants add to the already large numbers of paupers and criminals that may be found among the urban populace and provide anarchists and criminals with more "inflammable materials with which to work upon." In addition, it said, "most immigrants are inaccessible to the influence of Christian preachers and philanthropists and thus, immigration increases the already too large proportion of persons in the country who, besides being non-Christian, are below the general level of American civilization."[2]

Another example of the rhetoric about immigrants that appeared during this period in the *Literary Digest* is the following excerpt from the *American*, a newspaper in Chicago:

The decrease is wholly from Protestant countries (except for Ireland) in which the people have had the advantage of education and some share in their management of public affairs. The increase comes from countries where illiteracy and Romanism have conspired to retard knowledge and self government.[3]

"What Shall We Do with the Dago?" asked the title of a piece reprinted from the *Popular Science Monthly*. The article asks "What terrors have jails and prisons for such human beings? They live better and work about as much, have warmer clothing and better beds in the meanest jail in the United States than they experience out of it."[4] In the same issue, in a piece excerpted from the *Philadelphia Inquirer*, the reader is told, "The character of our immigration has also changed — instead of the best class of people, we are now getting the refuse of Europe — outcasts from Italy, brutalized Poles and Hungarians, the off-scourings of the world."[5]

More of the same rhetoric characterized 1891. The first piece on immigration was from an article by Henry Cabot Lodge in the *North American Review*, in which he dichotomized immigrants into good and bad; the former hailed from Britain, Germany, and Scandinavian countries and the latter from Italy and Slavic countries. The latter immigrants comprised, Lodge asserted, "the lowest and most illiterate classes among races. They are most alien to the body of the American people!"[6]

Rabbi Solomon Shindler, in a piece excerpted from the *Arena*, described three categories of immigrants, the best being those who came out of restlessness. The venturesome class "will always turn out to be a blessing to their new homeland." A less-desirable category, Shindler offered, were those who seek a better market for their working abilities. "[They] are not dangerous to the communities among whom they settle, although their arrival may tend to lower the rate of wages and thus bring apparent hardships upon those who have been want to consider their position a permanent one."

Immigrants in the third category not only were burdensome, Schindler contended, but also were likely to become dangerous. He explained that people who were driven from their homes by overpopulation, famine, religious or social intolerance, or unwise legislature would bring not talent, energy, or will with them but would bring only despair and discontent. "They are not the picked soldiers, they are the torpid mob which lacks push and pluck," he claimed.[7]

The next seven pieces on immigration, which appeared in the *Literary Digest* between March and the middle of June 1891, reiterated the same themes. Immigrants were characterized as coming in hordes, as having low intelligence and morals, and as not deserving of citizenship. The need for immigration restriction was portrayed as urgent. The June 6, 1891 issue of the *Literary Digest* reported that the Treasury Department had appointed an immigrant investigating commission whose purpose was to enable Congress to pass the most effective laws for restricting immigration to what it deemed a desirable class. The *Literary Digest* carried a survey of newspaper views on immigration. The *Minneapolis Journal* warned of the forthcoming invasion of hordes of Russian Jews and claimed that "even the Hebrew Aid Society" was apprehensive about them. The *Washington Star* wrote,

It is the later immigration from Southern and Eastern Europe and from Asia of persons of low intelligence and morals, not desiring to become and incapable of becoming good and useful citizens which has excited a determination in the minds of the people of America without regard to class, race, party or section to have the immigration laws greatly modified.[8]

The *Chicago News* observed,

Jews expelled from Russia, whom no European country wants to receive, are assisted to immigrate to the United States in spite of protests of members of their race residing here that they are not the kind of people to become Americanized because of their clannishness and bigotry.[9]

During the next two weeks, there was some relenting in the positions expressed above. In the June 13 issue, for example, the *Literary Digest* quoted the *New York Tribune* as saying "Honest immigrants, though poor, are desirable," and on June 20 Representative William McAdoo (of New Jersey) was quoted as saying he was not against immigrants generally, but he opposed "admitting the very poor who come to the United States seeking temporary relief with the intention of returning to their homeland with wealth accumulated in the United States." The July 18 issue reported a reassuring message from the *Philadelphia Times*, "there is nothing to fear from the Japanese; they are not coming in great numbers and they are a likeable people."

Of the remaining five articles on immigrants that appeared in the *Literary Digest* through the end of 1891, three carried positive accounts and two were negative.

The Jewish Alliance of America was reported to have formulated a plan for taking care of Russian Jews with the aim of making them self-supporting. A long excerpt from *Donahue's Magazine* titled "Shall Immigration Be Restricted?" concluded that,

> Worldly possessions should not be the prerequisite for admission, providing the immigrants have sufficient funds to keep themselves until they can recoup the fruits of their labor. Their labor is potential capital. Illiteracy alone should not be a barrier. Immigrants have settled our country.[10]

Twenty articles about immigration appeared in 1892, the large majority of which contained strong and bitter attacks against immigrants. For example, on January 30, an article titled "Chinese Immigration Again — A Plea for Severe Restrictions" was excerpted from the *Toledo Blade*. The article noted that the Chinese Exclusion Act of 1883 was due to expire on May 6 and called for its reenactment. It said,

> The Mongolian race should no more be allowed to come here and displace our labor, to lower our civilization, to contaminate our people with disease and to build up a brotherhood of murderers and criminals than should we welcome an armed mob of Fiji islanders bent only on spoil and plunder. The Chinese must stay in their own country. Our experience with the Chinese has not been pleasing. They have added nothing to our wealth, given nothing to science, been concerned in no enterprises and only in rare instances embraced the Christian religion or donned the garb of civilization.[11]

On March 26 the *Literary Digest* excerpted a piece from the *New York Sun* that noted that 21 exconvicts had just arrived from Italy and commented "a more undesirable looking lot would be hard to find." The article continued, "Immigration officials privately say that they are only a sample of the lot that every country in the world is foisting on America daily. Italy is the worst offender. Murderers and thieves arrive from there every day."[12]

Three pieces on Chinese exclusion appeared in April. Quoting the *New York Times*, it reported passage in the House of Representatives of the Geary Bill, which "would maintain exclusion of Chinese immigrants from the United States." The *New York Times* had observed "there is no sign of a demand or support of it [the bill] in public sentiment except possibly on the Pacific coast."[13] The following week the *Literary Digest* quoted the *San Francisco Chronicle* as asking, "Why should the United States confer upon the Chinese, any other, or greater, privilege than China has granted to the citizens of the United States resident in the empire of China?"[14] A few weeks later it quoted the *San Francisco Argonaut*, "Great is the good derived from keeping the Chinese out of this country. The next step will be the establishment of moral and property qualifications for all immigrants no matter what their blood or the part of the world they come from."[15]

Concern about foreigners buying up U.S. land did not originate in the 1970s and 1980s. As early as 1892, *Harper's* published an article, excerpted by the *Literary Digest,* describing the practice. It listed 11 foreign corporations that owned 17 million acres of U.S. soil. The article pointed out, however,

It is not denied that there may be some case of excessive land ownership by aliens, but it is not necessary to burn a house to roast a pig. If individual aliens or Americans hold too much land, the size of permissible holdings may be regulated by law. . . . It is to be regretted, perhaps, that foreign wealth has the ability, the courage, the foresight, the belief in our future, to buy our land. But, on the other hand, the imagination shrinks from the conception of the blow to our prosperity which would follow the withdrawal of this very real and very necessary help to our development.[16]

In May the *Literary Digest* excerpted from the *Forum* in New York a piece titled, "Incalculable Room for Immigrants," which praised immigrants and declared, "it seems almost pusillanimous to refuse a refuge to the oppressed and to the industrious and capable of other lands for fear that the institutions of this country may suffer."[17] The writer claimed that there was plenty of available land and resources in this country. "During the past 27 years, since May 1865, we have had a steady advance in the rate of wages, a steady reduction in the cost of labor per unit of product, and a correspondent reduction in the price of goods of almost every kind to the consumer."[18]

Over the summer of 1892 the *Literary Digest* carried four pieces on the Chinese Exclusion Act, which had been enacted into law on May 5. Almost all of the newspapers surveyed in the *Literary Digest* (19 over two issues, May 14 and May 21) favored passage of the bill. In August the *Literary Digest* excerpted a piece by former Congressman Sidney Dean from the *American Journal of Politics* that strongly attacked the bill, claiming it was "unworthy of a great, powerful, enlightened country."[19]

September marked the appearance of two pieces by Professor Francis Walker, excerpted from the *Yale Review*. Both were vintage Walker in their scathing denunciation of the new immigrants from eastern Europe. They were, in his words,

> Peoples that have [had] the worst of it in the race-wars of centuries, peoples that have the least possible adaptation to our political institutions and have shown neither the capacity nor the disposition to rise above the lowest plane of industrial life. As conditions are, there is nothing to prevent any stagnant pool of population in Europe, from Ireland, to the Ural mountains, from being completely drained off into the United States.[20]

Of the Poles, Bohemians, Hungarians, Russian Jews, and South Italians, he wrote,

> Ignorant, unskilled, inert, accustomed to the beastliest conditions, with little social aspirations, with none of the desire for air and light and room, for decent dress and home comfort, which our native people possess and which our earlier immigrants so speedily acquired, the presence of hundreds of thousands of these laborers constitutes a menace to the rate of wages and the American standard of living, which to my mind is absolutely appalling. . . . Taking whatever they can get in the way of wages, living like swine, crowded into filthy tenement houses, piecing out their miserable existence by begging and by picking over garbage barrels, the arrival on our shores of such masses of degraded peasantry brings the greatest danger that American labor has ever known.[21]

He outlined a law he would find satisfactory, whereby "the United States should proclaim that for ten years from November 1, 1893 a deposit of $100 shall be required from every alien entering its ports." If a person were to leave within three years, he should get his money back. At the end of three years, the money should be rewarded upon presentation of satisfactory evidence that the person is a law-abiding and self-supporting citizen. According to Walker, "such a measure would at once cut nine-tenths of immigration. It would not prevent tens of thousands of thrifty Swedes, Norwegians, Germans and men of other nationalities coming here at their own expense."[22]

In the remaining three months of 1892 the *Literary Digest* continued to publish stories that favored exclusion of the Chinese and opposed the "new immigration" from southern and eastern Europe. A rare exception was a piece excerpted from the *New York Journal of Commerce,* which said,

> There can be nothing more injurious to the prosperity of the American people than this senseless clamor against free immigration. . . . They are a real addition to the wealth of the country — With the broad acres of this country yet unsettled and all untitled, it is the most egregious folly to turn back the offered laborer who asks for a home and opportunity of self support on our unoccupied fields or in the channels of industry that need his labor.[23]

In 1893, the number of stories on immigration declined to 13, and then for the rest of the decade, the number per year never exceeded 6. Eight of the pieces in 1893 focused on Chinese immigration. The *Literary Digest* reported that with the exception of those on the West Coast, the press in the United States generally opposed the law (Geary Bill) that required Chinese laborers to register. Should the laborer fail to register, he was subject to arrest and deportation. Of the 11 non–West Coast newspapers quoted by the *Literary Digest*, 9 opposed the law, 2 favored it. Among the six West Coast newspapers surveyed, all favored the law. Articles that appeared in two issues in May reflected much the same distribution of opinion. The *Times of Brooklyn* harshly condemned the act when it wrote,

> There is nothing in the history of American legislature since the enactment of the Fugitive Slave Law to compare in infamy with the latest product of Kearneyism, the Chinese Exclusion Act, fathered by Congressman Geary of California. It is the rankest embodiment of caste and race prejudice ever enacted in a civilized country.[24]

The *Philadelphia Inquirer* asked, "If it is desirable to expel the Chinese, why is it not desirable to expel the scum of Europe?"[25]

The *Literary Digest* on September 23 reported that preparations for enforcing the Geary Act were suspended on orders of the attorney general, an action, they concluded, brought about by the Chinese government's response and by the U.S. Congress's "determination to reconsider the whole question."

Congressman Geary had his say in the *Literary Digest*. In a piece entitled "Should the Chinese Be Excluded?" excerpted from the *North American Review*, Geary wrote, "We are threatened with the loss of trade with China. We would be better off without any of it. It leaves a balance of 14 to 15 million against us every year."[26]

The other immigration stories that appeared during the year focused on the cholera epidemic in Europe and a bill introduced by

Senator William Chandler to suspend all immigrants for one year in order to keep out cholera and on whether immigration should be restricted because it was harmful to U.S. interests. In a piece titled "Shall Immigration Be Restrained," the *Literary Digest* quoted A. A. Halbrook from the *American Journal of Politics*:

> European labor is not crowding Americans out of work, though the Huns may be crowding our own people into a class of work which demands more skill and consequently higher salaries. True, the Poles and Hungarians are crowding out the Welsh and Irish in the coal regions, but they are only crowding them up, so open the gates and let them come in. They are only labor saving devices, and the idea that they interfere with the American work people is only the same false note which agitated labor circles in the years past; that a laborsaving machine is an injury because it appears to throw people out of employment.[27]

The opposite point of view appeared in a piece by William Jeffrey, excerpted from the *Journal of Political Economy*, that blamed immigrants for the increase in adult and juvenile crime rates. It recommended that Congress pass an act requiring every person who desired to emigrate to the United States to provide himself with a certificate of character from the chief executive officer of his city or town, stating the number of years that he had been a resident of the city or town.

> The law should require that the certificate have three endorsements — first by the Chief of Police, stating that the person named has not been brought before the court on any criminal charge for a period of not less than five years, and that no charges are now pending against the said person; second by the Chief Health Officer, stating that the person named is in good health, and that no contagious diseases have been reported in his household for a period of not less than one year; third by the Chief Officer of the Poor, stating that the person named has not received any assistance from the poor authorities for a period of not less than five years.[28]

Henry Cabot Lodge analyzed the census of 1890 in an article that originally appeared in the *Century Magazine*. In his analysis, Congressman Lodge argued along the same lines as William Jeffrey in claiming that immigrants composed a disproportionate share of the criminal and pauper classes. He repeated his call for legislation to restrict immigration.[29]

A tax on alien labor was an idea suggested by Charles Brown in an article in *New Occasion* that the *Literary Digest* excerpted on

January 27, 1894. The law would provide that the employer of any laborer who was not a U.S. citizen should pay the government a duty bearing a certain ratio to the duty upon the goods manufactured. Brown wrote,

> Just as a tariff on products tends to discourage importation and enhance the price of the home product, so a tariff upon alien labor would discourage immigration and enhance the price of American labor, and just as a Goods-Tariff brings revenues, so would a Labor-Tariff produce revenue.[30]

The only other piece on immigration that the *Literary Digest* carried in 1894 concerned the passage by the Senate of a new treaty with China whereby Chinese laborers would be totally excluded from the United States and which contained China's pledge to prevent such immigration to the United States. However, the treaty also allowed Chinese residents of the United States who visited China and left their near relatives or property in the United States to return to this country. The newspapers on the West Coast strongly attacked that clause.

The one piece on immigrants carried by the *Literary Digest* in 1895 reported on a movement in California that favored excluding Japanese laborers from the United States on the grounds that they were as dangerous to the whites as to the Chinese because they offered to sell their labor at 40 or 50 cents a day. The same unanimity that characterized the West Coast press attitude on the Chinese question appeared in their support of this movement. The newspapers in the East were largely opposed to it. The *New York Sun*, in referring to the Japanese as "the Yankees of the Orient," characterized the movement as "crazy, unnecessary and insulting."[31]

Broader issues pertaining to immigration were discussed in the six articles that appeared in 1896 than had been treated in the previous two or three years. For example, in January the *Literary Digest* excerpted an article by Sydney Fisher in the *Popular Science Monthly* that argued that immigration retarded the growth of native population and that "the rate of increase of our aggregate population is almost four percent lower than was the rate prevailing during the Revolution, when immigration was at its minimum."[32]

The first of many literacy tests for immigrants passed the House of Representatives on May 20, 1896. The provisions of the bill passed by the House excluded all males between the ages of 16 and 60 who could not read or write English or any other language. (Female illiterates of all ages were apparently welcome.) Press coverage of the bill, as reported in the *Literary Digest* on June 6, was mixed. The *Journal* in Minneapolis wrote, "This bill ought to pass the Senate. The country demands restriction of immigration because of the great deterioration in character of a large percentage of the inflow from abroad. Illiteracy is the protoplasm of crime."[33] The *Republic* of St. Louis, on the other hand, declared, "There are men in this country today who have barely succeeded in learning to write their name and who are nevertheless among the most enterprising citizens in the communities in which they live."[34]

The annual report of the commissioner general of immigration, Herman Stump, was the subject of an article in the *Literary Digest* on December 5. The commissioner reported that "statistics do not justify the conclusion that our alien population is growing in undue proportions." He also reported that he knew of no immigrant who had landed in the previous year who was now a burden upon any public or private institution; that the influx consisted for the most part of hardy people, skilled and unskilled laborers, and that they brought at least $5 million with them into the country.

By 1897, a bill requiring a literacy test for immigrants had also passed the Senate. The press speculated about whether President Cleveland would sign or veto it. It did not have long to wait. On March 2, President Cleveland, in one of his last official acts, vetoed the measure. In his message to Congress he explained why he acted as he did:

> In my opinion it is infinitely more safe to admit 100,000 immigrants who, though unable to read and write, seek among us only a home and opportunity to work than to admit one of those unruly agitators and enemies of governmental control who cannot only read and write but delight in arousing by inflammatory speech the illiterate and peacefully inclined to discontent and tumult.[35]

The president, in responding to a claim that the quality of recent immigrants had been undesirable, said that the same criticism was made of past immigrants who, with their descendants, had come to comprise the best citizens of the United States.

A survey of the German-American press's views on immigration was reported in the March 27 issue of the *Literary Digest*. The *Literary Digest* concluded that all of the German and American papers, "whatever their religious or political creed, unanimously opposed all efforts to restrict immigration."

Quoting Treasury Department statistics, the *Literary Digest* reported in August that "the tide of immigration is at the lowest point since the federal government assumed jurisdiction over the subject in 1882." The *Philadelphia Ledger* had analyzed the data as follows:

> The gratifying features of the report are first the general decrease of immigration and second the diminution of the

number of the most undesirable classes of immigrants. . . . It is not reassuring to know that immigrants from Germany, England, Ireland, Sweden and Norway are becoming fewer each year and that their places are being taken by Russians, Italians, Poles and Huns.[36]

In the last two years of the nineteenth century, only two articles about immigration appeared in the *Literary Digest*. In January 1898, the *Literary Digest* ran another survey of the German-American press, which proclaimed its support for unrestricted immigration and its strong interest in the subject. The last piece commented on the steady drop of German immigration to the United States.

Dire predictions about how the immigrants from southern and eastern Europe were likely to fill U.S. prisons and almshouses were the first stories on immigration in the *Literary Digest* in 1900. In addition, the *Literary Digest* reported,

The swelling tide of immigrants from Southern Europe and the Orient who can neither read nor write their own language and not even speak ours, who bring with them only money enough to stave off starvation but a few days, is a startling national menace that cannot be disregarded with safety.[37]

"Chinese Labor for the South" was the caption on a story that described a leading Southern newspaper's attitude toward the Chinese immigrants. This paper (the *Mobile Register*) urged, specifically, "a million active Chinese in the South to wake the negro population into activity." The *Macon Telegraph* agreed and wrote, "exchange of the negro for the Chinese would be in many respects a blessing."[38] These views were particularly timely because the Geary Chinese Exclusion Act, passed in 1882 and reenacted ten years later, was due to expire on May 5, 1902.

In 1902, the three stories that the *Literary Digest* carried on immigrants all focused on the Chinese exclusion issue, as did a piece that appeared November 30, 1901. Much of the support for continuing the policy of exclusion came from the West Coast. Newspapers elsewhere in the country advocated abrogating the exclusionary rule. In one excerpt, the Chinese were described as "the best educated people in the world" and "honest to a degree unknown in this country."[39]

The *Literary Digest* in 1903 quoted Frank P. Sargent, commissioner general of immigration, as saying, "immigration under present conditions presents a most serious problem. . . . Unless something is done to check the unprecedented influx of an undesirable foreign element, a very grave danger threatens our country."[40]

In that same issue, the *Philadelphia Record* attacked Sargent's position. The *Literary Digest* reported it as stating:

> Mr. Sargent is needlessly alarming a lot of people and is maligning a great many honest, even if not highly educated immigrants by foolish talk about the danger to American institutions of a great horde of population drawn from the scum of Europe. The fact that a man immigrates to better his condition creates the presumption that he has some enterprise and some pluck and there is a very small part of the immigrant who can with any degree of propriety be called scum. . . . The corruption of the ballot box and the control of cities by political rings is rather the work of the native Americans than of the foreign banks. Lawlessness and acts of violence are most common in those states where there is the least admixture of foreign population. The really dangerous classes in this country are not imported; they are natives.[41]

In June 1904 the *Literary Digest* excerpted newspaper debate on the rate cuts recently inaugurated by the steamship companies. The newspapers condemned the action because, in the words of the *Philadelphia Inquirer*,

> One important result of the war on steerage rates between the steamship lines is that we have a tremendous influx of undesirable immigrants. This country is big enough and undeveloped enough to care for many times its present population, but we have enough of the scum of Europe here now. . . . They recruit the criminal classes, flock to the almshouses, and are a burden on the community. . . . Those who arrive now do not have on the average more than $3.00 in their pocket, which simply argues that many of them will have to be supported.[42]

An article titled "Immigration Blunders," excerpted from the *Arena*, provided an antidote to the mainstream of anti-immigration messages carried by most of the print media in 1904. The *Arena* piece argued,

> Our boasted power of Yankeefying all the races that come hither is doing them and us more harm than good. . . . We are beginning to discover that the lynching and murder districts of the country are the native districts, and are told by Mr. Austin, of the government bureau of statistics, that a larger percentage of the children of the immigrants, as a whole, attend school during the years between five and fourteen than is the case among the children of native whites; and that there is a

smaller percentage of illiterates among those born in this country of foreign parents than among those born of native white parents.

The labor leaders who object to immigration forget that the imported workingman is also a consumer and creates a demand for labor, as well as a supply.[43]

A more familiar theme appeared in the next article, that is, a plan to divert immigrants out of the slums of large cities and scatter them over the country, especially in the South. The commissioner of immigration proposed to give Congress the power to establish an employment information bureau at Ellis Island, where arriving immigrants could obtain information about job possibilities in different parts of the country. The newspapers quoted (*Chicago Post, Chattanooga Times, Atlantic Constitution, New Orleans Times-Democrat*, and others) were all enthusiastic about the proposal. Only Robert De C. Ward, writing in the *Popular Science Monthly*, attacked the plan. He wrote,

Scattering our alien population of the more ignorant races simply spreads more widely the evils which result from exposing our own people to competition with the lower classes of foreigners. Again, in the case of the agricultural distribution of Italian and other alien laborers through the South, while it is perfectly true that these aliens will supplant the negroes in many — probably in most occupations, the effect will undoubtedly be to cause a migration of the negroes to the cities — a result which those familiar with the conditions of negroes now congested in cities cannot fail to view with the greatest alarm. Lastly, the more widely we scatter the newer immigrants, the more widespread will be the effect of the competition with the lower grades of aliens in causing a decrease in the birthrate among the older portion of our population.[44]

Over the next two years, the four pieces on immigration carried in the *Literary Digest* reiterated familiar themes. The *San Francisco Chronicle* played a crucial role in stirring up animosity against the Japanese in California. The Japanese, the paper warned, "are as much of a menace as the Chinese ever were."[45]

"During the last fiscal year undesirable immigrants arrived at the rate of two a minute," wrote the *New York World*, whose account appeared in the *Literary Digest* on June 3, 1905: "Tens of thousands of them were criminal, tens of thousands of them were dissolute women and hordes of them carried diseased baggage bearing counterfeit certificates."[46]

From 1907 through the end of the decade, with two exceptions, all of the 15 articles on immigration focused on the Japanese and the West Coast reactions to them. Newspapers in Washington and Oregon wrote at length to disassociate themselves from the "California" position, which sought to prohibit Japanese immigration completely and to bar Japanese children from the public schools of San Francisco. Newspapers in the East (*New York Mail*, the *New York Post*, the *Boston Globe*, the *Herald Tribune, Washington Post, Hartford Courant*) joined in condemning what they perceived as California's extreme reaction. However, California was not without its supporters; for example, Senator George S. Nixon of Nevada wrote to the governor of his state:

We are finding it difficult to assimilate even the immigrants of the white race, and have been obliged to carefully restrict such immigration. We have drifted into a condition regarding the black race which constitutes the great problem and peril of the future. Confronting our Pacific coast lies Asia, with nearly a billion people of the brown race, who, if there were no restrictions, would quickly settle upon and take possession of our entire coast and inter-mountain region. The time has come, in my judgment, when the United States, as a matter of self-protection and self-preservation, must declare by statutory enactment that it will not tolerate further race complications. Our country should by law, to take effect after the expiration of existing treaties, prevent the immigration into this country of all peoples other than those of the white race, except under restricted conditions relating to international commerce, travel, and education.[47]

The decade ended, however, with the defeat of anti-Japanese measures in the legislatures of three far-western states: California, Oregon, and Nevada. The Californian newspapers were almost unanimous in condemning the legislature for their action. The *New York Evening Post* captured much of the East's reaction with the following editorial:

One large reason for comfort rests in the present situation. Never again will California, on this question of the Japanese, easily rattle the nerves of the nation. The game has been worked once too often, and with the feeling of general relief that accompanies the cessation of the dreadful din, there is mingled a goodly measure of disgust. The amazing disproportion between California's grievance and the noise she made; the stupid clamor against conditions which, entirely apart from the question whether they are evil or not, are being done away with as rapidly as difficult conditions can be dealt with; above all, the impression that such sincere anti-Japanese sentiment as prevails in California is being worked by the politician and the newspaper demagogue for their own ends; all this has sorely tried the nation's patience, the nation's sense of humor, and the nation's sense of international right and wrong.[48]

Literacy requirements for entry into the United States were the major topic of the *Literary Digest*'s coverage of immigration issues in the second decade of the twentieth century. In 1912 it reported on the Senate's passage of literacy requirements (the Dillingham Bill) and the reactions of the press; approximately as many of the newspapers the *Literary Digest* quoted supported the bill as opposed it.

In its review of *The Immigration Problem* by Professors Jeremiah Jenks and W. Jett Lauck, the *Literary Digest* quoted the authors as perceiving the poor immigrant "as a wrong to the economic and social development of our race." They argued that the immigrant "cheapens labor, lowers the ideal of labor, and makes the lot of the American laboring man impossible." Their solution was "restrict immigration."[49]

"The Period of the Immigrant" is a proimmigrant piece that chided Americans for their treatment of the foreign born by demeaning and despising him and referring to him as "dago, sheeny, or bunkie." The article quoted Robert Walchorn, former commissioner of immigration at Ellis Island, who said, "If you gave the Hungarian and the Russian Jew half a chance, he will make the English and the Irish look like thirty cents."[50]

President Taft's veto of the Dillingham Bill was the first story on immigration the *Literary Digest* carried in 1913. It was followed by discussions of another Dillingham Bill that would have limited the number of aliens of any nationality to 10 percent of the number of persons of that nationality already in the country (a liberal forerunner of the 1921 Quota Act). The *New York Sun* reported that if the Dillingham Bill became law, it would reduce the immigration from southern and eastern Europe by approximately 130,000 annually and increase by approximately two-thirds the number from northeastern and western Europe.[51]

In October 1913 the *Literary Digest* reported a plan put forth by a newly formed Mississippi Valley immigration association, whose purpose was to try to divert European immigration from Northern to Southern ports on grounds that the South needed more labor and the (North)Eastern cities had too many immigrants. It also carried a report describing the fiscal year that ended June 30 as being the year in which more immigrants arrived in the United States than in the previous 10 years.

"Sieves for Immigrants" was the title of a long piece that the *Literary Digest* carried as the first of its five stories on immigration in 1914. It was a review of the various bills before Congress, all of which were aimed at "keeping out those coarser elements from Asia and Southern Europe which are so irritating to labor unions and Pacific Coast citizens and at the same time allow finer elements which we can assimilate to pass through our gates."[52] There are bills, the article reported, that would demand a minimum height of five feet four inches and a maximum of six feet one inch, a minimum weight of 128 pounds and a maximum of 176 pounds. The article was written in a rather playful, whimsical style, but the bills it described were real. The *Literary Digest* carried an account of the Japanese press's anger at the anti-Japanese immigration bills that were pending in the U.S. Congress. It quoted one of the leading newspapers in Tokyo as saying, "The Japanese Government and people have been courteous to the point of hypocrisy in dealing with America. . . . The Japanese should learn to give vent to their feelings more freely, lest their good intentions may be misinterpreted by the inconsiderate."[53]

The last piece on immigration in 1914 appeared after the war in Europe had begun, and it described notable declines in the number of aliens seeking to enter the United States and an increase in the number who were returning to their homelands. Some, the *Literary Digest* reported, were responding to calls issued by the warring countries for reservists to return "to their colors."

In 1915 the *Literary Digest* carried seven stories about immigrants. Three of them dealt with the literacy question and whether the United States should establish requirements. In February it reported that President Wilson, following Cleveland and Taft, had vetoed another attempt by Congress to pass a literacy requirement. The article reported that all of the newspapers in New York City agreed with the president's veto.

Later in February 1915, the *Literacy Digest* carried another piece about the decline in immigrants and the increase in emigrants. That was followed by two pieces in March on the literacy issue. One article was based on a timely census bureau publication that reported the rates of illiteracy among various immigrant communities. "The countries of Northwestern Europe," the bureau reported, "have comparatively few illiterates and have sent the United States few illiterates. This is not the case," the report continued, "for Iberian and Slavic immigrants, where the rate of illiteracy is over 30 percent."[54]

Two weeks later the *Literary Digest* carried a piece titled "Illiteracy 'Made in America'" which showed that there was "vastly more native than naturalized illiteracy" and "that the children of immigrants were the most generally literate class in the population."[55]

The last two articles on immigrants in 1915 concerned the alien's right to work. The *Literary Digest* reported that the U.S. Supreme Court had struck down an Arizona law that said "every employer of more than five persons had to employ not less than 80 percent of qualified electors or native born citizens of the United States."[56] In December it reported the Supreme Court's decision to let stand a New York law that required the state to hire nonaliens for public work projects.

The *Literary Digest* carried four stories on immigrants in 1916. On April 1 it described the Bureau of Naturalization's plan to involve public schools nationwide in a citizenship program directed at the new immigrants. The *Literary Digest* was skeptical that the people toward whom the program was directed would benefit from it. It observed,

> The sentimentalists who ask whether we should close the doors of hope that were open to our fathers are overlooking the fact that the early comers to this country took care of themselves. They were a charge on no one. They needed no special treatment. We can take as many such now as will come, but there is a limit to the number of the somewhat helpless folk that we can decently attend to, and to take more is neither to their advantage nor ours.[57]

A long piece summarizing reactions to the Dillingham (Literacy Test) Bill that recently passed the House of Representatives appeared in the April 22 issue. Samuel Gompers, president of the American Federation of Labor and a strong supporter of immigration restriction, pointed out that the literacy test would not affect political refugees and those seeking to come to the United States because they were victims of religious persecution.

Finally, after three Presidential vetoes, Congress successfully overrode a fourth veto by Woodrow Wilson and passed a literacy requirement. The *Literary Digest* reported that during the debate, Congressman Burnett shouted, "Not the South alone, but the labor elements in the North, the A.F. of L., the farmers' organizations and millions of citizens demand restricted immigration."[58]

The *New York World* sided with President Wilson and declared the test to be un-American. It claimed that organized labor was a major force in getting Congress to act favorably on the bill. Several of the other newspapers cited (for example, *San Francisco Chronicle*, *St. Louis Republic*) agreed with the *New York World*, but most also agreed that the literacy test had popular support.

By the autumn of 1917, the United States was actively involved in the war. The "alien slacker" was the subject of two stories in August and September of that year. The view that aliens of military age should be drafted received wide support among the press sampled by the *Literary Digest.*[59]

More than most other years, 1919 witnessed sharp swings in the pendulum between sympathetic, positive views about immigrants and hostile, negative opinions. On February 8, the *Literary Digest* carried a story advocating a halt to immigration, mostly on the grounds that it wanted to keep the "Huns" from coming over. The story noted that passage of a bill that would bar all immigration for four years had the support of the *Christian Science Monitor*, the *Philadelphia Inquirer*, *St. Louis Republic*, *Grand Rapids Herald*, *Seattle Post-Intelligence*, and the *Baltimore Sun*. One editorial stated,

> Our law-makers and immigration authorities should know that the American people feel a resentment toward the devastating, murderous Hun, that is implacable and will never cool. We want none of his kind in this country. And if the Government fails to keep him out, there is a danger that America's ex-veterans of the Great War will take the law into their own hands.[60]

One month later, in an article titled "How We Abused the Loyalty of Our Foreign Born," the message was, "for every spy, even for every alien of doubtful allegiance, we have thousands of industrious and patriotic citizens anxious to get on his trail."[61]

Frederick C. Howe, commissioner of immigration, predicted the arrival of 5 million persons after the war because, in Howe's words, "of the ideal of Americanism" presented to them "by the American private soldiers."[62] An excerpt from *Moody's Investment Service* that the *Literary Digest* carried in the same issue also anticipated the arrival of millions of immigrants but mostly because of the opportunities for unskilled labor. It wrote, "There is more reason than ever why common labor should leave Europe. . . . War taxes are bound to be enormously heavy and to have a depressing effect upon labor for many years to come."[63]

In a piece titled "To Clap the Lid on the Melting Pot," the *Literary Digest* reported on the various bills that had been introduced into Congress to halt immigration completely for some years. The press were quoted as very favorably disposed toward such an action. The *Cincinnati Times Star* wrote, "This proposal has the active support of the American Federation of Labor; it should have the energetic and enthusiastic support of Americans of all sorts who have a reasonable and proper interest in their country's future."[64]

The *Literary Digest*'s next and last piece on immigration for the year sounded a different note. Appearing in the "Investment and Finance" section, the article claimed that "an exodus of aliens is growing like a mania. Twelve hundred foreigners are leaving New

York every day." The article asked, "What would have happened if, during the century and a half of our national life, we had received no immigration?" It concluded,

> Above all the unregulated influx of foreigners, ignorant of our ways, has brought a loss in the vigor and integrity of our native institutions. Our lofty sentiment and our materialism are alike wounded by the proposal to limit immigration by means of selective tests. But if the result is to convince our middle class respectables of the dignity and worth of hard labor and at the same time to guard the integrity of our free institutions, there will be a compensation.[65]

Immigration in 1920 provided a schizophrenic experience for the United States, as reflected in the *Literary Digest*. During the first half of the year, the *Literary Digest*'s articles bemoaned the lack of immigrants and expressed fear that those who had recently arrived would soon depart forever. Two-thirds into the year, articles expressed fear that the United States would be unable to limit and control "the deluge" from Europe. For example, in reporting on the activities of the National Conference on Immigration, the caption above the article read "America Short 4,000,000 Workers." The conference urged the lifting of all restrictions on immigration. It adopted a resolution that stated:

> No other country is so profoundly interested in the problem of immigration as is the United States. Its industrial and economic history is, in effect, a history of immigration. There are in the country today sixteen million foreign-born people, and they are the parents of more than twenty million American-born children, and in so far as our national development depends upon the labor of its people, one-third of that progress is due to the immigrant and his immediate family.
>   There is a shortage of labor to the extent of at least five million men in this country. It is due to that shortage that the high cost of living has reached the point that it has. Unless there is an additional man-power there is no limit to the increase of the cost of living. Without that man-power we cannot produce.[66]

In June 1920, the *Literary Digest* carried a story that described the negative picture of the United States held by immigrants who were returning to their native country. Life in the United States was too hard; there was no time for play. They were disillusioned with the United States and did not plan to return.

A change of emphasis appeared in the *Literary Digest*'s September 11, 1920, story that reported an increase in the number of immigrants to 5,000 arrivals a day, 800,000 in the year that ended on June 30. Quoting the *Boston Transcript*, "Continuation of the present wave of immigration will do much to relieve the shortage of labor by which industry and enterprise generally are severally handicapped." The *Literary Digest* commented that the views expressed were representative of many newspapers.[67]

A drastic change occurred by October, when the *Literary Digest* reported on the battle in Congress "between employers of unskilled laborers who approve the swelling tide of immigrants and labor leaders who fear the same tide will bring down wages." The article reported that immigrants were arriving at the old prewar rate of 1 million a year and that organized labor was apprehensive lest the newcomers undermine the present living standards of the U.S. working man. The *Chicago Tribune* sounded the alarm by warning of the spiritual and mental deficiencies of the people who were currently being admitted:

In plain English, we mean that the renewed influx is from regions in Europe where political and social and economic conditions are almost as remote from our own as can be found anywhere. The men and women who are coming to us are not only entirely ignorant of our history and of the spirit of our society and institutions, but they have conceptions of progress, of politics, of social organization, widely different and even opposed to our own.[68]

The *Grand Rapids News* warned,

It is all well and good to have men among us who are not afraid of any kind of toil. But it is far more essential to have among us men who do not despise our system of government. Far better that we left some of the work undone than that we should be overwhelmed by an alien horde with fantastic notions about government, liberty, social intercourse and economic rights.[69]

A shift in the opposite direction, toward positive attitudes about immigrants, was reflected in a piece that appeared on October 30 titled, "Enter — The New Immigrant." The general theme was that the current cohorts were wiser and less gullible than earlier arrivals. The commissioner of immigration was quoted as saying that most of the aliens did not find the literacy test too arduous and were able to pass the other requirements as well.

The fight between the state of California and the Japanese immigrants made headlines again when the people of that state ratified a law barring aliens from holding or leasing California lands. Commenting on their actions, the *Sacramento Bee* wrote,

> California as a frontier state is making the nation's fight against the incoming rush of an alien unassimilable race which would engulf our civilization. Some Japanese announced their intention of leaving California for Texas and other states having no restrictive laws. Such immigration would prove the most effective method of convincing other states of the propriety of California's attempt to prevent the economic problems of today becoming the racial problems of tomorrow.[70]

The non-Californian newspapers quoted in the same article were critical of the state's actions and believed it acted irresponsibly and without proper regard for the impact its actions would have on U.S.–Japanese relations generally.

"The Threatened Inundation from Europe" was the headline for a *Literary Digest* piece on immigrants in December 1920. Having started the year by describing the great concern over the lack of immigrants, the *Literary Digest*'s final story reported that the American Federation of Labor was "entreating Congress to put a two year ban on all immigration." The clamor for restrictions on immigrants was not limited to organized labor. A U.S. banker was quoted as saying "unless this new wave of immigrants from desolated Europe is stopped or controlled, it will hurt both industry and labor, reduce wages and lower our standard of living."[71]

The *Chicago Tribune*, as reported in the *Literary Digest*, summed up the social and cultural anti-immigrant argument as follows:

> The powerful influences which make it possible for the United States to take in many, if not all, races and nationalities and still keep it from becoming a polyglot nation, can be overtaxed.
>
> We believe the United States is nearing its point of saturation. We believe this country can take care of a trickle of immigration, but not a flood.
>
> America must protect its strain, its blood, its breeding, and its political culture. It must breed true. The base was laid centuries ago by English, Scotch, Irish, Swedish, French and Dutch pioneers. Upon that base the American nation has built its structure, which is not to be changed by new inhabitants, but which is to change them to inhabit it.[72]

Thus, in a period of 12 months, the *Literary Digest* reflected the nation's change in mood from one of anxiety because of the lack of immigrants to one of fear of being besieged by an excess of immigrants.

Greater consistency of attitude returned in 1921. The nine stories on immigration that appeared in the *Literary Digest* were all negative in tone or, at best, skeptical of the value of immigrants. The first one described a movement whereby the United States, Canada, Australia, New Zealand, and South Africa would unite to exclude Japanese immigrants from their shores.

Scholarly views on current immigration trends and their implications were presented in an article that appeared later in January. The issues were posed thus: "Twenty-five million foreigners, the alarmists say, are determined to come to America. Where can we house them? How can we employ them? Why need we admit them?" Francis Walker responded as follows:

All the good the United States could do by offering indiscriminate hospitality to a few million more of European peasants, whose places at home will, within another generation be filled by others as miserable as themselves would not compensate for any permanent injury done to our Republic. Our highest duty to charity and to humanity is to make this great experiment, here, of free laws and educated labor, the most triumphant success that can possibly be attained. In this way we shall do far more for Europe than by allowing its city slums and its vast stagnant reservoirs of degraded peasantry to be drained off upon our soil.

It is claimed that the influx of foreigners of a low standard of intelligence and of life depresses wages, lessens available employment for native labor, and is a distinct hardship to the American workman. In some industries, such as the manufacture of clothing and the mining of coal, native laborers have been practically driven from the field. Moreover, it is maintained by those who desire further restriction of immigration that the influx of ignorant, inefficient and poverty-stricken aliens increases the public burden through pauperism and crime, while the bulk of the money which the more thrifty immigrants accumulate is returned to their native country.[73]

Sociologist E. A. Ross explained:

Overseas migration drops people down in cities, and most of them abide there, prisoners of ignorance and inertia. In a settled country receiving immigrants the cities become more polyglot and foreign than the rural districts. After our agricultural frontiers came to an end foreign immigration saturated American cities with foreign-born and contributed more to urban growth than the tide from the farms. The foreign stock which is represented on the farms by a fifth, makes up seven-tenths of the metropolitan myriads.[74]

Also, economist W. Jett Lauck observed:

The literacy test has been in existence too short a period to measure its full effectiveness. Evidence to date, however, offers little hope that it will prove a sufficient barrier to that type of immigration which is undesirable on economic grounds. In 1919 only 1,455 out of a total immigration of 141,132 were excluded on account of inability to meet the literacy tests.[75]

None of the experts quoted above offered positive views about the benefits of immigrants.

The Dillingham Bill, which would drastically restrict immigrants from southern and eastern Europe to 5 percent of the number of foreign-born persons of that nationality who were residing in the United States as of 1910 and at the same time accelerate immigration from northern and western Europe, was positively reviewed by all of the newspapers quoted in the article. Only the foreign press representing Jewish, Czechoslovak, and other eastern and southern European ethnic communities opposed the bill.

Half of the remaining six stories in 1921 described the incidence of typhus among immigrants who were arriving at Ellis Island and the precautions to prevent its spread into U.S. cities, as well as the deplorable conditions that existed at Ellis Island.

The last three stories of 1921 focused on the Quota Act, proposed by Representative Albert Johnson of Washington, which had already passed the House and was expected to pass the Senate. The Quota Act would restrict aliens to 3 percent of the total of each nationality in the United States at the time of the 1910 census. Of the newspapers quoted, almost all, especially those from the large East Coast cities (the *Brooklyn Eagle*, the *Newark Ledger*, the *Boston Globe*, the *Philadelphia Bulletin*, and the *New York World*) opposed the measure. Support for it came from the *Dayton News*, the *Seattle Post-Intelligence*, the *Buffalo News*, and, the exception to the big city Eastern papers, the *Baltimore Sun*. A flavor of the debate is provided below.

To the charge that the United States was threatened with a flood of immigrants, many of whom were of an undesirable character, the *Boston Globe* challenged with the question, "Who's undesirable?" "The undesirable of one generation is the desirable of the next," the *Boston Globe* maintained, as it pointed to the Irish, who it said were undesirable 70 years before. "On the other hand, we are told, the Germans, who, prior to 1914, were considered a highly desirable element, came to be regarded by a part of our population as highly undesirable. So," concluded the *Boston Globe*, "the standard of desirability is not a fixed standard in the public mind."

In the opinion of the *New York World*,

> That plan [the Johnson Bill] would be grossly unfair and impolitic and would not bar undesirables. On the 1913 figures it would shut out thousands of French, Swiss, Dutch, Spanish, and Portuguese however intelligent and industrious. It would admit all the British, Germans, and Scandinavians likely to apply, but it would bar more than 200,000 Italians.[76]

In support of the bill:

> Congress now is engaged in the enactment of emergency legislation to protect commerce and industry by preventing the dumping of foreign goods upon the American market, but the opponents of the immigration bill would deny like protection to the working people and would permit the dumping of foreign labor in unlimited quantities upon the American market.
>
> Certain European countries are encouraging the departure of undesirables to America. Those countries are taking advantage of the neglect of the United States to guard its people from a stream of impurity. Why should this nation become a dumping-ground of human material any more than a dumping-ground of cheap-labor goods?
>
> Americanism must not be either adulterated or diluted by a mixture with ingredients whose very nature is to irritate the body politic and cause at least its deterioration, if not its ultimate destruction. The principle of self-preservation protests. That is not selfishness. It is the guarding of that which is good against the assault of that which would injure it. Judicious restriction of immigration is simply American self-protection.[77]

In a follow-up piece that appeared three weeks later, the *Literary Digest* aired the views of the foreign-language press about the Johnson Bill. The *Literary Digest* summarized their opinions as follows:

> In general, however, we do not find so acrid a tone, but rather a consensus of opinion that the immigrant gives due value for value received, and the history of the United States shows the contributions in brawn as well as brains. These spokesmen of our foreign-born population apparently do not want to be coddled nor clubbed, and some rather humorously remind us that "America is a nation of immigrants," and venture to

suppose that when Columbus and his men set foot on San Salvador, doubtless one of the first ideas of the Indians was to put up bars against immigration.[78]

The Johnson Quota Act was enacted into law in June 1921.

The *Literary Digest* included only three pieces on immigration in 1922, in contrast to the eight and nine that appeared in the two previous years. The first was a report by the famous singer Lillian Russell, in her capacity as a matron of Pittsburgh, to the secretary of labor upon her return from Europe, where she was sent to investigate the immigration problem. Her report, among other things, recommended that immigration be suspended for five years. "Our melting pot has been overcrowded, it has boiled too quickly, and is running over. . . . If we don't put up the bars and make them higher and stronger, there will no longer be an America for Americans."[79]

Alien hatred of the Anglo-Saxon was the subject of an article excerpted from the *New York Times Book Review and Magazine*. In it, Professor Brander Matthews analyzed the situation as follows:

This process of satisfactory assimilation persisted up to the middle of the nineteenth century. There were in the United States only a few compact settlements of immigrants from any one country; and most of the newcomers, no matter whence they came, were soon scattered in American communities. The various stocks intermarried; and whatever the parents, the children were Americans, often with little sentimental affection for the remote land from which their fathers had migrated. The little Irish boy in Boston pointed out Bunker Hill to his father and said, "That's where we beat you!" The little German boy explained that he wept after his father had thrashed him, not because of the pain, but because of the humiliation of being licked by a damn Dutchman.

That German boy and that Irish boy were anxious to assert their solidarity with older stock of Americans. They wanted to be like us; they accepted our traditions; they acquired our folkways; they shared our opinions and even our prejudices. They wished to become "Anglo-Saxons" and to be recognized as "Anglo-Saxons." Nearly all of the newcomers from abroad preserved this attitude toward our civilization until comparatively recently. In fact, I think that most of them still preserve it.[80]

Although the 1921 Quota Act had been in effect only six months, the November 18 issue of the *Literary Digest* carried a piece about how Congress was likely to handle its revision. The National Industrial Conference Board complained that the character of the immigrant had changed such that many fewer skilled workers were arriving and a larger proportion of women and children — non-wage earners — were coming.

Economist Roy L. Garis in a *Scribner's* magazine article warned, "A return to the old custom of free immigration is impractical." He believed that the people would approve a law that would reduce immigrants from southern and eastern Europe to a few thousand each year and would admit all those from western Europe who wanted to come. In the end he warned, "the doctrine that America must be thrown open as the home for the oppressed of all nations, good and bad alike, is a false doctrine."[81]

Most of the 22 stories on immigration that appeared in the *Literary Digest* in 1923 and 1924 focused on the congressional debate over revising the Quota Act passed in 1921. The debate resulted in the passage of more restrictive legislation in the form of the 1924 Quota Act. As early as February 23, 1923, a proposal was made to restrict immigration from 3 percent to 2 percent and to use the 1890 census rather than the 1910 census as the base for determining the number to be admitted from each country. Such a change would exclude Japanese and other Orientals and would sharply reduce Italian, Greek, Russian, and Polish quotas.

In a long piece titled "Opening Guns in the Immigration Fight," the *Literary Digest* quoted a spokesman for the U.S. Steel Corporation as denouncing the current immigration law because

It keeps husky laboring men twirling their thumbs in Europe while American factories keep their "help wanted" signs nailed out. . . . America is forced by a shortage of labor, due principally to the laws restricting immigration. The laws as passed are the worst things that ever happened to the country economically.[82]

The American Federation of Labor responded to U.S. Steel as follows: "The A.F. of L. is not opposed to immigration with this exception. It is opposed to the bringing of Orientals here. Our civilization cannot survive if Orientals are permitted to come here and take the place of our workers."[83]

In its "Science and Invention" section, the *Literary Digest* reproduced an article from the *Journal of Heredity* that described the low mental age of the foreign-born soldiers drafted into the U.S. army in 1917 and 1918. The author allowed that greater familiarity with English and length of stay in the United States affected the scores, but concluded, "When all considerations are balanced, it seems to me likely a priori, that the difference here shown is to a marked extent one of the differences in the inherent quality of the immigrant."[84]

Terrible conditions at Ellis Island were described in detail in two articles toward the end of 1923. They were followed by two stories describing the U.S. Supreme Court's decision that resulted in upholding laws of the states of California and Washington forbidding aliens ineligible for citizenship to own land.

In January 1924, a new immigration bill was submitted to Congress by the secretary of labor. Debate over it began in earnest shortly thereafter. A major change in the bill was the secretary's proposal to extend quota restrictions to all of the countries in the Western Hemisphere, although he made no recommendation concerning the figure to be fixed as the quota limitation. The proposed bill sparked a flood of stories in the press, and the *Literary Digest* carried 14 over the year. More details about what the bill might contain appeared in two articles in its February issues. The magazine reported that Representative Albert Johnson, chairman of the House Committee on Immigration (and principal author of the 1921 Quota Act), wanted to halve the number of aliens permitted to enter, from 357,803 to 168,837. In addition, he advocated using the 1890 instead of the 1910 census as a basis, and he would reduce the quota from 3 to 2 percent. The press, as reported in the same *Literary Digest* issue, were quick to point out that "the two races whose numbers would be greatly reduced are the Italians and those who come from Russia and Poland — chiefly Jews." The *Literary Digest* excerpted reactions from *The Day (Der Tag)*, a Yiddish language New York daily, and the *Corriere D'America*, a New York Italian newspaper. *The Day* wrote,

This action means that those millions who since their arrival in the last thirty-four years have added immensely to American prestige, American civilization, American wealth; the millions who have given their full proportion to the armies of the Great War, who have built up institutions which might be a model to the whole country, are an inferior type. It means that America wants as little of them as possible. It means that the country is divided into two parts — inferior and superior, desirable and undesirable.[85]

The *Corriere D'America* said,

From statistics published by the American Government, we have gleaned figures showing the immense value of Italian immigration to America. The number of Italian immigrants excluded and deported is the smallest, which goes to show that the Italians are the healthiest in body and mind. The Italians contribute only a minimum percentage of those affected by tuberculosis and insanity. The Italian woman is the only one who does not appear among those sentenced for immorality. The percentage of criminality among Italians is one of the lowest. On the other hand, the Italian immigrant of all other races, give the highest figure for productive labor and the lowest for mendicancy. The Italians are now in the forefront of the movement toward agriculture, while this field is being deserted by others.[86]

Of all the groups that came under discussion in anticipation of the passage of the revised Quota Act, none received more attention than the Japanese. Of the 14 stories about immigration, 4 focused on the Japanese. The *Literary Digest* reported that Secretary of State Hughes was opposed to the present version of the bill, which would "bar out aliens who are ineligible to citizenship."[87] Instead, Hughes urged what he believed would be a better method of regulating the number of "little brown men" coming into this country by placing the Japanese on the same quota basis as other nations, namely, 2 percent of the number of their nationals already here according to the census of 1890 plus the 200 that is the minimum quota for any nation. This would have allowed the Japanese a quota of 246 per year. Hughes's proposal was not adopted. The 1924 Quota Act contained a clause intended to exclude Japanese immigrants.

On May 26, 1924, President Calvin Coolidge signed into law the immigration bill. Commenting on its passage, the *Literary Digest* wrote, "the law, which reduces the number of immigrants from 357,803 to less than half that number using the census of 1890 as a basis and by reducing the quota from 3 to 2 percent, is designed to reduce the number of Italian and Jewish immigrants." The *Chicago Tribune* referred to the signing of the bill as "the most momentous domestic event since the Civil War. It is a Declaration of Independence not less significant and epoch making for America and the world since the Declaration of 1776."[88]

However, the *New York Herald Tribune* warned, "the country as a whole will regret that the unnecessary affront to Japan was not avoided as the President desired."[89]

Following passage of the bill, a new issue captured the attention of the press: aliens entering the country illegally. The secretary of labor declared that "for every five immigrants who entered legally," one gained entrance in defiance of the code of his intended adopted country.[90] Japanese and Chinese appeared to be the worst offenders. A few months later, the numbers must have increased considerably, because the *Literary Digest* quoted the *Washington Post* as saying, "more aliens, we are told, are now smuggled in than are regularly admitted by law."[91] They came across the Mexican and Canadian borders and from Cuba to the Florida coast and were carried as far north as Baltimore, New York, and New Jersey. "Quotaize Canada" as a way of controlling illegal immigration from that border was recommended by the secretary of labor.

Bootlegging of immigrants, like the bootlegging of liquor, was producing a new class of millionaires. In a piece titled "The Higher Bootlegging — Assisting Immigrants," the *Literary Digest* reported that in contrast to immigrants, liquor was small game. For example, the story reported, "Where a boat [from Cuba] could formerly transport 200 cases of Scotch at a net profit of about $3,000, the same boat now can make an almost identical run with immigrants at a profit of $12,000 to $20,000 with no worry about distribution."[92]

The remaining four of the six pieces on immigration that appeared in the *Literary Digest* in 1925 focused on the pending shortage of unskilled labor as a consequence of the 1924 Quota Act. "For the first time in our immigration history we lost, in the fiscal year which ended June 30, more unskilled workers than we gained." So began one story that appeared on October 10, 1925. Quoting from the *Journal of Commerce*, the article continued,

> Figures for the first full year of the operation of the existing Immigration Law, particularly when coupled with the rather evident intention of the American Federation of Labor to go to further lengths if it can in excluding foreign labor, certainly suggest some very real dangers.[93]

Manufacturers and other employers were complaining that the greatest immigration problem was not too much immigration but, rather, too little.

A new immigration bill was debated and passed in 1926. The Wadsworth-Perlman Bill, aimed at putting "a little human kindness and gratitude into our present immigration legislation," allowed husbands, fathers, and mothers of U.S. citizens and wives, husbands, and unmarried minor children of aliens who had declared their intention to become citizens to enter on a nonquota basis.

The first piece on immigration in 1927 described the new immigrant quotas that were due to go into effect later that year. Their major effect would be to cut German and Irish admissions by 30,000 and 20,000, respectively, and to increase the British quota by 50,000, unless Congress acted to halt the change.

The other four articles in 1927 raised the question of applying quotas to immigrants from Mexico and Canada. Excerpts from the press that appeared in an August 27 piece separated the two countries, with many more urging quotas for Mexico, but not Canada. For example, "It would be humorous if it were not tragic, in the opinion of Assistant Secretary of Labor Husband, that we admit an annual immigration from Mexico that equals the entire quota of Great Britain, Northern Ireland, Sweden, Denmark, and Italy."[94]

The *Pittsburgh Sun* saw in the bootlegging of immigrants across the Mexican boundary "another phase of a situation that is certain to call loudly for quota control and border patrol in the next Congress."[95]

The *Milwaukee Journal* pointed out that the quota for Mexico under the law would be 1,600 instead of 68,000, and if this reduction deprives the Southwest of cheap labor, that does not give the Southwest a right to howl. The best of the country has cheerfully accepted a restriction of cheap labor from Europe, and the Southwest can do the same for the national welfare with regard to its Mexican sources.

However, the *Houston Post-Dispatch* and other newspapers in the Southwest argued,

It would curtail or destroy one of the main sources of cheap labor for South-western farms and ranches and bring ruin to thousands of citizens. In view of the extensive migration of negro workers to cities of the North and East, the effort to shut off the labor supply from Mexico assumes an even more alarming aspect. In addition to the fact that it would seriously cripple the farmers and stockmen of the Southwest, the quota scheme for Mexican immigrants deserves to be condemned on general principles. An outlay of millions of dollars annually would be required to enforce it.[96]

The *Brooklyn Eagle* saw the issue in more cultural and social terms. It wrote, "The Mexicans gather in little colonies and resist assimilation. While the Canadians are our own kind of people and become good citizens at once."[97]

In 1928, a presidential election year, the candidates' views on immigration were reported and debated. As early as December 1927, the governor of Maryland used the immigration issue in his bid for recognition as a national figure. In his address before the American Historical Association and the American Political Science Association, Governor Ritchie questioned the wisdom of rigid restrictive immigration laws. He attributed the growth of the United States in wealth and population to immigration.

We have been receiving full-grown or, at least, nearly adult workers, and so have escaped in considerable measure the heavy cost of raising, educating and feeding them through infancy and childhood, and the economic loss of infant mortality.

The United States could not have grown as it has, from the establishment of its sovereign independence to our own time, had not the adult manpower of Europe crossed the Atlantic, become animated with patriotism for its new-found home and loyalty to our flag, and helped develop the resources of this Continent.[98]

The *Arkansas Gazette*'s response to Governor Ritchie's proposals was to point to the types of people who were coming or had wanted to come and show how different they were from those who had come earlier.

Those immigrants were predominantly from the north of Europe. What we have cut off chiefly by our more rigid laws are immigrants from Southern and Eastern Europe, who began about twenty years ago to come in heavy volume, and who established in American cities what amounted to permanent foreign colonies.

America still offers welcome and opportunity to "adult European man-power" of the type America deems desirable. But we were not ready to receive innumerable hordes from other areas which experience has taught us do not send a large proportion of assimilable material. Between being a melting-pot and a dumping-ground, there is a vast difference.[99]

The *Cincinnati Times-Star* echoed similar sentiments:

The immigration law of 1924 is about the most important single piece of legislation ever enacted by Congress. It saved the United States from an alien flood of such overwhelming proportions that it would have changed the whole aspect of the country in a decade. The law was passed just in time. It is working well, without unfairness or cruelty to any one. It should not be weakened in any direction.[100]

No other press reactions were reported.

Both Republican presidential candidate Herbert Hoover and Democratic candidate Governor Al Smith talked about immigration in their nomination acceptance speeches. Both said they supported revisions of the current law, which separated families. Hoover, however, favored maintaining the existing quota system as provided in the 1924 act, while Smith would have changed the base year from 1890 to 1910 or 1920; such a change would have decreased the quotas from Germany, the Irish Free State, and Great Britain and increased them from Italy, Poland, Greece, and Russia.

The ordinarily Democratic *New York World* and *Newark News* opposed the governor's views, as did all the other newspapers quoted: the *Buffalo Courier Express, Detroit Free Press*, and *Hartford Courant*.

The other two immigration themes in 1928 were a plan to require aliens to obtain identification cards from U.S. consuls at the ports of departure and the establishment of quotas for Western Hemisphere countries. The purpose of identification cards was to discourage illegal entry into the country. The secretary of labor claimed that "Some of the large employers of labor in the United States would refuse to employ aliens except on evidence that they have been legally admitted for permanent residence."[101] On the matter of quotas for the Western Hemisphere, most of the press took the position that Canada and Mexico should be treated differently. "Canadians are home folks and there's no sense in trying by law to make foreigners of them. But Mexicans are ethnically different. They are of alien blood and not at all assimilable."[102] On the other hand, some argued, "the Southwest, especially its railroads and farms, is so dependent on Mexican labor that it isn't easy to see how it can possibly get its rough work done without the help of the peons."[103]

All six of the articles dealing with immigration in 1929 focused on the quota issue, on national origins as the basis for determining entry, and on the establishment of quotas for Canada and Mexico.

The most radical immigration proposal was one passed by the Senate early in 1929 that restricted incoming aliens to the same sort of people who made up our population in 1790. The major groups that would be positively affected by such a proposal were residents of Great Britain and Northern Ireland, but as the press was quick to point out, the British interest in emigrating to the United States had dwindled. In 1928 the British did not even come close to filling their quota of 34,000. The quota from Germany and the Scandinavian countries would be cut drastically. None of the press quoted in the *Literary Digest* supported the Senate's action. A follow-up story continued to denounce the national origins plan, with most of the newspapers attacking its proposed curtailment of German, Irish Free State, and Scandinavian immigration. However, on June 29, the *Literary Digest* reported that the Senate, in a special session, voted 43 to 37 for the national origins quota clause, over the strong objections of President Hoover. On this theme ended a decade that had seen more immigrants entering the United States than any preceding or subsequent decade.

The *Literary Digest* ceased publication in 1937. From 1930 until its last issue, it carried 17 stories about immigration. Like the other magazines surveyed, the dominant themes were the economic depression and the fear that alien labor would compete unfairly against U.S. workers for the few jobs that were available and the sharp drop in the number of immigrants coming to the United States.

Of the four stories that appeared in 1930, two concerned proposals and actions whereby the United States would close its doors to immigrants, especially those who were not economically self-sufficient. The *Literary Digest* reported a State Department decision not to provide passports unless applicants could convince authorities that they were unlikely to become public charges. The article reported that the *New York Journal of Commerce* was critical of State Department actions and claimed "we shall pay a very high price in ill-will for the privilege of excluding a few thousand individuals." To the *Chicago Daily News*, however, the ruling was "sensible and in no degree unfair to would-be immigrants of the desirable types."[104]

In an article titled "American Jobs for Americans," the *Literary Digest* reported the national coverage given to Senator Reed's proposal to suspend all quota immigration, plus the Philippine immigration, for two years. The senator was quoted as having said, "Every arriving alien who comes here to earn a living in times like the present either displaces someone now at work or becomes in some degree a public charge." According to the *Literary Digest*, editorial opinion around the country supported the senator's proposal. Slogans and statements like the following were the dominant tone: "Shut the gates to immigration and thus help solve the unemployment problem," or "Congress can make no more effective contribution to the solution of unemployment than by passing the Reed resolution."[105]

Of the other two pieces on immigration that appeared in 1930, one reported the amount of money immigrants remitted to relatives back home, and the other provided an account of the Chinese and Japanese press's outrage at the U.S. denial of entrance to 18 Japanese businessmen who had traveled first class from Japan but who were ordered shipped back to Japan by the U.S. government. The *Literary Digest* quoted from the *China Truth*:

> If a war should break out, which we do not wish to see, between Japan and America over the Exclusion Law, the Island Empire could undoubtedly count on the wholehearted support and cooperation of this Republic, for China is in the same boat as Japan.[106]

The four stories that appeared in 1931 dealt with the need to bar aliens from taking jobs away from U.S. workers, the dwindling number of immigrants coming to the United States, the presence of smuggling rackets specializing in illegal aliens, and the alien's eye for real estate. On the last topic, the *Literary Digest* summed matters up as follows: "The American who grows up next door to a thriving subdivision and never thinks of investing in the land should profit by the example of these strangers in our midst who so often see these opportunities first."[107]

The editorials quoted in the *Literary Digest* in response to Labor Secretary Doak's efforts to crack down on alien smuggling rackets were all praiseworthy. The *New York American* wrote that he was "performing a distinguished public service." The *Washington Post* wrote "The situation emphasizes the need for an alien registration law."[108]

No stories on immigration appeared in the *Literary Digest* in 1932. In 1933, two pieces focused on Japanese immigrants. The first reported, "Japan is rejoicing at the possibility that the next session Congress may repeal the Asiatic Exclusion Act."[109] The proposed quota for Japanese immigrants, should the law be lifted, would permit the yearly entrance of 185 Japanese and 105 Chinese. Minimum quotas of 100 would also be allowed to India, Afghanistan, Nepal, Siam, Bhuta, Hejaz, the Arabian Peninsula, and New Guinea. The second piece described Californian reaction to the proposed lifting of the ban as split.

> The two stories that appeared in 1934 noted that almost at the same time that the United States adopted national prohibition it also shut its door on immigration. The former event occurred in 1919, the latter in 1921. The fact that these two reversals of policy came so close together is not a mere coincidence. . . . They have a common source — namely, in the jealousy of the country toward the city, which in turn was largely the product of racial antipathy.[110]

The second piece also commented that from 1933 to 1934, immigration fell far below quota limits.

The one story on immigration that appeared in 1935 reported approvingly the efforts of the California council on Oriental relations to repeal the state's Japanese Exclusion Act.

The results of a study by anthropologist Franz Boas was reported in one of the two pieces on immigration in 1936. In 1930, the U.S. Senate had commissioned Boas to study "What effect the influx of foreign peoples has had on the country's future." The article reported that Boas began by measuring skulls and branched into a study of language, custom, and racial features. "Doctor Boas's studies," the article continued, "show that foreign born adults do not change appreciably while their children do. In generations of American life, racial origin often is entirely lost."[111]

A bill that would restrict the entrance of foreign performing artists seemed likely to pass the House of Representatives. The bill gained the support of leading U.S. artists and their organization, the American Guild of Concert Artists.

In one of its last issues, the *Literary Digest* carried a long piece on "Uncle Sam's Gate-Crashers: The Illegals." The message of the article is summarized below.

We have within our gates a vast and rather sinister army of aliens who, for reasons of their own, thought it best to avoid the officials posted at our port of entry. We are giving millions of them jobs. We are supporting millions more in charity. They will never become citizens and few could pass the requirements for naturalization. Many are mentally deficient — many more are sworn to overthrow democratic government.

Out of gratitude to a country which has welcomed them, is it too much to ask the properly qualified to register, in order that his fraudulent countrymen may be detected and sent home?[112]

NOTES

1. *Literary Digest*; May 17, 1890.
2. Ibid., August 12, 1890.
3. Ibid., August 23, 1890.
4. Ibid., November 29, 1890.
5. Ibid.
6. Ibid., January 10, 1891.
7. Ibid., March 7, 1891.
8. Ibid., June 6, 1891.
9. Ibid.
10. Ibid., August 29, 1891.
11. Ibid., January 30, 1892.
12. Ibid., March 26, 1892.
13. Ibid., April 5, 1892.
14. Ibid., April 16, 1892.
15. Ibid., April 22, 1892.
16. Ibid., March 5, 1892.
17. Ibid., May 7, 1892.
18. Ibid.
19. Ibid., August 27, 1892.
20. Ibid., September 10, 1892.
21. Ibid., September 17, 1892.
22. Ibid.
23. Ibid., December 7, 1891.
24. Ibid., May 27, 1893.
25. Ibid.
26. Ibid., July 15, 1893.
27. Ibid., February 25, 1893.
28. Ibid., August 5, 1893.
29. Ibid., October 28, 1893.
30. Ibid., January 27, 1894.
31. Ibid., September 28, 1895.
32. Ibid., January 18, 1896.
33. Ibid., June 6, 1896.
34. Ibid.
35. Ibid., March 13, 1896.
36. Ibid., August 21, 1897.
37. Ibid., November 10, 1900.

38. Ibid., July 27, 1901.
39. Ibid., November 30, 1902.
40. Ibid., August 8, 1903.
41. Ibid.
42. Ibid., June 1904.
43. Ibid., December 10, 1904.
44. Ibid., December 31, 1904.
45. Ibid., March 25, 1905.
46. Ibid., June 3, 1905.
47. Ibid., February 13, 1909.
48. Ibid., February 20, 1909.
49. Ibid., February 3, 1912.
50. Ibid., October 26, 1912.
51. Ibid., October 12, 1913.
52. Ibid., February 7, 1914.
53. Ibid., March 28, 1914.
54. Ibid., March 6, 1915.
55. Ibid., March 20, 1915.
56. Ibid., November 13, 1915.
57. Ibid., April 1, 1916.
58. Ibid., February 17, 1917.
59. Ibid., September 12, 1918.
60. Ibid., February 8, 1919.
61. Ibid., March 8, 1919.
62. Ibid., April 5, 1919.
63. Ibid., May 24, 1919.
64. Ibid., July 5, 1919.
65. Ibid., July 26, 1919.
66. Ibid., August 11, 1920.
67. Ibid., September 11, 1920.
68. Ibid., October 9, 1920.
69. Ibid., October 23, 1920.
70. Ibid., November 20, 1920.
71. Ibid., December 18, 1920.
72. Ibid., December 27, 1920.
73. Ibid., January 1921.
74. Ibid.
75. Ibid.
76. Ibid., May 7, 1921.
77. Ibid.
78. Ibid., May 28, 1921.
79. Ibid., April 22, 1922.
80. Ibid., September 9, 1922.
81. Ibid., November 18, 1922.
82. Ibid., May 5, 1923.
83. Ibid.
84. Ibid., February 23, 1924.
85. Ibid., February 2, 1924.
86. Ibid.
87. Ibid., April 12, 1924.
88. Ibid., June 7, 1924.
89. Ibid.
90. Ibid., July 5, 1924.
91. Ibid., October 18, 1924.

92. Ibid., April 11, 1925.
93. Ibid., October 10, 1925.
94. Ibid., August 27, 1927.
95. Ibid.
96. Ibid.
97. Ibid.
98. Ibid., January 21, 1928.
99. Ibid.
100. Ibid.
101. Ibid., July 14, 1928.
102. Ibid., December 22, 1924.
103. Ibid.
104. Ibid., October 4, 1930.
105. Ibid., December 13, 1930.
106. Ibid., November 8, 1930.
107. Ibid., June 6, 1931.
108. Ibid., September 26, 1931.
109. Ibid., September 2, 1933.
110. Ibid., February 24, 1934.
111. Ibid., May 9, 1936.
112. Ibid., December 11, 1937.

7

Harper's, Scribner's, Atlantic Monthly, and The Nation

Consider now *Harper's*, *Scribner's*, the *Atlantic Monthly*, and *The Nation*, each of which began publishing around the time of the Civil War and, except for one, has continued to publish to the present. From their foundings, each has been a magazine for the middle and upper middle classes who perceive themselves, and are viewed by others, as having taste, culture, manners, and interest in literature, national affairs, and social issues.

HARPER'S

The oldest of the four, *Harper's*, carried no articles on immigration in the 1880s. In March 1891 it carried the first of two articles to appear during the 1890s. "The Chinese Leak" described the manner in which Chinese aliens were smuggled into the United States from Canada, even though the Chinese Exclusion Act had been in effect for eight years.[1] In 1898 *Harper's* sent one of its writers, Kirk Munroe, to North Dakota to write a story about the Russian, Finnish, and Icelandic immigrants, covering their eating and sleeping habits, cleanliness, and friendliness. Munroe wrote in February's issue that he was sent by *Harper's* "to investigate if all the ugly things that were being said about these people were true." His impressions, however, were positive, and he concluded, "there is nothing to be feared, but everything to be hoped from such immigrants."[2]

The next decade (1900–1909) also contained two stories on immigrants. One was a first-person account of the scene at Leipzig railroad station as immigrants were beginning the first part of their journey to the United States; the second, "The Judgment of the Steerage," was also a first-person account, this time of the experiences of Italian immigrants aboard a transatlantic steerage class ship.[3]

During the decade of World War I, the number of *Harper's* articles on immigration increased from two to six. Five of the six, like the pieces that had appeared in previous years, were first-person accounts of immigrants' voyages to the United States. In four consecutive issues in 1917, *Harper's* printed flowery, romanticized accounts of the adjustments that poor immigrants from eastern Europe were making to big cities of the United States. The theme of these stories was that only from the humble immigrant can we learn just what the United States stands for in the family of nations.[4]

An exception to this genre was Walter Weyl's article, "New Americans." Weyl's piece examined how immigration had contributed to certain broad developments in the character and habits of the people of the United States. In comparing the United States of 1914 with the country it had been 50 years earlier, Weyl concluded, "the United States is far richer today, it is more stratified socially and economically, and it is more urban." He also reported a change in the social and moral emphasis of the society, which he attributed to the large immigrant population. He described the change as "an impulse based on social rather than individual ethics, unaesthetic, democratic, headstrong." He concluded with this message:

America's attraction is not to the good or to the bad, to the saint or to the sinner, but to the young, the aggressive, the restless, the ambitious. The Europeans in America are chosen men, for there is a rigorous selection at home and a rigorous selection here, the discouraged and the defeated return by the ship loads.[5]

The 1920s marked the appearance of the first and last anti-immigrant articles to appear in the pages of *Harper's*. Of the four articles the magazine carried in the 1920s, two were harshly critical of the immigrants themselves and of U.S. policy that permitted such large numbers to settle here. Grace L. Irwin, a schoolteacher, wrote of her experiences with immigrant children and their families. In "The Teacher and the Taught," she presented an ugly picture of the parents of immigrant children. She described them as ignorant, primitive, lacking in morality, and cruel to their children. She accused them of permitting, even encouraging, their children to drink. Irwin was sympathetic toward the children, but toward the parents she expressed contempt, anger, and disdain.[6]

In the other negative article, the noted geographer-writer Hendrik William Van Loon criticized those who had made it possible for large numbers of immigrants to come to the United States. He accused them of allowing "us Anglo-Saxons to be swamped beyond the saturation point by those who by nature of their inborn tendencies are hostile to our own civilization."[7]

Over the next 60 years, from 1930 to 1990, *Harper's* carried 12 articles about immigration: 2 in the 1930s, 2 in the 1940s, 3 in the

1950s, none in the 1960s and 1970s, and 5 in the 1980s. In 1931, Louis Adamic wrote a polemic against organizations such as the Ku Klux Klan, the Daughters of the American Revolution, and the Eugenics League and against government officials who were antialien.[8] Two pieces in the 1940s described why aliens made good citizens: they were less likely to commit crimes, they worked hard, they had a high rate of literacy, and they brought valuable professional and technical skills with them.[9]

Of the three articles about immigration in the 1950s, two concerned refugees and one described the impact of ethnic communities on the election. "The Perpetual Refugee" surveyed the number and locations of refugees worldwide. The author observed that like death and taxes, the world has always had refugees for political and economic reasons. In 1950 China had the greatest number, more than 50 million. The author of the article stated that India and Pakistan together had about 8 or 10 million, and Europe and the Middle East, about 13 million.[10]

The second piece on refugees condemned State Department officials for hamstringing the Refugee Relief Act of 1953 with restrictions and prohibitions that would make it impossible to really bring refugees to the United States. The article compared the number of refugees other countries admitted with the number admitted by the United States. Under the Displaced Persons Act, 400,000 were admitted to the United States between 1948 and 1952. Australia admitted 700,000; Argentina, 500,000; and Brazil, 200,000 in the same period. The Displaced Persons Act expired in 1952. The McCarran-Walter Act, which was passed later that year, made no provisions for refugees, and in *Harper's* opinion, "it was the most restrictionist piece of legislation ever enacted."[11]

Another aspect of immigration was treated in August 1951 in John J. Smertenko's review of the history of immigration to the United States and the reactions of Americans to each new group. The author claimed that "all immigrants, no matter how undesired upon their arrival, manage to assimilate into American culture and eventually become accepted." He argued, "Assimilation in the 1950s is being retarded by hyphenated organizations originally designed to help groups maintain their roots during their initial period of discrimination." Smertenko perceived these groups as dangerous to the cohesion and unity of U.S. society.[12]

Between 1955 and 1984, *Harper's* did not publish any pieces on immigration. In June and July 1984, it carried two articles. Each attacked a blacklist that *Harper's* reported had been maintained by the Reagan administration to deny visas to individuals seeking entry to the United States and to exclude U.S. citizens from obtaining government-sponsored speaking engagements abroad.[13] Both lists were maintained for ideological reasons, to keep "dangerous persons" out or in. The basis for the government's actions was the McCarran-Walter Immigration Act of 1952, which grants the government authority to deny visas on ideological grounds.

Three pieces in 1986, 1987, and 1988 focused on illegals mainly from El Salvador and Guatemala. *Harper's* took the position that immigrants from these countries should be granted refugee status on the grounds that they were fleeing politically oppressive regimes. David Quammen, author of the 1986 piece, advocated support for "Sanctuary," a movement backed by Catholic, Protestant, and Jewish congregations who were seeking to prevent Salvadoran and Guatemalan immigrants from being deported back home, "where they may face imprisonment, torture, and death."[14] The author argued that "political asylum is not granted to the majority of Salvadorans and Guatemalans who apply for it" because they come from the wrong kinds of countries. Quammen writes, "If you flee to the United States from a Soviet-backed regime in disfavor with Washington, your chances of being officially welcomed are much greater than if you flee from one of Washington's clients."

The 1988 piece had much the same theme, but it focused on a single case, that of a Salvadoran human-rights activist who was requesting political asylum in the United States. At the time the article appeared, the United States had denied her request on grounds that she had "Communist connections" and she was not at risk in El Salvador.[15] The story that appeared in 1987 also described illegal Hispanic immigrants mostly from El Salvador, Mexico, and the Caribbean Islands but focused on their economic status; *Harper's* favored amnesty for them on the grounds that they were good for the U.S. economy and for humanitarian reasons.[16]

SCRIBNER'S

From its founding as *Scribner's Magazine* in 1887 until its demise 55 years later in 1942, *Scribner's* carried 14 articles about immigration. With one exception, a pop-ethnographic account of a "Honkie family,"[17] all of the articles were anti-immigrant and prorestrictions. The first article in 1913 warned that "New York City was being taken over by Oriental-looking foreigners," who actually hailed from eastern and southern Europe. The author was talking about groups such as Italians, Jews, Poles, and Greeks, whom he characterized as energetic, ambitious, and crafty, warning that "unless Americans are careful, they will take over."[18]

During World War I, *Scribner's* prophesied that one of its aftermaths would be an "enormous number of immigrants who will want to come to the United States."[19] The article made dire predictions but contained no policy recommendations.

In 1917 *Scribner's* carried a long essay titled "Our Future Immigration Policy," which contained extensive statistics about the foreign born who live in major U.S. cities. It argued that the "new immigrants" from southern and eastern Europe were a burden "to our workers, our housing and our democracy." On the other hand, "the new immigrants," the article acknowledged, "create new markets and bring qualities of mind and temperament that may enrich the more severe and practical minds of those who belong to the race of Northern Europeans." In concluding, it recommended that after the World War, immigrants who were willing to settle farm land should be allowed to come to the United States.

The U.S. Government should open up idle land for use by settlers by providing easy credit terms. Those who are willing to move West and farm would be welcome; those who want to settle in the cities as their countrymen before them opted to do should not be admitted.[20]

Like many of the magazines in this survey, *Scribner's* hit its stride on the immigration issue in the 1920s. It ran nine articles in that decade, three of which were written by Vanderbilt University professor of economics Roy Garis, a favorite of the *Saturday Evening Post* and a strong advocate of quotas more restrictive than those passed by Congress in 1921 and 1924.

The major theme of a 1921 article titled "Some Biological Aspects of Immigration" was that "from the amalgamation of good races, good results may be expected; but fusion with inferior races will pull the higher ones down." The piece included some results from army mental tests administered during World War I. On the basis of these results, the writer predicted that "half of the U.S. population will never develop mentally beyond the stage represented by a normal twelve year old child, and only 13 million will ever show superior intelligence." In order to raise the mental level of society, the author concluded, "we must exclude immigrants because they [the new type] have low intelligence and a propensity for crime." The author acknowledged, "No race has a monopoly of good or bad qualities. All that can be said is that certain traits are more frequently found in one race than in another."[21]

Following passage of the Quota Act in 1921, *Scribner's* carried two articles that applauded the law's passage and assessed its consequences. The first answered affirmatively the question, "Has the Westward Tide of Peoples Come to an End?" The major consequences to U.S. society would be

The molding of an Anglo-Saxon-Germanic race, a shortage of servants, a vacuum in the labor field, a diminishment in the production of wealth, a rise in the standard of living of workers and the possibility of reverse immigration — some of those who are in the United States may decide to return home.[22]

Scribner's published a critical response to this piece that challenged the author's claim that anything positive had been gained by the admission of the "new types of immigrants" and expressed the wish that "we would close our doors completely and permanently." Ray Garis's piece in the same issue, titled "The Immigration Problem," estimated that passage of the Quota Act prevented between 1.75 million and 2 million immigrants from coming to the United States in 1922. Garis advocated more stringent and permanent restrictions on immigration and urged the adoption of 1890 rather than 1910 as the base year for estimating quotas, thereby guaranteeing the admission of fewer peoples from southern and eastern Europe.[23]

In September 1923 and February 1925, *Scribner's* carried two sentimental pieces, one on the hard and sad life of immigrant children, the other a Horatio Alger story about a Polish immigrant who arrived in 1907, worked his way through college, and became a captain in the U.S. army during the World War.[24]

In another article, "How the New Immigrant Law Works" (the Quota Act of 1924, also known as the Johnson-Reed Act), Professor Garis declared that the 1921 Quota Act had discriminated in favor of the immigrants. "The Southern and Eastern Europeans were entitled to 44.6 percent under the 1921 quota. Under the new act, they would be entitled to 14.9 percent." Commenting on the possibility of extending quotas to other non-European peoples, such as the Japanese, Garis wrote, "for America, the Japanese are non-assimilable people, as are all Asiatics. It is not that they are inferior; they are incompatible."[25]

Garis's third article took the form of a national appeal, rather than a scholarly essay. His message was "Keep America American" (a quote from President Calvin Coolidge) by maintaining national origins keyed to 1890 as the basis for allowing immigrants to enter the United States.[26]

Between 1928 and the time it ceased publication, *Scribner's* carried two pieces on immigration. In 1931 it ran the collective profile of the "Honkie" family mentioned earlier, and in 1941 it carried a warning by Jane Ellsworth that the war in Europe would produce a backlash on the United States. The author accused the European refugees of coming "not for any noble purpose of improving or building our country — but for sheer survival." Earlier peoples, the author noted, came voluntarily. "These refugees are desperate," and desperation made them, in Ellsworth's view, bad risks for the United States. She also warned that they were a threat to U.S. academia — they were already taking over jobs at U.S. universities. "As more come, they will displace not only American intellectuals, but artists, scientists and craftsmen," and all because they are desperate, she asserted.[27]

Scribner's shared many of its sentiments about immigrants with the *Atlantic Monthly*. The latter included articles on immigration earlier than *Scribner's* and carried many more of them during the period that *Scribner's* covered, but the anti-immigrant tone, the denigrating of southern and eastern Europeans, the view that Asians were beyond the pale, and the view that immigrants were dangerous for the moral, social, and economic fabric of U.S. society were shared by both magazines.

ATLANTIC MONTHLY

During the first 40 years of the survey, the *Atlantic Monthly* vied with the *Saturday Evening Post* for carrying the largest number of articles on immigration. The vast majority of the articles were negative in tone, detailing menaces they believed would result from immigrants in U.S. society, warning of the eroding force of immigrants on U.S. character and the U.S. work ethic. Of the five articles that appeared in the 1890s (there were none in the 1880s), four were negative in tone, advocating restrictions and describing the immigrant's inferior personal and social characteristics and warning of the dangers to U.S. life that they presented. In one piece, titled "European Peasants and Immigrants," immigrants were described as "genetically inferior — as inferior as American negroes." The European peasants, the author claimed, did not aspire for personal advancement but merely accepted their status without seeking a higher position or more power. He wrote,

> Our original population [Aryan] have never been slaves. Their stock has been but little pauperized by the army or the church or ground down by centuries of life in the conditions of a lower caste. Compare the origin and nurture of these free men with those of the ordinary laborer of Europe and we see at once the gravity of the danger which the mass of European immigrants brings to us. The American commonwealth could never have been founded if the first European colonist had been of peasant stock. It is doubtful whether it can be maintained if its preservation comes to depend upon such men.[28]

The next piece advocated the adoption of procedures that would discourage immigrants from coming by making the process of naturalization more complex and more difficult. It would require them to appear before a local official once a year in the company of two witnesses who must testify as to their good character and actual residence during the year. This procedure would be repeated annually for five years. The final ceremony would involve the presentation of additional documents and witnesses to attest to the candidate's character and motivation. Francis Walker, commissioner general of the immigration service and a regular contributor to the *Atlantic Monthly*, was consistently critical of immigrants, warning of dire consequences for U.S. society if they were permitted to enter without restrictions. He wrote,

> What is proposed is not to keep out some hundreds or possibly thousands of persons, against whom lie specific objections — but to exclude perhaps hundreds of thousands. . . . The question today is not of preventing the wards of our almshouses, our insane asylums, and our jails from being stuffed to repletion by new arrivals from Europe, but protecting the American rate of wages, the American standard of living, and the quality of American citizenship from degradation through the tumultuous access of vast throngs of ignorant and brutalized peasantry from the countries of Eastern and Southern Europe.[29]

Walker combined and compared the need for conservation of our natural resources with the necessity for restricting immigration. In his words,

> Today all intelligent men admit that the cutting down of our forests, the destruction of the trees covering our soil, has already gone too far; and both individual states and the nation have united in efforts to undo some of the mischief which has been wrought to our agriculture and to our climate from carrying too far the work of denudation. In precisely the same way it may be true that our fathers were right in their view of immigration, while yet the patriotic America of today may properly shrink in terror from the contemplation of the vast hordes of ignorant and brutalized peasantry thronging to our shores.

Warning of the dangers to the U.S. work ethic, Walker said,

> But when the country was flooded with ignorant unskilled foreigners, who could do nothing but the lowest kind of labor, Americans instinctively shrank from the contact and the competition thus offered to them. So long as manual labor, in whatever field, was to be done by all, each in his place, there was no revolt at it; but when working on railroads and canals became the sign of a want of education and of a low social

condition, our own people gave it up, and left it to those who were able to do that and nothing better.

Finally, he cautioned,

The entrance into our political, social and industrial life of such vast masses of peasantry, degraded below our utmost conceptions, is a matter which no intelligent patriot can look upon without the gravest apprehension and alarm. These people have no history behind them which is of a nature to encouragement. They have none of the inherited instincts and tendencies which made it comparatively easy to deal with the immigration of the older time. They are beaten men from beaten races; representing the worst failures in the struggle for existence. Centuries are against them, as centuries were on the side of those who formerly came to us. They have none of the ideas and aptitudes which fit men to take up readily and easily the problem of self care and self government, such as belong to those who are descended from the tribes that met under the oak-trees of old Germany to make laws and choose chieftains.

Their habits of life, again, are of the most revolting kind. Read the descriptions given by Mr. Riis of the police driving from the garbage dumps the miserable beings who try to burrow in those depths of unutterable filth and slime in order that they may eat and sleep there. Was it in cement like this that the foundations of our republic were laid? What effects must be produced upon our social standards and upon the ambitions and aspirations of our people by a contact so foul and loathsome? The influence upon the American rate of wages of a competition like this cannot fail to be injurious and even disastrous.

The preceding passages capture the essence, color, tone, and intensity of the anti-"new immigrant" movement, and Francis Walker was among its most articulate spokesmen. To the movement's supporters, these newcomers represented the lowest forms of human life; they would remain in their depraved, loathsome state forever, because they were biologically and genetically inferior; and they would wreak havoc on the U.S. economy, values, morals, and living standards if they were allowed to continue to pour into our country.

In the same year, 1896, the *Atlantic Monthly* carried two profiles of ethnic communities: "The Irish in American Life" and "The German American." Of the former, the *Atlantic Monthly* wrote,

The only hope for the Irish lies in the mingling of their blood with that of native Americans. Even those of them who move up, rise to the level of saloon keepers. When they enter politics, they leave honesty behind, perhaps because they have always thought of governments as oppressors. They pose a danger of changing and turning the United States away from its friendly, close ties to the English.[30]

The Germans fared better in the *Atlantic Monthly*. Their positive characteristics were seen by the author as outweighing their negative ones. On the positive side, the Germans were described as having high respect for law and authority and being intelligent, patient, industrious, honest, and healthy. On the negative side, they were characterized as boisterous, rough, petty minded, and men who viewed their wives as beasts of burden. In sum, however, the *Atlantic Monthly* wrote, "there is more good than bad, more positive gains than negative drawbacks" in having them migrate to the United States.[31]

The articles that appeared early in the *Atlantic Monthly*'s publishing history proved to be accurate forerunners of the position that the *Atlantic Monthly* would hold about immigrants up to the end of World War II.

In the first decade of the twentieth century, the *Atlantic Monthly* published five articles on immigration. In the first piece, the author expressed her gratitude to immigrants because by their mere presence they contributed to a growth of religious toleration "that our ancestors praised in theory, but in practice knew very little about." The author, Kate Claghorn, was optimistic about the immigrants' desire for betterment and upward social mobility. She saw in them the same desire for self-improvement, for bettering their conditions, that is part of the general human tendency. She also sounded a practical note when she pointed out that "even as individuals Americans do not like immigrants, nevertheless this is a half-worked country in need of a larger labor force; across the sea is a labor force in need of employment. It will be impossible to keep these apart."[32]

Five years later, in 1905, the *Atlantic Monthly* published an article titled "Immigration and the South," in which the author argued that the South was in need of and would welcome honest, industrious, intelligent, thrifty, and physically fit aliens.[33]

In September 1907 and February 1908, the magazine ran a two-part series on immigrant women that was generally sympathetic to them and critical of the host society for its treatment of them. Immigrant women, the articles reported, were more likely to be in the labor force than were U.S.-born women. Many of those who came alone were victimized by steamship companies, exploited by employers, and waylaid by sinister men who preyed on innocent, ignorant newcomers, the series claimed.[34]

The last piece of the decade, "Races in the United States," was a testimony to Anglo-Saxon civilization. This appeared as a description of the "Anglo-Saxon burden," which is to "nourish, uplift, and inspire all these immigrant people of Europe, that in the course of time, even if the Anglo-Saxon stock be physically inundated by the engulfing flood, the torch of its civilization and ideals may still continue to illuminate the way."[35]

During the decade of World War I, the *Atlantic Monthly* carried 16 articles on immigrants. Five of them, from December 1911 through April 1912, were excerpts from Mary Antin's book *The Promised Land*, an autobiographical account of her experiences as an immigrant Jewish child from Russia. In it, she described the anti-Semitism she encountered in Russia and the difficult but rewarding and thankful early years she spent in Boston becoming an American.[36]

During that same period, the *Atlantic Monthly* also carried three articles (May, September, and November) by economist W. Jett Lauck on immigrant laborers and their impact on U.S. wage earners. The first piece described the changing labor force of the cotton mill operatives in New England from English, Irish, Scottish, and German workers between 1840 and 1880 to the current labor force of Poles, Turks, Portuguese, Greeks, and Lithuanians. The immigrants brought radical changes to the working and living conditions of all the workers because they had a lower rate of literacy, they lacked any prior industrial experience, and they were poorer and therefore more willing to take any kind of job. They sent their children into the mills as soon as they were of legal age, and they hoped and expected to be able to return to their native land after a few years of hard work with enough money to take care of them.

Lauck's next piece, "A Real Myth — The American Wage Earner," described the disappearance of that role among native Americans.

> They have been displaced by the Southern and Eastern Europeans, almost all of whom have come to the United States in the past 25 years. They have been displaced because they are willing to work for much lower wages than are the American workers.

The article concluded by damning the liberal immigration policy of the United States, which made possible the competition of immigrant laborers with U.S. workers.

> This competition has gradually become more and more direct; and because of mechanical inventions has within recent years

penetrated to occupations which were formerly skilled and exclusively held by Americans. In other words, we have had protection to commodities but free labor. This labor has been without industrial experience, but it has been possible by the adoption of improved machinery in industrial establishments to use it to displace American labor. As a consequence, labor unions and other organizations for collective action among wage-earners have been disrupted, the bargaining power arising from skill for training has been destroyed, and the American wage earner has not been in a position either to maintain his status or to demand his share of the output of industry.[37]

The third piece, "The Vanishing American Wage Earner," reiterated the same theme. It blamed U.S. immigration policy for lower wages and for unsafe and unsanitary working conditions, and it denigrated the quality of the new immigrants' labor skills. It also accused the new immigrants of plotting to take the money they earned in the United States and returning to their home country. In the opinion of the article's author, the only way to change and improve the situation would be to alter U.S. immigration laws by restricting the number of immigrants and by limiting the countries from which they could come.[38]

The *Atlantic Monthly* returned to the fray in September 1915 with another attack on the new immigrants. This one exposed what were perceived as the negative traits immigrants brought with them; the hopelessness of the expectations that immigrants would assimilate and internalize U.S. (read "Anglo-Saxon") values, modes of behavior, standards of cleanliness, honesty, industriousness, and good manners; and the danger that they posed to the U.S. political system, labor force, and way of life. The author, Agnes Repplier, cited authorities such as sociologist E. A. Ross and President A. Lawrence Lowell of Harvard University to substantiate her observations and opinions. Quoting Professor Ross, she wrote,

> The immigrant seldom brings in his intellectual baggage anything of use to us, . . . the admission into our electorate of backward men — men whose mental, moral and physical standards are lower than our own — must inevitably retard our social progress and thrust us behind the more uniformly civilized nations of the world.[39]

She characterized Jews as cunning, deceitful, filthy, and clannish and the Italians as dangerous, contemptible, inferior, and disloyal. She accused Mary Antin of sentimentality and false optimism about the immigrants' qualities and capabilities. Repplier claimed that the

Germans' and Italians' loyalties would always remain with their homelands. "The Jew has no loyalty to any country," she wrote, and Magyar, Pole, and Greek "will always blight our cities, drive away decent neighbors and bring property down to his level and purse."

In the January 1916 issue, Frances Kellor responded to the Repplier article mostly by claiming that the United States had altered its treatment of immigrants from hospitality to exploitation and that the immigrants should not be blamed for the "wretched conditions" under which they lived. Kellor cited immigrant communities in which "the water supply was unhealthy, the sanitary conditions dangerous, the prices charged for housing exorbitant." She reported that in almost every state, foreign laborers were being restrained and that by the standards of legal evidence, they lived under conditions of peonage. She asked of the host society:

> Does America make the slightest effort to teach him [the immigrant] the difference between liberty and license? No. At the very port of entry he is robbed by the cabman and by the hotel runner, the expressman, the banker who exchanges his money, the steamship agent and the hotel keeper. His first lesson on property rights in America is often the loss of his own small possessions. He is held in bondage by the hotel keeper, who takes up his through railroad ticket and keeps it until he has secured a fair return on the board bill. The padrone gets him a job, and for the privilege of housing and feeding him at a price and under conditions about which the immigrant has nothing to say keeps him in a job. If he rebels, he is promptly blacklisted. The employment agent gets him into debt with a prospective employer and peonage results. In time of scarcity of labor, contingents of immigrant workmen have been made drunk, shut up in box cars, and landed in labor camps from which there is no return until spring.[40]

Given these experiences, Kellor argued that it should not be difficult to understand and, indeed, to sympathize with the immigrant who listened attentively to the organizers of the International Workers of the World (IWW) when they spoke to him in his own language and sought his support and his loyalty, especially when the U.S. labor unions ignored him. She also showed that the least illiterate element in the population was the native-born children of foreign-born parents and that the immigrants moved from the squalor and dirt of the lower east side of Manhattan to Fifth Avenue as soon as their income permitted. The article concluded by asking both sides, the host country and the immigrants, to blame themselves for the sins of omission and commission and to join together to weld a united, strong society.

Although the United States was not yet directly involved in the European war, public sentiment and official opinion were anti-German. Three pieces published in the *Atlantic Monthly* in 1916 reflected the growing anti-German sentiment. In "Our Divided Country," immigrants, especially Germans, were categorized as disloyal even after they became citizens. The author argued that during wartime, the more homogeneous the country, the stronger it was likely to be. He bemoaned the U.S. policy of granting easy citizenship to people who were bound to their homelands by ties of blood, language, religion, law, and sentiment. Were they not citizens, "we could in the hour of need expel them or confine them in concentration camps; but as citizens, until they commit some overt act of treason they are entitled to all the rights of the native-born."[41]

In "The Failure of German Americanism," the eminent theologian Reinhold Niebuhr wrote, "We have found to our sorrow that our melting pot has not been able to undo in a decade what the process of centuries has wrought on the hard metal of racial consciousness." As he saw it, German sympathy for blood relatives was overpowering. Neibuhr argued that the German-American was not loyal to the United States and had not made any spiritual contributions to our national life. In his words, "Their virtues are individualistic rather than social. They played no prominent role in our political struggles and have been indifferent to our social problem. Also — they are against prohibition."[42]

In "Kultur in American Politics," Frank Perry Olds accused the German-Americans of similar shortcomings and attacked them for urging the United States to remain neutral in the current European war.[43]

In the same year the *Atlantic Monthly* published a piece by Randolph Bourne, titled "Trans-National America," that contained a strong pro-pluralism message. Bourne enthusiastically quoted Mary Antin, who wrote, "our foreign born are people who missed the Mayflower and came over in the first boat they could find."[44] Unlike the other three pieces published in 1916, Bourne's claimed that the English were most suspect on the loyalty issue. In Bourne's view, they had held most tenaciously to their English ways. His major theme, however, was that there was no distinctively U.S. culture: "we have a federation of cultures." It is in the concept of federation that the author envisioned the future of the world, with the United States as its model.

At the end of World War I, the *Atlantic Monthly* ran an article advocating a ten-year ban on all immigration for economic purposes. According to the article, if the U.S. labor supply decreased and the need for labor increased or maintained itself, programs and policies would be developed to expedite the expansion of industrial training and would thus inspire the efficiency of the U.S. labor population.[45]

Unlike most of the magazines in the survey, the *Atlantic Monthly* did not noticeably increase its coverage of immigration in the 1920s. It carried 5 pieces between 1920 and 1929 in contrast to 16, 5, and 5 in the previous decades. The major article appeared in July 1924 in the form of a commendation to Congress for its passage of the 1924 Quota Act. In voting as it did, the *Atlantic Monthly* believed that Congress had voted for the practical exclusion of foreigners and the total exclusion of Asiatics from settlement in the United States.[46]

A similar message appeared in "The Unarmed Invasion," a piece that described the smuggling of undesirable aliens as usually taking place with the approval of European governments, who encouraged emigration for their own self-interest. The author endorsed the Quota Act of 1924, claiming that "it is the only means whereby we can conserve our racial character, our Anglo-Saxon culture and our political ideals."[47]

Between 1925 and 1953, there were no pieces on immigration in the *Atlantic Monthly*. This silence was broken in May 1953 with an article by Oscar Handlin, who in 1951 had received a Pulitzer Prize for *The Uprooted*, his historical treatment of immigrants and their adjustment to the United States. The title and message of Handlin's piece in the *Atlantic Monthly* was "We Need More Immigrants."[48] He attacked the recently passed McCarran-Walter Act because it kept in place the national origins quotas of the 1924 act "with all of [their] racist consequences" and because it allowed only 150,000 immigrants per year. Handlin wrote that he was proimmigrant because immigrants have always helped to raise the standards of native labor and because a liberal and fair policy on immigration helped the image of the United States in the world. "It strengthens our struggle against Communism . . . it is human and decent for people who live in fear of poverty and want to emigrate," he asserted. Handlin proposed that the United States admit 250,000 immigrants per year without regard to national origins quotas but with a proviso granting the president the power to lower the number when necessary. For example, in periods of high unemployment and depression, the president might use this power. When appropriate, a portion of that total should be allocated to refugees who seek political or religious asylum, Handlin wrote. Following publication of Handlin's article, the *Atlantic Monthly* published two letters that attacked the piece.

The September 1953 *Atlantic Monthly* contained an editorial against the McCarran-Walter Act and in favor of a proposal to admit 240,000 immigrants as refugees from behind the Iron Curtain.[49] Another Handlin piece appeared in the *Atlantic Monthly* in 1956; "Immigrants Who Go Back" was based on interviews the author had conducted in Europe.[50]

In 1967, Walter Mondale, then senator from Minnesota, contributed an article that described the brain drain the developing countries were suffering as a result of the flow of professional manpower from poor to rich countries.[51]

In April 1978, for the first time, the *Atlantic Monthly* ran a piece on Mexican illegals, titled, "Immigrants: Whose Huddled Masses?" The author, Elizabeth Midgley, a staff member of CBS News in Washington, estimated that there were 250,000 illegal aliens in Chicago of whom officials had no record or knowledge. She reported that even though illegal aliens paid taxes, they were afraid to call the police if they were in trouble. They were also afraid to apply for credit cards. She claimed that the groups most opposed to immigrants were the labor unions, the environmentalists, and advocates of zero population growth, while fruit and vegetable industrialists and restaurant and other service employers favored their admittance. The author warned that the problem of illegal immigration to the United States would not go away and that the United States must establish a more coherent policy.[52]

In the 1980s, three articles on immigration appeared. One piece, in 1981, was about 6,000 Cubans, part of the Mariel migration, who were held at an army base in Arkansas because they did not have sponsors in the United States and because many of them were thought to be mentally ill or criminals. The thrust of the piece was that many of them only wanted a chance "to fit into the quiltwork of American life."[53] The article claimed that

> One of the untold stories of the Cuban refugee phenomenon was that many were rejected by their own families in the United States, not because they were dangerous but because they were vivid reminders of recent deprivation and threatened their sponsors with the loss of painfully acquired status.

A 1984 piece by Al Santoli, author of "Everything We Had: An Oral History War," described the plight of Vietnamese boat people who "face robbery, abduction, and rape at the hands of Thai pirates."[54] The article placed much of the blame on the United States because of a recent change in policy that lowered refugee quotas and made it increasingly difficult for the boat people to enter this country. Santoli reported that the U.S. Immigration and Naturalization Service disqualified thousands of potential refugees in Thailand by giving them "seemingly arbitrary classification like economic migrant." (The State Department discouraged acceptance of refugees who did not have immediate family members in the United States.)

The third piece, in 1987, attacked U.S. failure to grant refugee status to Salvadorans. It stated, "The point is that there are ongoing human-right violations in Central America, including classical persecutions that people are subjected to. Some of these people are entitled to political asylum if they manage to make their way here."[55]

The author argued that the 1980 Refugee Act was being implemented "in a manner that reflects American foreign policy."

The 1980s thus witnessed consistent support by the *Atlantic Monthly* for the admission of refugees to the United States and disapproval of policies that delayed or ignored requests for admission by country of origin.

THE NATION

The Nation is the most consistently proimmigration magazine in the survey and the one in which the earliest stories on immigration were found. In the 1880s, *The Nation* carried three articles on immigration, each one opposing restrictions.[56]

In "The Paupers and the Immigration Law," it discussed and challenged the requirements of a bond imposed by several states on the steamship companies.[57] This bond was a guarantee that the immigrants they brought would not become public charges within a certain term of years. In this manner, legislators had hoped to enjoin steamship companies in their quest for quality control of immigrants to be admitted. The law was declared unconstitutional by the Supreme Court. In August 1887 the magazine attacked the Virginia Democratic party platform, which urged Congress to pass a law that would prevent foreign pauper labor into the country. The article claimed that such a position was worse than the Know-Nothingism of 30 years before. The magazine also opposed a proposal for prolonging the period of naturalization for anarchists and other aliens who were political agitators of one sort or another.[58]

In "The New Immigration," *The Nation* provided a detailed, statistical analysis of the countries from which immigrants originated and who had come prior to and after 1868. It included statistics on types of skills the immigrants brought as well as their age and sex distributions.[59]

In 1893 there was a worldwide cholera epidemic. Congress was debating a proposal to suspend all immigration until the disease scare was over. *The Nation* opposed the measure on the grounds that disinfection could handle the problem. Given space to locate infected people and money to buy their necessary medication, the problem could be solved. "The difficulties are not greater," the article argued, "than the maintenance of the health of a regiment of recruits."[60]

In March 1896 it attacked Senator Henry Cabot Lodge's position for instituting a literacy requirement for prospective immigrants, and in 1899 it applauded President Grover Cleveland for his veto of a bill mandating literacy test for immigrants, which Senator Lodge and his colleagues had passed in Congress.[61]

Commenting on a reported cut in steamship rates from $25 to $10 a head between England, Scotland, and New York, *The Nation* sought to quiet the fears of those who expected such a reduction to induce a "large influx of undesirable aliens." The article claimed that "our laws are adequate to protect against such an eventuality." Specifically, it referred to a law that excluded idiots, epileptics, the insane, and those suffering from loathsome or contagious diseases. It referred also to a recently passed act that had forbade steamship companies from advertising "except in the most perfunctory way," subjected them to a fine of $1,000 for every illegal immigrant they attempted to land, and made them cover the maintenance and transportation costs of all those whom they brought in against the law.[62]

Between 1905 and 1907, *The Nation* ran three pieces on immigrants and the South. The first two called for more immigrants to settle in the South, where the opportunities for the development of agricultural and mineral resources were boundless. Such a migration would be "good for the Negro, too," one of the articles reasoned, because he would work side by side with earnest, steady workmen who would serve as a model for him.[63] However, in order to attract large numbers of immigrants, the South would have to improve its image: "Each lapse of justice and unpunished mob rule will keep thousands of people from coming to work the land," it charged.[64] Its third piece was an exposé by an assistant attorney general who claimed that in some parts of the South, Italian immigrants were kept in conditions that bordered on peonage. The article commented that in some places the "dagoes" were regarded as about on par with "niggers" and treated accordingly.[65]

The Nation questioned President Theodore Roosevelt for first seeming to support the right of Japanese to become citizens and then doing an about-face to oppose that right. The editorial attacked the president for supporting a treaty that would exclude Japanese laborers.[66]

"The Tide of Migration," in August 1908, showed that for the fiscal year ending June 30, 1908, the number of people leaving the United States would exceed those coming in by 200,000. The article went on to explain that with decreasing birth rates among the native-born population, "we may yet find in these strong stocks of the Old World, a very real element of our national strength."[67]

The 17 stories on immigration that *The Nation* ran between 1910 and 1920 were the largest number for any decade in its history. Two letters by history professor Henry Fairchild appeared in *The Nation* in 1911. The first charged that a story on the final page of the *New York Evening Journal* about brutality toward immigrants at Ellis Island was false.[68] The second charged that the riotous demonstrations in which the "new type of immigrants" participated and that resulted in the breaking up of a peace meeting at Carnegie Hall demonstrated that their loyalty was not to the United States but to their home countries. The professor claimed that

Unlike the old stock of immigrants [German, the Irish, and the Scandinavian], all of whom have inherited for generations back, sentiments, principles and habits of mind similar to the early settlers of this country, the new stock do not share the same values and thus the solidarity of our country is placed in a precarious position.

The letter ended with a warning to the new immigrants:

If these adopted elements of our population wish to win and keep the sympathy of the American people as a whole, they will wisely refrain from exhibiting, publicly at least, views and opinions based on any other allegiance than that of an American citizen.[69]

In "Metaphysical Standard of Living," *The Nation* asserted that U.S. workers had risen to positions of foremen and directors of foreign laborers. "They have not suffered as a result of foreign competition. Indeed, the presence of immigrant laborers probably raised rather than hurt the position of the American workers." A letter to the editor published two weeks later disagreed and argued that a scarcity of laborers would improve the U.S. workers' standard of living and that immigration ought to be restricted.[70]

An early move to pass a national origins quota act was reported in *The Nation* in 1913, when Senator William Dillingham of Vermont introduced a bill that would have limited the immigration of any one nationality in a given year to no more than 10 percent of the total number of residents of that particular nationality in the United States. Having failed on at least four occasions to pass a bill requiring a literacy test for immigrants, Dillingham dropped that section from the current bill. The bill, which was much more liberal than the Johnson Act, which would be passed eight years later, did not get through Congress.[71]

Horace Kallen wrote a two-part article for *The Nation* in 1915 in which he attacked and responded to sociologist E. A. Ross's new book, *The Old World in the New*. Ross considered the new immigrants as inferior peoples and a danger to the U.S. way of life. Kallen went to the heart of the matter when he wrote, "Hence what troubles Mr. Ross and so many other Anglo-Saxon Americans is not really inequality; what troubles them is *difference*."[72] "The Exclusionist Spirit," the second part of the Kallen article, deplored the fact that during the entire debate on the Dillingham Bill that had just passed the Senate, the "exclusionist spirit" was assertive and triumphant. It also reported that an amendment had been adopted that excluded persons of the black or African race. The article commented, "No one not obsessed with the exclusionist spirit could possibly believe that the United States needed any safeguards against the immigration of colored men. They have come in such small numbers." In the end, the author urged the president to veto the bill if it passed the House.[73]

In November 1914, *The Nation* reported with approval that the U.S. Supreme Court had declared unconstitutional an Arizona law that forbade private employers from having more than 20 percent aliens among their employees.

During World War I, *The Nation* urged its government to do away with the Chinese and Japanese Exclusion Act or Agreement on grounds that it was wrong and was against U.S. self-interests. "From a business point of view," the author argued, "We should want to cultivate friendly relations with China and Japan. They are potentially, very big markets."[74]

The Nation's major immigration article of the decade appeared on February 8, 1919. It was a strong attack on an immigration bill that had just passed the House that would practically suspend immigration into the United States for the next four years. As for what it considered an enlightened immigration policy, *The Nation* stated "with the obvious exception of criminals, defectives, paupers, and other such types, immigration should be free for all who wish to come whether they work with their hands or with their minds." The article condemned the House bill as "thoroughly vicious." It argued that a prohibition on immigration would not add to the well-being of the wage earner or the employer; it would, at best, "only give to the laborers a little more chance to go on working under conditions which he increasingly denounces as intolerable." For the employer, it would provide a little less opportunity to exploit the immigrant, the article stated.[75]

The Nation returned to its attack of U.S. policy toward the Chinese and Japanese in a piece about a recently passed California law that forbade Japanese and Chinese from owning land in that state.[76]

The 1920s was a decade of restrictionism and isolationism. When World War I was over, the United States opted not to join the League of Nations, and later in the decade, Congress passed two major quota bills. *The Nation* thought both actions wrong and against the best interests of the United States. It also continued to berate California in particular, and the United States in general, for its policy vis-à-vis the Chinese and Japanese. It carried another story on the California law that did not permit Japanese to own or lease land in the state. The item pointed out that there were 87,279 Japanese in the state with a population of 3,200,000. The Japanese cultivated 278,000 acres of a total of 18,000,000.[77]

The following month, the magazine warned again of the large numbers of people who were leaving the United States and the relatively small numbers who were arriving.[78] In 1921 it reported the results of a referendum that had been held in California. The referendum passed, and as a result, Japanese parents would no longer have legal guardianship over the property rights of their children who had been born in the United States. The California secretary of state had pushed for such a referendum because the Japanese in the state had been successfully evading the law that prohibited them from holding property by vesting the title to their land in their U.S.-born minor children who were citizens. The article emphasized the negative impact of the referendum on Japanese-American relations.[79]

The same issue contained a piece that spelled out *The Nation*'s position on immigration policy. In essence, it advocated the adoption of a policy that would be free of all racial discrimination and that would admit as many people annually as the United States could incorporate "into its body politic and its economic life."[80]

The Nation linked anti-Semitism and immigration policy in an article charging that U.S. consuls in Warsaw and Rumania were withholding visas from Jewish applicants on the grounds that they were "a class of economic parasites, tailors, small business men and butchers" and that they were not "productive laborers."[81]

In October 1922 and again in May 1923, two articles appeared warning of the dangers of too few immigrants and of the prospect of a shortage of manpower. Both articles included statistics that showed that more "able-bodied men" were leaving than were entering the United States. The articles warned against the upsurge in a 100 percent Americanism campaign that was developing, increasing anti-Semitism, and the anti-immigrant activity of U.S. labor unions.[82]

It pursued the same themes in an article titled "Land of the Noble Free." Relying largely on data supplied by Congressman Meyer Jacobstein of Rochester, New York, it showed that the percentage of foreigners in the United States was exactly the same as it was in Lincoln's time. In New York City, the percentage was lower: 36 percent of New York's residents were foreign-born compared with 47 percent in 1860. The article included a table comparing the yearly immigration quotas allowed under the 1921 Quota Act compared with the pending Johnson-Reed Quota Bill, which would virtually exclude eastern Europeans.[83]

In a piece critical of the use of the intelligence test on army recruits, anthropologist Melvile Herskovitz analyzed the results reported by army psychologists. He claimed that the crucial factor in explaining the distribution of scores was length of time in the United States, not country of origin. He also argued that the tests were culturally biased in favor of Anglo-Saxons.[84]

The final piece of the decade was an editorial urging a shift in the national origins quotas that would reduce the immigration from Germany, Norway, and Sweden and increase it from southern and eastern Europe.[85]

In 1930 the Mexicans became the subject of interest for *The Nation.* In an article entitled "Mexico and the Harris Bill," it reported anger felt by the Mexicans because the bill would restrict Mexican immigration but not Latin American immigration. The author compared the U.S. treatment of the Japanese with the way legislators were proposing to treat the Mexicans. He added that such legislation treated Mexicans and Japanese as if they were inferior or undesirable.[86]

Of the five stories on immigrants that *The Nation* carried in the 1930s, three reported U.S. violation of aliens' civil liberties. Two appealed for admission of refugees, especially children, from Nazi Germany.[87]

Portraying the plight of refugees was *The Nation*'s immigration theme of the 1940s. It was particularly critical of the State Department for using what *The Nation* viewed as obstructionist tactics in admitting political refugees. The article insisted that fewer than 200,000 immigrants were refugees. It also asserted that the refugees from Nazi Germany were rich in human capital and could make important positive contributions to U.S. society.[88]

In a piece entitled "Nazifying Our Law," *The Nation* claimed that the Hobbs Bill represented another step in the campaign to make the United States as unpleasant a place as possible for aliens, to discourage immigration, and to use limitations on the rights of aliens as an "entering wedge" for restricting the rights of citizens. It foresaw the creation of detention camps for persons who were unable to obtain travel documents to foreign countries.[89]

After World War II, *The Nation* carried two stories that strongly supported admission of displaced persons. In June 1947 it urged passage of the Stratton Bill, which would have admitted 400,000 refugees over a four-year period.[90] An August 1949 editorial praised members of the Senate who were attempting to remove the Displaced Persons Bill from the judiciary committee headed by Senator Pat McCarran. The editorial attacked Senator McCarran, claiming that he was acting against the desires of his own committee, the president, and the Senate. It charged McCarran with keeping thousands of people in displaced persons' camps for more than four years after the war had ended and with sabotaging efforts to raise the total number of displaced persons to be admitted to the United States from 205,000 to 339,000.[91]

The Nation devoted more space to the McCarran-Walter Bill than any of the other magazines surveyed. Through articles and editorials, it praised efforts to defeat passage of the bill, it attacked the provisions and overall objectives of the bill, and it called upon Congress, the president, and the country to repudiate it. All 14 pieces on immigration that it carried in the 1950s referred to the McCarran-Walter Bill by warning against its passage, spelling out the negative consequences that would ensue, and (after it was passed) showing the harm it had perpetuated.

The first piece appeared in the form of an editorial, "To the Credit of the 81st Congress," that praised Congress for expanding the inadequate and discriminatory Displaced Persons Bill of 1948. The editorial interpreted the substitute Kilgore Bill as a rebuke to Senator McCarran, who had, it claimed, fought tenaciously against any liberalization. Specifically, the Kilgore Bill would admit 139,000 more refugees, provide refuge for 20,000 orphans rather than the 5,000 previously allowed, and give congressional approval to the establishment of a displaced persons' commission.[92]

The next piece was an editorial titled "Ministry of Fear," which described the McCarran-Walter Bill (still being debated) as "obnoxious, dangerous, un-American, formidably exclusive, cruelly suspicious, and offensively arrogant." The editorial accused McCarran and his supporters of using quotas to retain "the archaic and baseless ideas that some races are superior to others." The editorial concluded by urging readers to write to middle-of-the-road representatives who were against the bill but who had not pressured McCarran and his supporters into permitting liberal amendments.[93]

Alex Brooks, a lawyer active in civil rights, compared the Lehman Bill with the McCarran-Walter Bill. The former would eliminate racial discrimination, update the quota system by using the 1950 census as the base, and permit the pooling of quotas to allow for unused quotas. Brooks attacked the McCarran-Walter Bill for its retention of the 1920 census figures, its low quotas for Japanese, and its discrimination against blacks.[94]

The same issue of the magazine also carried an editorial that urged its readers to write to their congressmen, asking them to vote for remittal of the McCarran-Walter Bill. Before the year was out, there were four more editorials in *The Nation* opposing the McCarran-Walter Bill.

The Nation's lead editorial in its first issue of 1953 discussed the negative effects of the recently passed McCarran-Walter Act on the attitudes and policies of foreign countries toward the United States. The editorial suggested that unless Eisenhower took steps to have the act revised, European governments might take actions of their own. "America," it concluded, "is already the hardest Western nation to enter," and rigorous enforcement of the act would make it a "forbidden land."[95]

Later in the month it carried a piece by Maurice Visscher, professor of physiology at the University of Minnesota, who accused

McCarran and his supporters of subjecting the nation to intellectual slavery. Visscher stated that "McCarran and others like him are paranoid in their unfounded fear of the unknown or the different. It is the duty of scientific organizations to educate people about the truth."[96]

Reviews of two books, *Civil Rights in Immigration* by Milton Konvitz and *The Golden Door: The Irony of Our Immigration Policy* by J. Campbell Bruce, provided another opportunity to attack the McCarran-Walter Bill. The reviewer was David Fellman, a political scientist at the University of Wisconsin. Fellman concluded that the bill was a badly crafted statute.[97]

The last piece of the decade on the McCarran-Walter Act, by J. Campbell Bruce, described the problems that the law was causing for foreign scientists who were refused visitors' visas to the United States. He claimed that over half who applied had been denied, for reasons known only to the consul denying the admission, with no appeal possible, and pointed out that as a result, many scientific organizations were holding their meetings in other countries. Moreover, the Soviet Union was admitting visitors who had been refused entry to the United States.[98]

Only two stories on immigrants appeared in *The Nation* in the 1960s. One dealt with the brain drain problem. The article carried statistics on the number of scientists, engineers, and physicians who had immigrated to the United States from less-developed countries. For example, it quoted data from the National Science Foundation that showed that between 1952 and 1961, more than 30,000 engineers and 14,000 physicists had come to the United States.[99]

The other piece, titled "Wetbacks, Growers and Poverty," described the illegal Mexicans as poor men who were trying to get ahead.[100] The measures that were suggested for solving the problems, such as having immigrants carry identification cards, proceeding with formal deportations, and imposing fines on employers of illegals, were not likely to be effective, according to the writer.

Mexican immigration monopolized all discussion of immigrants in *The Nation* in the 1970s. The magazine opposed attempts by Congress to sanction employers who knowingly hired illegals; it deplored conditions under which illegals were carted across the border into California; it applauded the change in the International Ladies Garment Workers Union policy for the illegal workers in California. A piece titled "The Earnings Gap" cited economist Barry Chiswick's data showing that on the average, immigrants required approximately 13 years to catch up in earning power with U.S.-born Americans of comparative age, schooling, and years of residence.[101] After that, immigrants earn more than natives largely because of the selective factors at work in migration, that is, migrants tend to be young, ambitious, energetic, and highly motivated. However, according to Chiswick, Mexicans were an exception to this pattern. Controlling for years of schooling, age, and other factors, Chiswick reported that immigrants born in Mexico initially averaged 33 percent lower wages than U.S.-born white males and that it took 15 years before their incomes matched those of persons with Spanish surnames who were born in the United States and who subsisted at levels substantially below those of the average. The major thrust of the article was that the lag in earnings for Mexican immigrants represented an enormous subsidy to U.S. employers, the more so because Mexican immigrants also included illegal immigrants, for whom the 33 percent initial gap and the 15-year cycle kept repeating.

The Nation's last piece in the 1970s, "Unmeltable Immigrants," reviewed the work extending over 30 years of Carey McWilliams, a former editor of The Nation, on how the United States ill-treated the Chinese, the Japanese, and most recently, the Mexican immigrant.[102]

The Nation included more articles on immigration in the 1980s (20) than it had in any previous decade of its publishing history. Sixteen of the 20 pieces attacked U.S. policy vis-à-vis immigrants from Central America and the Caribbean, especially Haiti, and praised the efforts of the Sanctuary Movement to help Hispanic, Haitian, and other immigrants from the Americas find safety in the United States. The following provides a sample of the tone and content of The Nation's coverage: "No area of government action defines the character and destiny of our nation, who and what we are, more directly than our handling of immigration."[103] That is the opening sentence of an article by sociologist Geoffrey Fox that appeared in September 1981. The author continued,

> Overall, then, the Reagan program legalizes employer access to a vast pool of low-wage workers with no accompanying dependents and almost no rights; rather like the system in South Africa. For the tens of thousands of Salvadorans and Guatemalan fugitives from state terrorism who are now in Los Angeles, New York, and other U.S. cities, the right to asylum is of little use. When the Immigration and Naturalization Services apprehends them, it generally discourages them from applying for asylum.

In December 1981, an article entitled "Refugee Gulogs" stated,

> Since the internment of Japanese-Americans during World War II, there have been few episodes in American History as disgraceful as the treatment of the Cuban and Haitian "boat people." Although no charges have been brought against them, more than 4000 of these refugees are currently in American prisons.[104]

Referring to the imprisonment of 49 Haitians by the U.S. government, a 1982 article by a staff attorney for the American Civil Liberties Union stated,

There is no sinister reason why the Brooklyn 49 were not included in the release order. By reviewing the evidence, Federal District Court Judge Robert Carter concluded that the Haitians had been locked up by the I.N.S. "because they were black and/or because they were Haitian." In support of that finding, Judge Carter noted that non-Haitians who applied for political asylum in New York were routinely released, while Haitians who applied for political asylum were routinely detained. It is difficult to characterize the government's decision as anything but punitive and vindictive. It is certainly not supported by public policy considerations. In the words of a third Federal Judge who reviewed the government's Haitian program, "INS officials have acted as haphazardly as the rolling seas that brought these boat people to this great country's shores."[105]

More on the Haitians appeared in 1985:

Of all the horrors visited on poor black Hispanic or Asian refugees seeking shelter in the United States, none are as egregious, gratuitous and well documented as those inflicted on the survivors of Haitian tyranny. Denied the comfort — cold enough, it's true — given immigrants from countries where U.S.-backed regimes have been overthrown, the Haitians must enter the United States illegally, often arriving at great peril, in small boats on the Florida Coast, where they are treated as pariahs by immigration officials. Many Haitians are sent to desolate detention camps in the barren quarters of Texas or along the frigid Canadian border in upstate New York. There they find no interpreters, no lawyers, no funds.[106]

Still more on the unfair, inhumane treatment given to Haitian and Central American immigrants and support for the Sanctuary Movement appeared in an editorial published in November 1985:

When a Rumanian sailor jumps ship in Florida, the government gives him a hero's welcome as the day's defector from Communist tyranny. When a Ukraine teen-ager would rather stay with relatives in Illinois than accompany his parents home, the U.S. authorities grant him resident refugee status. . . . No such welcome attends the arrival of thousands of victims of oppression in Central America who make their way to el Norte only to find sanctuary denied. They are not even afforded semantic haven as defectors, refugees, or emigres; the government calls them illegal aliens and charges those who help them with smuggling and "criminal enterprise." In the savage logic of Administration immigration policy, they have no human right because they come from the wrong side of the ideological tracks: America's imperial client states to the south. The Sanctuary movement has its power to organize both conscience and consciousness beyond the government's determination to destroy it. The Administration may think it can stop the "underground railroad" in an Arizona courtroom, but it will find that it is using a lot of heavy machinery on what is essentially a sidetrack.[107]

Two months later, another editorial described Sanctuary:

The church led Sanctuary campaign has been the most important form of protest against the U.S. government's intervention in Central America. The Administration refuses to recognize the aliens as political refugees and maintains that they are merely fleeing the poverty of their land to enjoy the riches of El Norte. The moral witness of the sanctuary activists is unassailable in its own terms, and the Administration has been forced to use vulgar police tactics and hypercritical legal maneuvers to oppose it.[108]

More on Sanctuary appeared in April 1986:

The six month sanctuary trial has been marked by the most bitter ideological arguments heard in a U.S. courtroom since the tumultuous proceedings of the late 1960's. Lawyers for the clergy and lay activists have likened the defendants to Abolitionists who gave refuge to runaway slaves on the Underground Railroad before the Civil War; and to Christians who aided Jews escape the Gestapo. The prosecution sees the accused as racketeers and subversives engaged in a conspiracy to smuggle aliens who want to enter the country only for the well-known economic benefits of life in the Hispanic barrios of the Southwest.[109]

Other themes of *The Nation*'s coverage of immigration in the 1980s included attacks on the Simpson-Mazzoli Bill along the following lines:

Every thirty years or so, the United States undergoes a xenophobic convulsion in the name of "immigration." The Simpson

Mazzoli Immigration Reform and Control Act, now before the House is a product of the latest such spasm. Allegedly to preserve the cultural integrity of this nation of immigrants from the consequences of a brown, black, and yellow invasion, Senator Simpson and Representative Romano Mazzoli of Kentucky introduced a bill that would tighten controls on immigration in a way calculated to encourage discriminatory practices and union busting of U.S. companies.[110]

The following week, *The Nation* carried an editorial that characterized the Simpson-Mazzoli Bill as legitimizing "an approach to immigration that has its roots in racism and xenophobia." After the Immigration Reforms and Control Act of 1986 passed, *The Nation* stated the law would have "a direct discriminatory effect on minority persons seeking employment."[111] The law, it claimed, would have the effect of pitting the foreign born against the native born and make immigrants the scapegoat for economic problems. "Hispanics are currently playing a role in the American social imagination that was filled in turn by the Irish, Italians, Chinese, and Slavs."

The Nation has remained consistent for the 110 years we have followed it: immigrants are good for this country, and they should be welcomed and appreciated.

NOTES

1. *Harper's*, March 1891.
2. Ibid., February 1898.
3. Ibid., September 1908.
4. Ibid., July 14, 1914; September 14, 1914; March 17, 1917; April 17, 1917; May 17, 1917; June 17, 1917.
5. Ibid., September 14, 1914.
6. Ibid., March 22, 1922.
7. Ibid., November 25, 1925.
8. Ibid., November 1934.
9. Ibid., September 1940; January 1943.
10. Ibid., July 1950.
11. Ibid., April 1955.
12. Ibid., August 1951.
13. Ibid., June 1984; July 1984.
14. Ibid., December 1986.
15. Ibid., July 1988.
16. Ibid., August 1987.
17. *Scribner's*, February 1931.
18. Ibid., April 1913.
19. Ibid., November 1915.
20. Ibid., May 1917.
21. Ibid., March 1921.
22. Ibid., September 1922.
23. Ibid., August 1924.

24. Ibid., September 1923; February 1925.
25. Ibid., March 1925.
26. Ibid., January 1928.
27. Ibid., June 1941.
28. *Atlantic Monthly*, May 1893.
29. Ibid., June 1896.
30. Ibid., March 1896.
31. Ibid., November 1896.
32. Ibid., October 1900.
33. Ibid., November 1905.
34. Ibid., September 1907; February 1908.
35. Ibid., December 1908.
36. Ibid., December 1911.
37. Ibid., September 1912.
38. Ibid., November 1912.
39. Ibid., September 1915.
40. Ibid., January 1916.
41. Ibid., February 1916.
42. Ibid., July 1916.
43. Ibid., September 1916.
44. Ibid., July 1916.
45. Ibid., April 1919.
46. Ibid., July 1924.
47. Ibid., January 1925.
48. Ibid., May 1953.
49. Ibid., September 1956.
50. Ibid., April 1956.
51. Ibid., December 1967.
52. Ibid., April 1978.
53. Ibid., February 1981.
54. Ibid., February 1984.
55. Ibid., February 1987.
56. *The Nation*, July 5, 1883; August 11, 1887; December 29, 1887.
57. Ibid., July 5, 1883.
58. Ibid., August 11, 1887.
59. Ibid., September 17, 1891.
60. Ibid., July 19, 1893.
61. Ibid., March 26, 1896; October 19, 1899.
62. Ibid., July 16, 1904.
63. Ibid., May 17, 1905.
64. Ibid., May 17, 1906.
65. Ibid., December 19, 1907.
66. Ibid., February 21, 1907.
67. Ibid., August 14, 1908.
68. Ibid., June 8, 1911.
69. Ibid., July 6, 1911.
70. Ibid., November 7, 1912; November 21, 1912.
71. Ibid., June 5, 1913.
72. Ibid., February 18, 1915.
73. Ibid., June 15, 1915.
74. Ibid., March 28, 1918.
75. Ibid., February 8, 1919.
76. Ibid., April 12, 1919.
77. Ibid., August 7, 1920.

78. Ibid., September 18, 1920.

79. Ibid., February 2, 1921.

80. Ibid.

81. Ibid., June 22, 1921.

82. Ibid., October 18, 1922; May 23, 1923.

83. Ibid., April 23, 1924.

84. Ibid., February 11, 1925.

85. Ibid., April 3, 1929.

86. Ibid., July 9, 1930.

87. Ibid., December 30, 1931; January 13, 1932; April 10, 1935; December 18, 1935; July 1, 1939.

88. Ibid., August 2, 1941.

89. Ibid., September 6, 1941.

90. Ibid., June 14, 1947.

91. Ibid., August 20, 1949.

92. Ibid., April 15, 1950.

93. Ibid., March 29, 1952.

94. Ibid.

95. Ibid., January 3, 1953.

96. Ibid., January 24, 1953.

97. Ibid., April 10, 1954.

98. Ibid., November 26, 1955.

99. Ibid., April 3, 1967.

100. Ibid., October 10, 1969.

101. Ibid., May 14, 1975.

102. Ibid., December 22, 1979.

103. Ibid., September 5, 1981.

104. Ibid., December 12, 1981.

105. Ibid., September 25, 1982.

106. Ibid., April 6, 1985.

107. Ibid., November 30, 1985.

108. Ibid., January 25, 1986.

109. Ibid., April 19, 1986.

110. Ibid., August 21, 1989.

111. Ibid., August 28, 1989.

8

Christian Century, Commentary, and Commonweal

CHRISTIAN CENTURY

The *Christian Century* is a window into U.S. Protestant views and positions, just as *Commentary* provides insight into aspects of U.S. Jewish opinion and *Commonweal* provides the opportunity for examining segments of U.S. Catholic opinion. Until 1900, the *Christian Century* was known as the *Christian Oracle*. It has published continuously as a weekly from 1881 to the present. It included its first piece on immigration in October 1912.

In the second decade of the twentieth century, the *Christian Century* carried ten essays on immigration. Two assured its readers that the foreign born were loyal Americans (even the Germans born during World War I),[1] pointing out that many foreign-born young men were in France fighting to protect their adopted country. Another piece expressed concern over the high birth rate of immigrant families: "No religious worker can blink at the fact that the character of our population is being fundamentally changed, nor can it be ignored that the birth rate is far higher among Roman Catholic peoples than it is among Protestants."[2] The other seven articles focused on the role Protestant churches should play in helping Americanize the immigrants.

"The Making of a Nation" by Arthur Holmes pleaded with Christian Americans to help foreign-born children become assimilated into U.S. society. Holmes described the growing social problems in this country, pointing to one in ten marriages that ended in divorce and the 8,000 to 10,000 homicides that are committed annually.[3]

"The Disciples and the Immigrants," published in 1914, warned of the danger that these recent immigrants (Poles, Bohemians, Italians, and Jews)

Are becoming imbedded with Socialism and American radicalism of various brands; and the Catholic authorities now report that one-third of the Poles in this country are outside the Catholic Church. If the Protestant Church fails to sense this crisis, we shall probably have an anti-religious movement among the Poles that will far exceed that among the Bohemians. The immigrant cannot be evangelized in the old spontaneous and haphazard way by which we did so much work for the pioneer. Once we realize the significance of these newcomers, once we appreciate fully that their children are to be the future Americans and possess vast sections of our country, we shall see that if Disciples are to have standing room in the America of another generation, they must go seriously to the task of evangelizing the immigrant. . . . Through the length and breadth of the land, the sermon, the printed page and the missionary conference should make real to our brotherhood the peril and the opportunity of the immigrant invasion.[4]

"Learning to Walk — Among Immigrants" was both a plea and a proposed program to help understand the immigrant and to overcome "our own" prejudices. To find out

What are their instincts and what sort of behavior do they prompt? . . . What age old customs are their portion? Have they any fundamental defects of nature that are liable to be infused through heredity into our American life? What races do they belong to and what has race-character to do with their ability to become adjusted here? What values do they bring with them that are worth conserving here?

The author urged that special colleges be established by the Disciples to train "missionaries to immigrants."[5]

Like the other magazines in the survey, the *Christian Century* gave immigration a lot of attention in the 1920s. It published 28 articles and editorials on the subject during the decade. The major themes were "the new immigrants" (the reference was to the Mexicans), U.S. policy vis-à-vis Japanese aliens, and the debate about immigration restrictions. The major message in the five pieces on the Mexicans was the opportunity they afforded for evangelical religion. The *Christian Century* saw in the Mexican immigrants an "outstanding missing opportunity" for the Protestant churches to proselytize, because most of the Mexicans had "long cast off Catholicism" and were "needy religiously."[6]

The *Christian Century* censured California for its treatment and policies vis-à-vis the Japanese:

The dictates of our civilization and the imperatives of common fairness demand we treat all people who are legally and rightfully here with equal justice. To restrict immigration is one thing; to circumscribe and regulate with unnecessary strictness the lives of those now within our gates is quite another.[7]

In 1924, the *Christian Century* reported that the Federal Council of Churches deplored the quota bill under debate in Congress because the United States was behaving in an insulting way to the Japanese government. It favored restrictions but not exclusion of Asians. In 1927 it quoted Sidney Gulick, former missionary to Japan and secretary to the Federal Council of Churches, as follows: "The real harm and tragedy of the situation lies in the growing conviction of Japanese, Chinese, East Indians, all equally humiliated by the exclusion law, that Americans cannot be relied on for equal, just and honorable and courteous treatment."[8]

The *Christian Century* was slow to adopt a rigid restrictionist position, but it did support more stringent screening of potential immigrants and recommended use of the Stanford-Binet tests, used on recruits during the World War, to ferret out undesirable new-comers. It took President Wilson to task for vetoing an immigration bill that contained literacy requirements. It called for the establish-ment of quotas based on census statistics and for the regulation of immigration according to economic conditions in the United States.[9]

In 1923 the *Christian Century* likened the immigrants to robots, describing them as "mechanical men who can do all of the work of the world as unthinking, unfeeling automatons." It also compared immigrants with parts of a Ford car: "produced by the millions, easily replaceable, cheap, subjected to unbeatable wear and tear."[10]

Sidney Gulick, secretary of the commission on international justice for the Federal Council of Churches, proposed an immigra-tion policy that received positive coverage in the *Christian Century*. He called for the admission of only "such a number of immigrants as can be assimilated without shock to the industrial system" and urged that admissions be based upon the number of those who in the past became U.S. citizens by naturalization and the number who inter-married into families already resident. Gulick advocated a 2 percent immigration quota, using the latest census as the base. Such a system, he pointed out, would admit 9,249 Slavs instead of the 81,814 who arrived in the last period.[11] The *Christian Century* criticized proposals to use the 1890 census as the basis for the quota percentages.[12]

Sprinkled through the decade were four or five pieces that criticized U.S.-born Americans for not adopting a more Christian attitude toward the newcomers. The magazine editorialized against banning foreign language newspapers from the mail and requiring aliens to register.

The one blatantly anti-immigrant piece the *Christian Century* carried during the decade appeared in 1925. Attending an Episcopalian convention in New Orleans, the editor decided that the society was too heterogeneous. He reported that hotels, for example, were owned by Greeks, Italians, and Hebrews and the people who worked in them were of French, German, Irish, Mexican, and other extractions. He commented, "for the social, not commercial good of the society, it is necessary to slow down the immigrant tide in order to weld an entity worthy of the traditions which cluster around the name American."[13]

In its December 1929 issue, the *Christian Century* carried an article critical of current immigration policy because that policy did not permit "persons who are irrevocably committed to peace" (a group of Quakers) to become citizens.

The *Christian Century* in the 1930s carried five pieces on immigration; they appeared in 1930 and 1931 in the form of letters to the editor and editorials. One letter from a U.S. citizen in Japan and one editorial attacked as discriminatory U.S. policy vis-à-vis Japanese immigrants. Both urged the government to disavow the 1908 gentlemen's agreement whereby the U.S. and Japanese governments agreed that Japanese would not be admitted to the United States as immigrants.[14]

A second letter warned of the dangers to civil liberties if any one of the three alien registration bills currently before Congress were enacted. The author claimed that the registration requirement would put a weapon of intimidation into the hands of the police.[15]

An editorial criticized a bill recently passed by the Senate that singled out Mexicans from all Latin Americans and put them under a quota system. The editorial labeled such action as discriminatory and asked, "Why not put all Latin American immigrants under a quota system?"[16] A third editorial challenged the U.S. Supreme Court's decision to uphold a lower court in refusing to grant citizenship to Professor D. D. Macintosh, a Canadian subject on the faculty at the Yale Divinity School; the professor's application for naturalization was turned down because he said he would not bear arms in the event of war.[17]

The 1940s saw an increase to nine pieces on immigration. Three of the pieces attacked policies and legislation that discriminated against Asians. The *Christian Century* emphasized that justice for the Asians required more than permission for 105 Chinese a year to enter the United States; it required that all racial stigmas be removed from immigration policies. A Methodist spokesman in 1942 sought the repeal of all immigration bills that banned people on the basis of race; specifically, he called for the repeal of the Chinese Exclusion Act. That piece was followed by another article in February 1943 that also called for the dropping of all Asiatic color bias.

In 1940 and 1941 the *Christian Century* carried one article and three editorials about the registration of aliens. It viewed the requirement as a necessary evil but warned that registration might violate due process and be enforced overzealously. Two editorials commented unfavorably on the passage of legislation by individual states that forbade aliens to engage in certain types of work such as skilled trades, law, and medicine. "Aliens," the editors stated, "have a right to work and earn their livelihood."[18]

In 1947 the *Christian Century* urged support for passage of the Stratton Bill, legislation introduced by William Stratton, Republican of Illinois, that would liberalize U.S. policy vis-à-vis the displaced persons of Europe and the survivors of concentration camps.

Surprisingly, given its coverage of immigration until the 1950s, the *Christian Century* carried not a single article, editorial, or letter to the editor on the McCarran-Walter Act or any other immigration issue in the 1950s. It made its first comment on the McCarran-Walter Act in 1961 by calling for "a basic overhaul of our immigration law" and by describing the act as "racially and regionally, as well as nationally discriminating." The article favored an immigration policy based "solely on the ability of this nation to absorb immigrants as needed."[19]

Over the remainder of the decade, the *Christian Century* carried three other pieces on immigration. The author of "Bigotry's Shifting Patterns" commented, "It will be an ironic and especially tragic twist of our history if the ethnic groups which have been most abused by the WASP's and which are engaged in a common struggle for a full share of the nations's blessings now let loose upon each other the deadening sting of the WASP." The article pleaded with white Catholic and Jewish ethnics to support a more liberal immigration policy.[20]

Mexican immigrants were the major target of the *Christian Century*'s coverage of immigrants in the 1970s. Three of its four pieces sympathized with the plight of the illegal aliens and were critical of U.S. policy toward the Mexicans. Each piece emphasized moral as well as pragmatic issues. In an editorial titled "Personae Non Gratae," the *Christian Century* approvingly noted the U.S. government's welcome to thousands of Vietnamese refugees but observed that

Immigrants of another sort are still grimly regarded as unwelcome visitors — the illegal Mexican. Perhaps as we in the affluent United States accept our responsibility to Vietnamese who are refugees of a war and a new regime, we should also give due consideration to nearer neighbors — those Mexican nationals who are refugees of hunger and jobless-ness. More especially, it is time to take a realistic view toward those aliens in this country who, even after many years' residence must still live in fear of being deported and separated from their United States families.[21]

Nothing more concerning immigration appeared in the *Christian Century* until 1978, when the magazine published a letter from a staff person with the International Refugee Committee about the boat people. The letter was a plea to Christians "to make a vital witness of human compassion" by urging the U.S. government to cut quickly as much red tape as possible in order to admit "these latest victims of war and tyranny in a land stained by American blood and responsibility."[22]

In its Christmas issue of the same year it published an article on "The Challenge of the United States–Mexican Border." The author, a Mexican immigrant who was a physician at Cook County Hospital in Chicago, reviewed Mexico's domestic problems (corrupt government, high unemployment, poverty), claimed that the United States had a long record of treating Mexicans unfairly, attacked biologist Garret Hardin (University of California, Santa Barbara) for his advocacy of a "sealed border," and called upon those who hold Christian values to do something to ease the plight of Mexicans seeking to come to the United States.[23]

"Human Rights Fenced Out," in the same issue, announced that the moral dilemma of the 1980s will be "the way the United States treats the millions of refugees from hunger entering the country without a legal status." The article also pointed out that undocumented immigrants pay taxes in the host country but are entitled to few social and educational services.

True to its prediction, in the decade of the 1980s, the *Christian Century* carried 20 pieces on immigration, 17 of which discussed the plight of refugees (mostly those from Central America and Haiti) and all of which were critical of U.S. policy for its failure to grant official refugee status to Salvadorans and Haitians. Only 1 of its 20 articles had an anti-immigrant theme, that written by Professor William G. Hollingsworth from Tucson College of Law on "Controlling Illegal Immigration" (July 1985). Hollingsworth warned of the importance of regaining "sovereignty over its own borders." Until we do so, "the outlook for jobless and low income U.S. citizens will remain bleak." The author also warned of the dangers of overpopulation:[24]

The most idealistic opponents of securing our borders are those who think that every one wishing to escape poverty should be able to immigrate to the U.S. But since the Third World population is expected to double to more than 7 billion people within approximately 40 years, American-idealists need to connect their hearts with their heads. There are better responses to ever-expanding world poverty than permitting its overflow into the U.S.

He also asserted that "The majority of Latino and black voters want illegal immigration to end. They well know that the prime victims of uncontrolled immigration are the unemployed and the low income workers — who are very often themselves."

In October 1985, the *Christian Century* carried one reader's response to the Hollingsworth piece, which stated, "An immigration policy that focuses exclusively on control, and protects United States citizens while the rest of the world is starved and slaughtered, has no claim to the support of the religious community."[25]

In all of the 15 pieces on Haitian, Salvadoran, and other Central American immigrants, there were strong arguments for granting these immigrants formal refugee status. The United States was charged with racial discrimination for its "refusal to treat the Haitians in the same way as Cubans, Vietnamese, and others in flight from political repression and economic despair." A 1981 editorial on the Haitians stated,

December 12 will mark the tenth anniversary of the arrival of the first boat load of Haitian refugees — and they continue to come, more than 1000 a month. And for a decade, a succession of U.S. administrations, from Richard Nixon's to Ronald Reagan's has viewed "illegal aliens" with indifference if not hostility, clinging to the myth that their motivation is economic rather than political. It is true that Haiti is the most impoverished country in the Western hemisphere. . . . Some of the Haitian refugees are seeking to escape malnutrition and starvation, but they are also seeking to escape terror. In Haiti the two motivations are not unrelated. The effort to emigrate in itself makes one an enemy of the state.

Reasonable limits to immigration do have to be set; the intake capacity of the United States is not infinite. To state the anti-immigration argument in strong terms: if all the people in the world who would prefer to live in America were actually to come here, sooner or later — and probably sooner — this country would become the kind of crowded, poor, oppressive place those people were eager to flee. That argument is not without a certain pragmatic merit, however exaggerated and inhumane it may seem. But at this point the United States, proportionately speaking, is not nearly so populous — or so repressive — as are a good many other countries. The troublesome burden of inflation, recession, and unemployment not withstanding, surely America is not yet so crowded, so economically distressed or, one hopes so uncompassionate that we must make a mockery of the words of Emma Lazarus inscribed on the Statue of Liberty. Certainly the Haitian refugees are "tired," "poor," "wretched," and "tempest tossed" as other refugees we have readily welcomed (and scolded other countries for not welcoming).[26]

In the more than half-dozen pieces that the *Christian Century* carried on the Sanctuary Movement, none stated its position more eloquently than the following excerpt from a 1983 editorial:

If we as Christians value human life, if we seek to be compassionate, if we oppose injustice, if we repudiate torture and terror, then we really have no choice but to offer sanctuary to people whose lives are in jeopardy. And if to do so proves illegal? Whatever the things that we are to "render unto Caesar," our consciences are not among them. The biblical moral order transcends the morality of the civil order, and on those infrequent occasions when the two come into conflict, the biblical imperatives have a greater claim on us.[27]

Several articles compared U.S. policy vis-à-vis refugees from Communist governments with its policies vis-à-vis right-wing governments. In an editorial in 1985, the *Christian Century* stated,

Not only has the U.S. Immigration and Naturalization Services routinely enforced regulations against undocumented people fleeing from Central America, but it has aggressively sought to thwart every attempt of religious forces to assist these refugees.

Referring explicitly to the case of a Soviet seaman who jumped ship and sought asylum, the editorial continued,

The fundamentals of present policy are: If you are running from a Communist state, come in; if you are fleeing from a state with a U.S. backed government, go back. The just opposition of these two cases reveals a policy that is not only mean spirited but also far more interested in political ideology than fairness or justice.[28]

In sum, over a period of 78 years from 1912 to 1990, the *Christian Century* carried 53 pieces about immigration policy and immigrants. Most of the pieces expressed support and concern for immigrants and advocated increasing the number permitted to enter. The groups selected for especially favorable notice were Asians, Mexicans, Salvadorans, and Haitians. About the Asians, the magazine reminded its readers of its government's historic policy of discrimination and strongly advocated repeal of all stigmatic legislation against Chinese, Japanese, and other Asian people and the liberalizing of quotas for those people. About the Mexicans, it also invoked history, namely, the U.S. policies of expansionism vis-à-vis its southern neighbor, and noted the contributions that Mexican immigrants make to the U.S. economy in the form of taxes and in their reluctance to avail themselves of social, economic, and educational benefits. Regarding the Salvadorans and Haitians, they are oppressed, impoverished, and deserving of the same refugee status as people who flee the Soviet Union or Vietnam. The *Christian Century*'s concerns about immigrants were often couched in Christian symbolism, and its support for policies and programs was often done in the name of Christianity.

COMMENTARY

From its founding in 1945 until 1990, *Commentary* published four articles and three book reviews about immigrants and U.S. immigration policy. All of the pieces appeared in the first half of the 1950s: "America's Ethnic Pattern" by Nathan Glazer, "The Scientific Basis of Our Immigration Policy" by William Peterson, "The Triple Melting Pot" by theologian Will Herberg, and "Our Broken Promise to the Refugees" by James Rorty. The three book reviews all appeared in 1954. The books were *Civil Rights in Immigration* by Milton Konvitz, *The Golden Door: The Irony of Our Immigration Policy* by J. Campbell Bruce, and *The American People in the Twentieth Century* by Oscar Handlin.

During the period when the McCarran-Walter Act was under debate, *Commentary* was conspicuous by its silence. Almost all of the organizations and points of view comprised by the American Jewish community spoke out against the McCarran-Walter Act, made it an important issue in the 1952 elections, and proposed various alternatives, especially to the provisions concerning refugees and displaced persons. The failure of *Commentary*, a publication of the American Jewish committee, to run even a single article on the McCarran-Walter Act specifically, or on immigration policy generally, during the first eight years following World War II seems extraordinary.

Commentary's first piece on immigration focused on cultural pluralism versus the melting pot as modes of immigrant adjustment to and participation in U.S. society. Sociologist Nathan Glazer argued that the earliest immigrants to the United States, the Irish, Germans, and Scandinavians, did not melt any more readily than did the new immigrants — those who came from the 1880s until World War II.[29]

In 1955 *Commentary* ran a piece by sociologist demographer William Peterson, titled "The Scientific Basis of Our Immigration Policy," in which Peterson critically reviewed the role of the Eugenics League and other groups within the anti-immigration movement.[30]

Will Herberg's "The Triple Melting Pot" in August 1955 picked up some of the same themes discussed by Glazer, except that Herberg claimed that a "triple melting pot" type of assimilation was occurring as a result of the high rates of intermarriage among Catholics, Protestants, and Jews.[31]

The only piece in *Commentary* on the McCarran-Walter Act was in the form of a book review. J. Bruce Campbell's book, *The Golden Door: The Irony of Our Immigration Policy*, was a polemic against U.S. immigration policy from the 1920s on and especially against the McCarran-Walter Act.[32]

In "Our Broken Promise to the Refugees," James Rorty condemned Congress and the Eisenhower administration for dragging their feet on issuing visas to displaced persons in Europe. Rorty asserted that Edward Corsis had been hired as a special assistant to Secretary of State John Foster Dulles to placate proimmigrant groups but that the State Department tied his hands. After Corsis quit, he made public his frustration and anger at the State Department and, in doing so, reported that 18 months after the enactment of the Refugee Relief Act, fewer than 25,000 visas had been issued and fewer than 1,000 of the 214,000 refugees authorized by the act for admission to the United States had actually been admitted.[33]

Between 1955 and 1980 *Commentary* did not carry a single article on immigration, despite the arrival of more than 500,000 Cubans in 1959 and 1960, the arrival of the Vietnamese boat people, the negotiations leading up to and subsequent admission of almost 100,000 Soviet Jews, the passage of the Hart-Celler Act, and the presence of several million illegal aliens in the country.

One piece appeared in *Commentary* in the 1980s, and it carried an anti-immigrant message. The author, Samuel Rabinove, legal director of the American Jewish Committee, quoted a recent Gallup poll that showed that 91 percent of the respondents favored halting all immigration to the United States until the national unemployment rate dropped to 5 percent. Rabinove directed much of his attack against granting amnesty to illegals on the grounds that "it would condone the flagrant violation of our laws on a massive scale." He concluded that "immigration is out of control" and favored enactment of a federal law forbidding employers from hiring illegal aliens, adopting a national identification card, and sealing of the "now porous Mexican border."[34]

COMMONWEAL

Commonweal is the third magazine in the survey supported by a religious community. Founded in 1922, *Commonweal* is published by, and appeals primarily to, educated, liberal Catholics. Of the three, *Commonweal* is older than *Commentary* by 21 years and younger than the *Christian Century* by almost 40 years. Over the same time period, 1924 to 1990, *Commonweal* carried approximately six more pieces on immigration than did the *Christian Century* and, from 1945 on, more than five times as many as *Commentary*.

Its first piece on immigrants appeared in 1929 in an essay entitled "America for Americans." The article criticized the national origins basis of the Quota Acts of 1921 and 1924 and pointed out that the leading supporters of such legislation were the Ku Klux Klan and the Daughters of the American Revolution.[35]

In the 1930s *Commonweal* carried six articles, one book review, and one letter to the editor on immigration. The articles covered fingerprinting of aliens (a requirement in the Blease Bill); U.S. policy vis-à-vis the Japanese, immigrants, and crime; the numbers that ought to be admitted; immigration trends; and refugees from Nazi Germany. It opposed the Blease Bill, which would require all aliens to be fingerprinted, on the grounds that fingerprinting would be a violation of due process. It commented sadly on the unjustness of our policy vis-à-vis Japanese who might wish to immigrate to the United States but acknowledged that Congress should or could act to redress the discriminatory policy only if public sentiment on the West Coast changed radically from what it was and what it had been.[36]

The author of the piece on "Immigration and the Crime Wave" argued that "the great majority of criminals in this country are American born" and indeed are the "products of our schools, sensational press, movies and speakeasies." "Indeed," the article continued, "the Southern states, which are distinctively native American and favor prohibition, take the palm for murder and other crimes." It listed the cities that had the highest murder rates, showing that all of them were Southern and incidentally were in locales in which the percentage of foreign born was much lower than that in Northern cities such as New York, Chicago, Boston, and Philadelphia.[37]

In 1933 *Commonweal* returned to the quota issue with a long essay that started out, "We cannot admit all newcomers without examination or thought. . . . When there was room for all, all were welcome, [but] times have changed." The author went on,

> The number of people in this country has increased, and the economic conditions have worsened. There must therefore be some bar set up against the great number of people who are

desirous of coming to share our diminishing prosperity. But the immediate remedy that has been offered up by noisy propagandists is inspired primarily by religious intolerance and fortified by imaginary science. The result is the present Quota Bill — which with the exception of the Volstead Act [prohibition] is about the most nonsensical method ever adopted by any country to achieve a worthwhile objective.[38]

Two months later, *Commonweal* carried a letter to the editor that disputed the intentions of those who favor quotas as racists. The letter stated,

Nor is it a reflection on any group of nations in Europe to say that in the past the immigrants from Northwest Europe have adapted themselves to the American scene more quickly than is the case with the average newcomer from other regions of the continent. Furthermore, it is a fact that the countries of Northern Europe have sent us a far greater proportion of their better element than is the case with Southern and Eastern Europe, as proven by the records of prisons, insane asylums, and alm houses, as well as by the intelligence tests of the United States Army during the World War.[39]

Although the letter was directly antagonistic to *Commonweal* editorial policy, it drew no published response.

The 12 pieces on immigration that appeared in *Commonweal* during the 1940s focused on two issues: war refugees and U.S. policy toward Asians. On the first issue, *Commonweal* consistently favored admitting as many of the European refugees and displaced persons as wanted to come. It emphasized how much the United States would gain from such people because of the talents and skills they would bring with them.[40]

Following the end of World War II, it strongly supported President Truman's proposals for the admission of refugees beyond the numbers allowed under the quota system.[41] It also gave strong backing to the Stratton Bill but claimed that such actions were not enough. It took the British to task for their treatment of Jewish refugees who wanted to immigrate to Palestine. (The British had placed a blockade around Palestine, making it impossible for ships carrying displaced persons and other refugees from Europe to land in Palestine.)[42]

In July 1947 the magazine published portions of testimony before Congress by U.S. Catholic clergy on behalf of the Stratton Bill.[43] In its November issue it presented the views of Pope Pius XII on the moral responsibility of the United States to admit Europe's displaced persons.[44] Before the end of the decade, it carried two more stories that urged admission of displaced persons to the United States.

During World War II, *Commonweal* had called for "Justice to Our Allies" by repealing the Chinese Exclusion Act and treating Asian immigrants as any other immigrant population.[45] After the war, it carried two stories that commented approvingly on the introduction and passage of the Judd Bill, which did away with previous legislation that excluded Asians.[46]

All 18 articles on immigration that appeared in *Commonweal* in the 1950s condemned the McCarran-Walter Act on the grounds that it was discriminatory and that it allowed too few immigrants. *Commonweal* urged admission of more refugees without regard for quotas.[47]

Commonweal published a summary of the report of the President's Commission on Immigration and Naturalization in January 1953, supporting the commission's recommendation that national quotas be abolished to admit 240,000 refugees over a two-year period and attacking the McCarran-Walter Act for not allowing refugees to enter the United States following World War II because of "supposed Communist ties."[48] The September issue carried a piece criticizing the red tape and inefficiency that accompanied the legislation to admit 214,000 refugees and orphans to the United States by the end of 1956; at the time of the story, only 5,000 had been admitted.[49]

Its pre–Christmas-1955 issue included an essay that was critical of the quota system first introduced in the 1920s. The article reminded readers of the United States' "hallowed tradition as a haven for the oppressed and freedom loving people of the world." It showed that the quotas from Britain and Northern Ireland of 65,000 a year were not being used and recommended that unused quotas be shifted to countries having people who wanted to come here. Greece, for example, had a quota of only 308, and Italy "desperately needs a larger allotment than the 6,000 it has currently." The article's author warned that current U.S. policy would trigger the loss of friends of the United States and work against the nation's chances in the Cold War. The article concluded, "the present law violates the basic Christian injunction to harbor the harborless."[50]

In March 1956 *Commonweal* carried another piece on the unfairness of U.S. immigration law. It strongly supported President Eisenhower's proposal to raise the ceiling on the number of immigrants admitted annually from 150,000 to 222,000 and to remove clauses discriminatory to eastern and southern Europeans.[51]

In "Fact and Fancy," *Commonweal* pointed out the irony of the U.S. Information Agency distributing pamphlets to 80 countries that described the contributions immigrants had made to this country and the warmth with which the United States had welcomed such immigrants to its shores. The McCarran-Walter Act, the article concluded, "makes a mockery of this pamphlet."[52]

A few months after the Hungarian Revolt, *Commonweal* ran a story asserting that the McCarran-Walter Act placed an "unnecessary obstacle" in the path of Hungarian refugees seeking sanctuary in the United States.[53]

The decades of the 1960s and 1970s witnessed a sharp decline in the number of articles on immigration compared with the number carried in the previous three decades. In the 1960s there were four articles, and in the 1970s, only three.

World Refugee Year was the designation of 1960. *Commonweal,* in its April issue, carried a piece, "Barriers to Immigration," that claimed "America's post war immigration policy has failed to measure up to contemporary human needs." As the leader of the free world, the piece held, it was incumbent upon the United States to make a substantial "extra contribution to the international refugee resettlement problem."[54]

During that decade, 1965 was the only other year that *Commonweal* included articles on immigration. It described a proposal that President Kennedy had sent to Congress shortly before his assassination in which he urged that the national quota system be supplanted by a policy based on "individual merit and ties to America of the applying immigrant rather than on his national and racial origin." The article noted with approval that President Johnson was pushing for its adoption and that there was a good chance he would succeed.[55]

A comprehensive article with extensive statistics about countries that were not filling their quotas appeared in the June 1965 issue. The article warned of a new danger when it said, "the other disturbing aspect of immigration reform is the certainty that the present prejudice on the basis of race will become a prejudice against the unskilled." Quoted was Republican Richard Schweiker, who said of immigrants, "We must seek the quality of their contribution to our nation, not the quality of numbers." The writer of the *Commonweal* article translated that remark as, "Give me your poor Ph.D.'s, your huddled graduate engineers."[56]

Immigrants from Latin America were the concern of a piece that appeared in October 1965. The article supported President Johnson's proposal to permit unrestricted immigration from Latin America. It urged the United States to "open itself to those people in particular need, and at the present time, Latin Americans are in this unenviable position."[57]

Of the three articles that *Commonweal* carried on immigration in the 1970s, two focused on the Mexicans. In June 1975, the U.S. treatment of Vietnamese refugees was compared with its treatment of illegal Mexicans with the conclusion that "many of those Mexicans who were swept up recently in Chicago and given a choice between a one way bus ticket to Mexico and two months in Cook County jail awaiting trial — with deportation almost inevitable." The author of the article pointed out that the illegal Mexicans paid taxes but were not eligible for welfare assistance.[58]

"A New Peril" by Abigail McCarthy in January 1977 likened the current attack on Mexican immigrants, both legal and illegal, to the attacks that had been made on immigrants from southern and eastern Europe in the late nineteenth and early twentieth centuries. The thrust of her argument was that such attacks were unwarranted then and they are unwarranted today.[59]

Commonweal also expressed strong support for the Vietnamese boat people and for the U.S. policy of allowing as many as could safely survive their escape to enter this country.[60]

The ten pieces on immigration that appeared in *Commonweal* in the 1980s focused on illegal Hispanics (mostly from El Salvador, Guatemala, and Mexico), Haitians, and the Sanctuary Movement. Each piece pressed the U.S. government to grant refugee status to the Salvadorans, Guatemalans, and Haitians, amnesty to illegals from Mexico, and support for the Sanctuary Movement. One of the articles compared the United States unfavorably with Canada in the two governments' treatment of El Salvadorans and Guatemalans. The author wrote,

> There will be no compromise on Canada's humanitarian courses. All persons fleeing persecution, as defined by the Geneva Convention as refugees whether they are Central Americans escaping from the U.S., whether they come from behind the Iron Curtain, or from the Middle East, whether they are from Asia or Africa, will be welcome in Canada.[61]

Comparing treatment of Haitians with that of Cubans, an article contained the following observations:

> The federal government's generous if erratic welcome to Cuban refugees is just. Its consistently hostile policy denying Haitian claims to political asylum is not. . . . The fact that Haitians denied entrance are black has not escaped the attention of American blacks in Miami.[62]

On the granting of amnesty to illegals, *Commonweal* argued,

> Those opposed to amnesty, even in a piecemeal fashion, argue that it condemns and encourages the breaking of the law and gives away costly tax payer benefits. But it appears to be the only humane option, unless the U.S. is willing to have massive roundups far exceeding in scale the deplorable exodus of four hundred thousand alien workers from Nigeria. Moreover,

legalization would recognize the contribution that many undocumented aliens make to the economy as well as eliminate some of the conditions that lead to exploitation and blackmail of a huge underclass within our borders.[63]

The following provides a taste of the substance of at least five pieces that appeared in the 1980s on the Salvadoran refugee status:

Why not grant the Salvadorans and other Central American refugees Extended Voluntary Departure status? Presently enjoyed by Ethiopians, Poles, Lebanese, Ugandans, and Afghans, this status grants refugees permission to stay in the United States, until such time as it is safe to return to their homeland. This gesture would support the recent call by both sides of the conflict in El Salvador to "humanize the war," and would fulfill our country's obligations under the Geneva Convention, as well as our duty as a spiritual and moral people to protect those fleeing war and persecution.[64]

The list of refugee admissions and grants of asylums are still dominated by those from Communist countries. Individuals fleeing from non-Communist countries have not fared nearly as well. Nowhere is this clearer than in the case of Salvadorans. Last year the State Department granted asylum status to only 200 Salvadorans. Many Salvadorans do not seek asylum, with good reasons. INS data show that in 1983 only six percent of the Salvadorans who appear for asylum were granted it. Compare this with the 67 percent acceptance rate for Afghans. The United Nations High Commissioner for Refugees has recognized Salvadorans as a group as refugees, and so have our neighbors to the north and south, Canada and Mexico. The U.S. has not.[65]

Commonweal and the *Christian Century* share a common view that has three major components: immigrants have been good for the United States in the past, they are in the present, and they will be in the future; using national origins quotas as a basis for admission is discriminatory and racist; the United States has a special responsibility toward refugees.

NOTES

1. *Christian Century*, December 13, 1917.
2. Ibid., October 3, 1912.
3. Ibid., April 9, 1914.
4. Ibid., October 3, 1912.

5. Ibid., November 2, 1916.
6. Ibid., May 6, 1920.
7. Ibid.
8. Ibid., October 20, 1927.
9. Ibid., April 18, 1921.
10. Ibid., June 7, 1923.
11. Ibid., June 27, 1924.
12. Ibid., November 14, 1924.
13. Ibid., March 10, 1925.
14. Ibid., April 16, 1930; September 10, 1930.
15. Ibid., May 28, 1930.
16. Ibid.
17. Ibid., June 30, 1931.
18. Ibid., May 3, 1961.
19. Ibid.
20. Ibid., September 30, 1964.
21. Ibid., August 6, 1975.
22. Ibid., May 3, 1978.
23. Ibid., December 25, 1978.
24. Ibid., July 10, 1985.
25. Ibid., October 13, 1985.
26. Ibid., October 8, 1981.
27. Ibid., April 27, 1983.
28. Ibid., November 20, 1985.
29. *Commentary*, April 1953.
30. Ibid., July 1955.
31. Ibid., August 1955.
32. Ibid., May 1954.
33. Ibid., October 1955.
34. Ibid., February 1984.
35. *Commonweal*, July 31, 1929.
36. Ibid., April 2, 1930; September 17, 1930; September 28, 1932; May 26, 1933; July 14, 1933; May 25, 1934; August 25, 1939; September 8, 1939.
37. Ibid., September 28, 1932.
38. Ibid., May 26, 1933.
39. Ibid., July 14, 1933.
40. Ibid., February 5, 1943.
41. Ibid., August 30, 1946.
42. Ibid.
43. Ibid., July 4, 1947.
44. Ibid., November 10, 1947.
45. Ibid., June 5, 1942.
46. Ibid., March 18, 1949; April 8, 1949.
47. Ibid., December 15, 1950; November 10, 1950; October 19, 1951; November 9, 1951; June 20, 1952; January 9, 1953; July 31, 1953; October 2, 1953.
48. Ibid., January 9, 1953.
49. Ibid., September 24, 1955.
50. Ibid., December 14, 1955.
51. Ibid., March 12, 1956.
52. Ibid., September 14, 1956.
53. Ibid., January 4, 1957.
54. Ibid., April 18, 1960.
55. Ibid., January 29, 1965.
56. Ibid., June 4, 1965.

57. Ibid., October 17, 1965.
58. Ibid., June 20, 1975.
59. Ibid., January 21, 1977.
60. Ibid., September 1, 1978.
61. Ibid., March 27, 1987.
62. Ibid., June 6, 1980.
63. Ibid., July 15, 1983.
64. Ibid., December 14, 1984.
65. Ibid., May 9, 1986.

9

Reader's Digest

From its founding in 1922 through 1989, the *Reader's Digest* carried 26 stories on immigration, 6 of which appeared in the 1980s. The first piece appeared in April 1938 in the form of an excerpt from William Seabrook's book, *These Foreigners*. It contained a lot of sentimental prose, but the essential message was that foreigners are not aliens when you get to know them; rather, they are people much like native-born Americans. The second and last piece of that decade took the form of a debate about whether we should "Open Our Doors to German Refugees." The question was whether the United States should alter its immigration quotas to admit larger numbers of European refugees from political and religious persecution. The pro side rested on two major points: immigrants bring skills, trades, and know-how, they make new jobs rather than take jobs away, and they expand the consumption base; it is the decent and humane thing for the United States to do. The author used the analogy of a ship's captain who would not refuse to lower his lifeboat because there might be more people in the water than he could hope to reach in time.[1]

The opposing argument was that the U.S. economy was in sad shape, with millions of people unemployed; the situation would only be worsened by the influx of refugees. On the moral issue, the contrary argument was that the United States had done its share, having taken in more than 38 million people in the course of its history, and other countries ought now do their share.

During World War II, *Reader's Digest* carried two articles that lauded the patriotism and loyalty of immigrants vis-à-vis their adopted land.[2]

New York city planner Robert Moses wrote a piece especially for the *Reader's Digest* that reviewed U.S. immigration policy and assessed the mood of the country about future policy. On one side, he saw church people and liberals in favor of unrestricted immigration; on the other side, he saw popular sentiment and Congress in favor of restricting immigration and cutting quotas from what they were in the 1920s and 1930s. In his review of the consequences of an open immigration policy, Moses argued that the great number of immigrants who entered in the first quarter of the twentieth century

> Clogged our economic, administrative, social and cultural systems in scores of ways. The effect was intolerable on our language, on the schools, on housing, on crime, on disease, on congestion of urban centers, and on labor and employment.[3]

Moses granted that the quota acts of the 1920s were crude and motivated by chauvinism, bigotry, and intolerance, but the results, in his view, were not unfair. He concluded that the mood of the country favored drastic restrictions on immigration.

Reader's Digest carried a debate between Senator Tom Stewart of Tennessee and Attorney General Francis Biddle on the theme "Should We Keep All Foreigners Out?" Stewart took the affirmative and argued that as long as there were 1 million unemployed, all immigration should be prohibited. If the unemployment figures dropped below the 1 million mark, then some immigrants should be admitted. Although he argued on the other side, Biddle's views did not differ much from Stewart's except that he would permit some immigrants to enter after the war because it would be good "international public relations."[4]

The *Reader's Digest*'s first piece on Mexicans who enter the country illegally was titled "2,000 Miles of Trouble." The article predicted that the problem would worsen before it got better. The article urged the United States to spend a lot more money on expanding the border patrol and building fortifications and fences.[5]

After World War II, the *Reader's Digest* ran two articles that advocated the adoption of more restrictive immigration policies. It compared the United States with Canada, Britain, and Australia and urged Americans to behave as those countries do, which meant not allowing emotions and sympathy for the refugees and displaced persons to determine U.S. immigration policy. Economic interests should come first, and they pointed to restrictions.[6]

Senator James Eastland warned of the dangers of illegal entry, not from Mexico, but from sailors and visitors who left their ships once they reached U.S. ports.[7] Of the six pieces that the *Reader's Digest* carried on immigration in the 1950s, the major one was an interview with Representative Francis Walter (coauthor of the McCarran-Walter Act). In it, Walter accused U.S. Communists and left-wing organizations of making false and vicious attacks on the McCarran-Walter Act. He supported retention of the 1924 quota system because he believed that some races were closer to the United

States in culture, custom, standard of living, respect for law, and experience in self-government.[8]

In the midst of the Korean War, *Reader's Digest* published an article titled "Why Shouldn't They Be Americans?" that made a plea for allowing Orientals to become U.S. citizens. "Refusing Orientals citizenship damages American relations with the people of Asia," claimed the article's writer.[9]

"The Mystery of the Multiplying Sons" was an exposé of an immigration racket by which Chinese gained admission to the United States as false sons of naturalized citizens.[10]

The last piece in the 1950s was an ode to the rich harvest that the United States acquired in its admission of fugitives from Nazi and Communist oppression. The people, the article rhapsodized, brought skills, talent, and knowledge of "incalculable value" to their adopted country. It listed most of the famous artists, scientists, and writers who had come to the United States in the 1930s and 1940s.[11]

Between 1960 and 1980 *Reader's Digest* carried only five pieces on immigration. One was devoted to the brain drain, which it saw as a hardship and danger to the developing countries because physicians, engineers, and scientists who received their training in the United States opted to remain in this country rather than return to the countries where their services were needed more.

Historian Oscar Handlin's article in 1966, "At Last: A Fair Deal for Immigrants," applauded passage of the Hart-Celler Act (1965) for doing away with the national origins quotas, which he viewed as racist. Handlin wrote that, under the new law, prospective immigrants anywhere in the world would receive visas on a first come–first served basis within the limit of the number of places available annually.[12]

In the 1970s the *Reader's Digest* published two pieces on immigrants, both focused on illegal aliens. An article in the December 1973 issue estimated that as many as 5 million persons were entering the United States illegally and that the annual income loss to displaced U.S. workers was $10.4 billion. It called for employer sanctions and urged prohibiting the payment of welfare benefits to illegal aliens.[13] The same themes appeared again in October 1976, when *Reader's Digest* excerpted an article by the commissioner of the U.S. Immigration and Naturalization Service, Leonard Chapman, who wrote that illegal aliens "milked" the U.S. taxpayers out of $13 billion annually by taking jobs from legal residents and forcing them into unemployment, by illegally acquiring welfare benefits and public services, and by avoiding the payment of taxes. Chapman estimated that 10 percent of Mexico's total population was in the United States illegally. He called for employer sanctions, alien identification cards, and the appropriation of funds to increase the size of the border patrol force.[14]

Two of the six pieces in the 1980s described and applauded the Cuban migration and adjustment to the United States. The Cubans were characterized as "freedom seeking refugees" who had and would continue to "make it" in the United States. George Gilder described the Cuban-American miracle as follows:

Often exiles, outcasts, or rejects, entrepreneurs learn early the ecstasy of struggle, the lessons of life. And it is from this knowledge, this experience that they forge success.

Castro, like so many other tyrants before him, believed he had seized the wealth of Coca-Cola when he expropriated the firm's assets in Havana. But the spirit of enterprise that Goizuete and other Cubans like him brought to America would turn out to be far more valuable that the material possessions they left behind.[15]

Another story about how hard immigrants work and how industrious they are described Koreans in the grocery and produce market business in New York City.[16]

Juxtaposed against these stories were three strongly anti-immigrant pieces that appeared in the *Reader's Digest* in 1980, 1983, and 1985. The strongest one, "Our Immigration Nightmare" by Carl T. Rowan and David M. Mazie, argued that immigrants take jobs away from U.S. citizens and place a heavy burden on the government for health care, welfare benefits, housing, and other services. They add to the already burdensome number of people in this country, threaten the environment, and are difficult to assimilate. The article concluded with policy recommendations for restricting immigration that included a national identification card, punishment for employers who knowingly hired undocumented workers, and additional manpower and equipment for the Immigration and Naturalization Service to guard our borders.

Far beyond any other country, America has been generous in accepting refugees and legal immigrants. However, we cannot accept all the world's "huddled masses." Our national interest requires more controls. There will have to be compromises in search of a humane, reasonable, enforceable policy — one that recognizes past traditions and present needs and seeks durable solutions, not quick fixes. The "golden door" should not be locked — but it cannot be left open, either.[17]

"Should We Limit Immigration?" was a piece condensed from a longer article that *Newsweek* carried earlier in 1980. The theme was that the United States had to strike a balance between "our traditionally generous impulse and our instinct for self protection."

The article stated that "On the whole, Americans seem to have outgrown racism in their reactions to the newcomers." It quoted Roger Conner as follows: "The over-riding issue in immigration policy is not race, not ethnicity. It is sheer numbers."[18]

The numbers theme is central to the last piece the *Reader's Digest* carried on immigration in the 1980s, "America's Refugee Mess": there are too many and they cost the United States too much.[19]

NOTES

1. *Reader's Digest*, May 1939.
2. Ibid., November 1941; March 1943.
3. Ibid., March 1943.
4. Ibid., November 1944.
5. Ibid., July 1945.
6. Ibid., August 1947; October 1948.
7. Ibid., October 1948.
8. Ibid., May 1953.
9. Ibid., August 1951.
10. Ibid., December 1956.
11. Ibid., January 1957.
12. Ibid., August 1966.
13. Ibid., December 1973.
14. Ibid., October 1976.
15. Ibid., December 1985.
16. Ibid.
17. Ibid., January 1983.
18. Ibid., November 1980.
19. Ibid., June 1985.

10

The Big News Weeklies: *Time, Life, Newsweek,* and *U.S. News and World Report*

A group of magazines fitting under the same umbrella are the mass-market news weeklies: *Time, Life, Newsweek,* and *U.S. News and World Report. Time* is the oldest, having been founded in the 1920s, approximately a decade earlier than *Newsweek* and *U.S. News and World Report. Time's* circulation is almost equal to that of *Newsweek* and *U.S. News and World Report* combined. *Life,* which, like *Time,* was founded by Henry Luce and began publishing in 1936, suspended publication in December 1972 and started again in October 1978.

The news weeklies provide a third type of coverage of immigration issues. They differ both from the essays and opinion pieces in the monthlies and from the excerpts and condensed reprints reported in the *Literary Digest* and *Reader's Digest. Time, Newsweek,* and *U.S. News and World Report* are news magazines. Each week they summarize and highlight the major events of the past seven days. They also have columnists who write on special topics (the nation's economy, sports, book reviews), as well as those who write about special issues or problems they consider important. Their style of reporting is more akin to the news section of a daily paper than it is to a magazine.

TIME

The only two stories that *Time* carried about immigrants in the 1930s concerned testimony given by musicians and actors before the U.S. House of Representatives committee on immigration, urging its members to enact legislation that would make it more difficult for artists from abroad to perform in the United States. In 1939 it reported testimony by Helen Hayes and other well-known theater people before the Senate judiciary committee on behalf of the Wagner Act, a bill that would have permitted 20,000 refugees from Germany (about one-sixth of those trying to leave) to enter the United States.[1]

Five stories on immigrants were reported in the 1940s. The first appeared in 1940, and it summarized the 70 bills that were currently pending in Congress, all of which were against aliens. The bills sought to keep aliens out of the United States, to send those already here back where they came from, and to make life uncomfortable for those who remained.[2] During World War II it reported Japanese propaganda to the Chinese about the U.S. policy of excluding Chinese immigrants and about various bills the House committee on immigration was considering that would modify or repeal the Chinese Exclusion Act.[3]

On the subject of U.S. treatment of Asians after the war, *Time* reported, in 1946 that a quota had been established for immigrants from India that would permit 100 per year to come to the United States with the intention of remaining here. Countries still barred included Japan, Korea, Malaysia, the Netherlands Indies, the Philippines, Samoa, and Sumatra.[4]

Between June 1946 and June 1948, *Time* ran three stories on Europe's displaced persons who were permitted to enter the United States. Of an estimated 900,000 displaced persons waiting to come to the United States, only 36,000 had been admitted as of May 1948. Next to this news article was a story on six displaced families who had come to the United States and made a "wonderful" adjustment. The reporter also described a "racket" operated out of Scotland in which the Scots provided phony papers at $1,500 apiece to displaced persons in a hurry to come to the United States.[5]

The McCarran-Walter Act was the major immigration news event of the 1950s. *Time* quoted Senator McCarran on the floor of the Senate the day his bill was voted on:

Admitting D.P.'s would add to the number of unemployed, would take housing away from veterans and would jeopardize the economy. There will be only 11,000 real displaced persons left by June of this year; the rest are criminals, diseased and those who cannot take care of themselves.[6]

Time referred to the McCarran-Walter Act as the "McCarran Curtain," and in October 1952 it listed the eminent scientists who were barred from entering the United States as a result of the act. The article contained long quotes from scientists in the United States who protested the restrictions and warned of the harm the law was inflicting on the U.S. image.[7]

Seven more stories about immigrants appeared between 1953 and 1959.[8] All of them were about the number of refugees Congress was willing to admit and how expediently government agencies were processing refugee papers. On August 26, 1957, *Time* reported that under the leadership of Congressman Walter and Senator Eastland,

Congress turned down President Eisenhower's request for an increase in the annual number of immigrants from 155,000 to 190,000.

Time carried only five stories on immigration during the 1960s. The two big ones focused on the debate leading up to and the passage of the Hart-Celler Act in 1965. *Time* described the standing immigration law (the McCarran-Walter Act) as an abomination and welcomed the new bill,[9] especially the provisions that did away with the national origins quota system and offered visas on a first come–first served basis.

In 1968 *Time*'s article captioned "Death Trap for Wetbacks" described a locked truck that had been captured in San Antonio on a very hot day. The truck contained 47 trapped Mexican laborers; 1 was dead, 2 were dying, and 15 needed hospitalization. Each had paid $100 to be smuggled into the United States.[10]

Illegal aliens, mostly from Mexico, were the dominant theme in eight of the nine pieces on immigrants that *Time* carried in the 1970s. Quoting Immigration and Naturalization Service (INS) Commissioner Leonard Chapman, *Time* reported "about one million illegal Mexicans in the country are holding jobs that might be filled by unemployed citizens."[11]

As part of the July 4 issue in the U.S. bicentennial year, 1976, *Time* published a report titled "The New Immigrant: Still the Promised Land," which described the immigrants' positive contributions to U.S. society. It characterized all immigrants, irrespective of their country of origin or the period in which they came, as bringing with them an intangible quality of energy and hope. It applauded the Hart-Celler Act of 1965 for having done away with discriminatory national origins quotas and allowing the admission of more people from poor countries, particularly Asian countries.[12]

In 1977, *Time* supported President Carter's proposal of amnesty for many of the 8 million to 12 million illegal aliens from Mexico believed to be living in the United States.[13]

In November of that year, *Time* reported that New England fruit growers had to get special permission to import some 1,500 Jamaicans and Canadians to harvest apples in Massachusetts. The foreign pickers arrived just in time to save the crop. The story went on to explain that even though few Americans are willing to do the work, the U.S. Labor Department has made it harder to hire foreign pickers on the ground that farmers should provide jobs for unemployed U.S. citizens.[14]

"Its Your Turn in the Sun" was an in-depth profile of the 19 million Hispanics in the United States. Using census data, the article described various groups within the Hispanic community and located them in different parts of the country. It described their demographic characteristics (age distribution, marital status, number of children, participation in the labor force) and prophesied that they would become a powerful voice in U.S. politics.[15]

"Justice's Wall" is how *Time* described the 10-foot–high fences the INS decided to build along sections of the boundary between Mexico and California and between Mexico and Texas. The cost of the project was estimated at $2,015,000. Its purpose was to wall off those sections of the 1,950-mile U.S.–Mexican border most frequently used by illegal immigrants.[16]

Time's first story on the most recent groups of refugees admitted to the United States appeared in May 1979. It focused on the Indochinese and the Soviet Jews but emphasized that the worldwide refugee problem was worse in that year than at any other time since World War II. The writers estimated that there were more than 10 million refugees in various parts of the world. Current U.S. law permitted 17,800 to settle in the United States annually, but Attorney General Griffin Bell used emergency "parole" powers and permitted 251,000 Indochinese and 18,000 Soviet Jews to enter the United States during the first two months of 1979. In March he permitted another 25,000 Soviet Jews and 35,000 Indochinese. *Time* reported that Bell urged passage of the Refugee Act of 1979, which would raise the normal refugee allotment to 50,000 a year.[17]

In an article that appeared in October 1979, *Time* described an operation along a strip of the U.S.–Mexican border near Tijuana where it estimated that 3,000 people crossed illegally every night. Smugglers usually charged $250 per person.[18]

As in the other magazines, the 1980s was a big decade for immigration coverage for the mass-market news weeklies. *Time* and *Newsweek* each carried 33 stories, and *U.S. News and World Report* ran 58. Each of these weeklies included more stories on immigration in the 1980s than in the earlier four or five decades combined.

In the 1970s, *Time* focused its immigration stories on illegal aliens. In the 1980s, it divided its emphasis between illegal aliens and Cuban and Haitian refugees. Unlike the magazines reviewed in the earlier chapters, most of *Time*'s stories were neutral in tone. Of the 15 pieces on illegal aliens from Mexico and Central America, 9 had neither a positive nor a negative bias, 2 were sympathetic toward the plight of the immigrant, and 4 were anti-immigrant, each holding to the theme that we were losing or we had lost control of our borders. Several of the articles quoted Attorney General William French Smith or congressional leaders who claimed, "With the Mexican economy in a crunch, and with other countries in Central and South America rocked by political instability, the steady stream of illegal immigrants is turning into a flood. Simply put, we've lost control of our borders."[19] Covering the debate on the Simpson-Mazzoli Bill, *Time* quoted President Reagan: "The bill's purpose is to regain control of our own borders and to prevent the further explosion of a shadow society composed of immigrants who live in the U.S. outside either the protection or the obligations of American laws."[20] In its two proimmigration articles, *Time* reported the arrest of 18 workers in New York City by armed INS agents on the mistaken assumption that they were illegal aliens. The writers commented,

Most Americans would probably agree with the INS's premise that illegal workers should not be stealing jobs from U.S. citizens. But last week's sweeping police victimization left a sour taste especially in view of its meager returns. The arrest of a few thousand people seemed a curious way to reduce the number of unemployed (ten million) or illegal aliens (some three million).[21]

The other pro piece focused on the good works of the Sanctuary Movement.

Christians who advocate lawbreaking for a higher good believe it is futile for the Central American exiles to apply for legal residency. Some 250,000 are in the U.S. illegally, and last year the INS approved only seventy-four applications for asylum from Salvadorans, rejected 1,067 and faces a backlog of 25,000 other cases.[22]

Nine articles on illegal aliens described "the underground workplace" in which illegal aliens formed "a vast pool of easily exploitable labor." Employed in such sweatboxes were Koreans, Cubans, and Mexicans who "make as little as $60 a week for seventy hours of work — less than a third of the minimum wage."[23] Another piece estimated the number of illegals coming into the United States at 1 million per year.[24]

In October 1986, *Time* reported on the major sections of the Immigration Act of 1986, focusing on employer sanctions (fines from $250 to $10,000 for each illegal alien hired) and "amnesty to illegal aliens who can show that they entered the country before January 1, 1982 and have lived here continuously since then."[25]

In June 1987, there was a story about "an unintended consequence" of the new Immigration Reform Act. *Time* reported a shortage of migrant workers, many of them "illegal aliens from Mexico, who are staying home or sticking close to the border this summer because they are afraid of deportation under the new law. In the meantime fruit crops are rotting in the fields."[26]

Most of the other pieces on illegal aliens discussed the likely impact of the new immigration act. Like the tenor of the pieces on illegal aliens, 13 of the 15 articles on Haitian and Cuban refugees were neutral, one favored granting political refugee status to the

Haitians, and the other deplored the "double standard that exists in the treatment of aliens seeking sanctuary in the U.S."[27] The other articles described the continuous struggle by groups seeking to gain official refugee status for the Haitians and concerns about the number of additional refugees from Cuba seeking admission. Three pieces described the successful resettlement of Vietnamese refugees in the United States.[28] A 1989 article entitled "The Immigration Mess" contained quotes from government officials who believed that the United States was on the verge of being swamped by a tidal wave of new arrivals from Central America and from the Soviet Union as a result of the Soviet Union's liberalized emigration policies. Wyoming Senator Alan Simpson (coauthor of the 1986 Immigration Act) commented, "We stand on the precipice of an enormous immigration crisis." *Time* authors wrote, "It is a crisis for which the U.S., despite its cherished history as a nation of immigrants is not prepared to cope." The piece concluded on an optimistic note:

Nevertheless, the beacon of hope for a better life in America burns brightest for those who endure the most profound debasement and despair in their native land. While the U.S. today is ill-equipped to take them all in, the dream lives on. Nor, despite the burden, is the U.S. likely to turn its back on its history by hanging out a sign that states No Vacancy.[29]

LIFE

Immigration was not a high-priority issue for the editors of *Life*. The magazine carried only ten stories on the topic in the almost four decades of its existence. Each article was proimmigrant and against restrictive measures. Its first piece, "Europe's Refugees Need a Place to Go and America Needs to Set a World Example," claimed that U.S. immigration laws were among the most discriminatory in the world and appealed to the generosity of the people of the United States to allow more displaced persons into the country. It argued that an annual quota of 153,000 should not seem too much for "a nation that had been built by immigrants."[30]

In 1947, Italian novelist Carlo Levi described Italian peasants' dream of the United States as an enchanted land of big cities and big riches. The United States to them was an earthly paradise. This myth, Levi wrote, was one of the chief incentives to emigration.[31]

Three of the six pieces on immigration that appeared in *Life* during the 1950s attacked the McCarran-Walter Act. One listed the names of world-famous intellectuals, scientists, artists, and writers whose visas were held up or who were denied entry because their political ties were questioned. Among the names were Michael

Polyani, philosopher; Alberto Moravio, novelist; E. G. Chair, Nobel Prize chemist; Graham Green, novelist. *Life* argued that it was counterproductive for the United States to behave as it did on the matter of whom we admit into the country yet spend $85 million per year on propaganda portraying itself as the land of the free.[32]

"Love or the Law" examined the problem of war brides who were having difficulty gaining entrance to the United States. One especially sympathetic case was dramatized: a Belgian war bride was not allowed to join her husband because of her criminal record — a record acquired as a result of resistance to the Nazis.[33]

A picture showing 50,000 aliens becoming citizens was the centerpiece for a story on how good immigrants have been and are for this country. "Immigration: The Real Issue," attacked the State Department for dragging its feet and not implementing effectively the Refugee Relief Act that President Eisenhower had described as a "new chance in life" for 214,000 people.[34]

The one piece on immigration that appeared in the 1960s supported the proposed Hart-Celler Act when it was debated in Congress.[35]

The 1970s included a piece on "America's Heritage" that contained a set of profiles (families and individuals) with brief biographical captions describing Swedes, Chinese, Irish, Greeks, and Germans.[36] Two pieces in December 1978 and September 1979 described the plight of the Vietnamese boat people and their search for a safe haven.[37] The 1978 story reported the arrival of a U.S. rescue vessel "just in time" to save the lives of many of the fleeing Vietnamese whose leaky craft was about to founder.

Life carried more stories on immigration in the 1980s than it did in any previous decade of its existence. Refugees and the new immigrants, mainly the Cubans, were the foci of most of the stories. The three stories on the Cuban-Mariel immigration showed sympathy and understanding. The stories did not focus on all of the negative characteristics that other publications reported this cohort of immigrants as having. For example, in its July 1980 piece "The Cuban Tide," *Life* wrote,

> Unlike those who fled Cuba in the years immediately following Castro's victory over Fulgencios Batista in 1959, the newcomers do not represent the upper strata of Cuban society. The great majority are craftsmen and manual laborers with only a smattering of professionals and businessmen. Fears that Castro emptied his prisons and insane asylums appear unfounded. Prison records are commonplace among the refugees, but they reflect a society that punishes its citizens for buying scarce food on the black market or for speaking too openly against the government.[38]

In November 1980, a piece entitled "No Haven for the Last of Cuba's Outcast" described the 10,000 Mariels imprisoned at Fort Chafee, Arkansas: "There are criminal and mental cases among them, but many are simply misfits, people with meager skills and little education — outcasts who have not found sponsors willing to guarantee their well being on the outside."[39]

Among the stories that appeared in 1981, one was a positive profile of recent immigrants to the United States. About the Cuban, Soviet Jewish, and Vietnamese refugees, *Life* wrote,

> However, newcomers generally do not tarry long on the public dole. Indeed, the same sense of initiative that inspired them to seek a new homeland seems to move them right along once they have arrived. Within a decade, immigrant families have begun to out-earn the native born, according to a recent federal study. Moreover, from the time they get their first job, immigrants promptly begin paying more in taxes than they take out in public services.[40]

One of the other two pieces described the status of illegal aliens, primarily young Mexican men who were smuggled across the border by coyotes. The piece described the hardships illegals endured in getting into the country and then focused on how hard they worked once they cross over. The article quoted a Los Angeles immgration officer: "We're not getting 'the weak,' 'the tired,' or 'those huddled masses' any more. We're getting eighteen and nineteen unemployed teenagers." Businessmen were quoted as saying, "I don't have to advertise for them, they just show up. I hire a guy and he either works his tail off or I go out and find another one." "No more Mexicans?" asked one plant foreman. "Why, we'd have to shut down. It's as simple as that." A Mexican illegal who came across the border five years previously was quoted:

> Within a few months we had saved up enough to pay a coyote to bring up the family — ten of them. He let us pay the $2500 in installments. With all the family here, we started our own little factory — we have four machines and everybody works. See that pile there? That's 500 pair of pants — at 50 cents apiece — and we have to finish all of them by tomorrow morning. For three days' work working all night, we'll make $250 — for all of us.[41]

Douglas Fraser, James Reston, Isaac Asimov, Elia Kazan, and Louis Nizer, all famous immigrants, were pictured at Ellis Island in a 1983 story that celebrated the restoration of the island and described plans to establish an immigration museum there. Of the remaining four stories about immigrants that *Life* carried in the 1980s, three described happy, successful adjustments by immigrant children in Florida schools, Ethiopians feeling at home in Indiana, and Taiwanese running businesses in Appalachia.[42]

The last piece of the decade appeared in April 1989 and focused on refugees all over the world. It portrayed refugee camps in Mexico, Pakistan, and Thailand and described the plight of some 14 million people struggling to find new homes and create new communities.[43]

NEWSWEEK

From 1936 to 1990, *Newsweek* carried 64 articles about immigration, approximately the same number as *Time* and approximately one-third less than *U.S. News and World Report*. The first appeared in 1939, and it described actions taken by Pennsylvania to track aliens more effectively by introducing identification cards.[44] The only other piece that year was an editorial by Raymond Moley urging admission of 20,000 German children who had escaped from the Nazis.[45]

Of the four stories about immigrants that appeared in *Newsweek* in the 1940s, three concerned displaced persons. Each of the three described the large number of such refugees (850,000) waiting to come to the United States, President Truman's desire to open the "Golden Doors," and the Stratton Bill.[46] The last piece told about the heavy flow of mail allegedly received by some congressmen whose constituents feared that the immigrants would take jobs and housing away from Americans.[47]

The McCarran-Walter Act occupied center stage in the *Newsweek* articles on immigration in the 1950s.[48] All but one of the nine articles dealt directly or indirectly with the bill itself or with the actions of its chief sponsor, the senator from Nevada.

Newsweek reported that in the final Senate debate on the McCarran-Walter Bill, Senator McCarran accused Senators Lehman and Humphrey, the two leaders of the opposition, of wanting to change the ethnic and cultural composition of the United States and flood it with Orientals.

The one article in 1951 that was unrelated to the McCarran-Walter Act concerned the brain drain from Canada to the United States. Canadian officials complained about the loss of 18,000 people a year to the United States, practically all of whom were of working age and a majority of whom were professionals or skilled workers.[49]

In 1956 *Newsweek* described the "good feeling" the United States had about permitting 25,000 Hungarian refugees to enter the country following the uprising against the Soviet Union. It reported that Senator John F. Kennedy of Massachusetts introduced a bill that allowed for the transfer of 60,000 unused quotas to any country where the demand exceeded the supply.[50]

The two pieces on immigrants that appeared in the 1960s both dealt with the new immigrant act that would do away with the national origins quota system. After the Senate passed the Hart-Celler Act, *Newsweek* reviewed the 1921 and 1924 Quota Acts, labeling them discriminatory against certain ethnic groups. It also reported that Senators Everett Dirksen and Sam Erwin had added an amendment to the bill that limited immigration from the Western Hemisphere to 120,000 per year.[51]

The five stories that appeared in the 1970s touched on a variety of issues. *Newsweek* reported on the anti–"colored"-immigrant attitudes in Great Britain, the Carter proposal to grant amnesty to illegal aliens who had been living in the United States for a long time, and another Carter proposal to admit 50,000 refugees each year with no ideological or geographical requirements.[52]

"Round Up of the People Smugglers" was the caption for a story that described arrests in Tijuana by the Mexican government of 136 people who organized the movement of Mexicans into the United States. The article reported that human smuggling was a billion-dollar-a-year business. It described the horrendous treatment that the Mexicans received at the hands of the smugglers.[53]

A short piece on the decision by the Immigration and Naturalization Service to no longer exclude homosexuals, even though the law forbidding their admission would remain on the books, ended the decade.[54]

In the 1980s, *Newsweek* also covered a broad array of issues about immigration. It paid less attention to refugees and illegals than did *Time, The Nation, Christian Century*, and most of the other magazines. Less than one-third of *Newsweek*'s coverage was devoted to refugees. Those stories that described refugees seemed focused on the Cubans and the Haitians along with one story apiece on Afghans and Soviet Jews. *Newsweek*'s other pieces on immigration reported on the experiences of illegal aliens from Mexico and Central America, the 1986 Immigration Reform Bill, the children of immigrants, brain drain problems, and European immigrants.

In April 1980 and October 1989, *Newsweek* carried articles about the worldwide refugee problem. The 1980 piece cited United Nation's figures that estimated the number of refugees in the world at 9 million.[55] In the 1989 piece the figure quoted was 15 million, with most of the refugees fleeing from regimes in Africa and Asia.[56] The 1980 piece discussed the recently passed Refugee Act of 1980 that dropped earlier geographic and ideological restrictions and provided a broader definition of a refugee as anyone fleeing racial, religious, political, or social persecution. The new law would admit 231,700 refugees in fiscal year 1980 and grant the president emergency authority to permit more if he saw fit. The 1989 article focused on the part of the world from which the United States was most likely to accept refugees. The article noted that,

> Washington rejects 97 percent of the asylum applications from friendly El Salvador despite the fact that more than 60,000 civilians have been killed there in the past decade. Haitian refugees get even rougher treatment. Since 1981, the U.S. Coast Guard has been intercepting boat loads of them in the high seas. Beyond the jurisdiction of U.S. courts, officers of the Immigration and Naturalization Service conduct shipboard hearings on asylum cases. INS claims the Haitians are merely economic migrants looking for a better life. Human right groups call the hearings a sham. Despite widespread political violence in Haiti, only six of the more than 20,000 Haitians intercepted so far have been allowed into the United States to apply for asylum. Africa's 4 million refugees are out of sight and out of mind. . . . The Soviet refugees' greatest asset has been the powerful support of the American Jewish community and voluntary resettlement organizations backing their causes.
>
> Unlike their counterparts in Africa or Latin America, refugees from Southeast Asia have powerful patrons in veterans groups, Congress, and the administration.

The pieces on the Cubans and Haitians that were included over the course of the decade covered the Cubans' reception in the United States (mostly Florida) and the numbers fleeing. About the Haitians, the focus was always on their failure to gain formal political refugee recognition. Most of the pieces on the Cubans had a negative tone: "Fidel Castro is taking advantage of the situation by exporting common criminals and other undesirables,"[57] but, the Haitian stories were generally sympathetic:

> At the heart of the matter is a dispute about whether the Haitians are fleeing oppression or poverty: are they in danger from the regime of Jean-Claude (Baby Doc) Duvalier, or are they, as the U.S. government argues, simply people who want to better their lot in life. For many Haitians, the victims of swindlers, extortion, and abuse at the hands of the Tontons Macoutes, the distinction is an artificial one.[58]

Illegal aliens mostly from Mexico and El Salvador were topics for some 15 of *Newsweek*'s pieces on immigration. Most of those pieces also had a positive tone vis-à-vis the immigrants. Concerning an INS raid and arrest of illegals, *Newsweek* stated, "Hispanic leaders charged that Mexicans were being singled out as scapegoats for the nation's economic woes." The article commented, "Indeed while Mexicans constitute only about half of the estimated 4 million to 6 million illegal aliens in the United States, more than eighty percent of those arrested last week were Mexicans and many of the remaining were Hispanics."[59]

That same month *Newsweek* devoted its "My Turn" column to the subject of illegal aliens and, under the title "Citizens in All But Names," had this to say about illegals in southern California:

They lived better than they had in their own country, but humbly and often in fear. They were afraid to make trouble and often would be afraid to look me in the eye when I spoke to them. They asked little of the government, received little, yet they paid sales tax every time they bought groceries. They went to free clinics for medical care, if they knew about them, or ignored their health problems.

Most of the undocumented workers I met and talked to lived quietly on the money when they could get it. The neighbors banded together and many of the women worked, leaving their children at one house during the day. They sent money home to family members still living in Mexico, always hoping they could save enough to buy the expensive passage across the border. They bothered no one and asked only to be left in peace.[60]

Other stories on immigration reported in *Newsweek* described "sham marriages for immigration purposes." *Newsweek* wrote, "Of the 111,653 aliens who married U.S. citizens last year, as many as 40 percent did so only to bypass immigration laws, the INS believes."[61]

It carried an account of a proposal to resettle all of the Amerasian children (estimated at between 8,000 and 15,000) who were left behind when U.S. troops pulled out of Vietnam in 1975. The children were shunned by the Vietnamese and often forced "to fend for themselves by begging, stealing, or worse. For almost a decade, they were either ignored or offered only limited hope of escaping their plight. But last week the United States finally moved to make amends to the left behinds."[62]

That new Americans were still pouring in by the millions and the natives were migrating to the South and West was the theme of a January 1983 story.[63] In the years 1977, 1978, and 1979, the article continued, more immigrants were admitted than during any other years since 1924. They were coming mostly from Asia and the Pacific Islands. For the decade from July 30, 1969, to September 30, 1979, the INS reported 4.3 million immigrants admitted to the United States. The tone of the article was neutral; no judgement was implicitly or explicitly made about the increasing non-European character of the U.S. population.

U.S. NEWS AND WORLD REPORT

Until the 1970s, the amount of coverage *U.S. News and World Report* allocated to immigration was on a par with that of *Time* and *Newsweek*. In the 1970s, *U.S. News and World Report* carried 21 stories on immigration, compared with 5 in *Newsweek* and 9 in *Time*. In the 1980s it carried 63 pieces on immigration, almost twice as many times as *Time* and 50 more than *Newsweek*. Many of the 1980 pieces were editorials with anti-immigrant overtones. Unlike *Time* and *Newsweek*, many of its stories were long, in-depth analyses of some aspect of the immigration issue. They were more interpretative, they contained more debate, and they appeared more scholarly.

Such, for example, were the six pieces *U.S. News and World Report* carried on displaced persons following World War II.[64] Unlike *Time* and *Newsweek*, each *U.S. News and World Report* story offered an in-depth analysis of the issue. "U.S. Issues in Refugee Plight: Shall We Alter Immigration Law?" contained tables and graphs describing from where the demand for entry was coming, the countries whose quotas were not being used, and what the trends over time were.[65]

Two articles in 1947 reviewed the various options that Congress was considering concerning immigration law. A U.S. official stationed abroad was quoted as having said, "Almost everybody in Europe would move to the United States if given half a chance." It reported that Representative Emanuel Celler's plan would let in an additional 2 million refugees by exhausting all of the unused immigration quotas since 1924.[66] Another proposal, put forth by Representative Stephen Pace of Georgia, which was described as an extreme response to the Celler plan, would have banned immigration whenever the number of unemployed Americans exceeded 100. In addition to the Celler and Pace plans, there were approximately a half-dozen others that called for admitting from 150,000 to 850,000 displaced persons.[67]

The same issue also carried an editorial by David Lawrence that appealed to the Christian charity of Americans and urged that the United States open its doors to the victims of totalitarianism.[68]

In 1948 *U.S. News and World Report* published an article on "How the U.S. Would Absorb 200,000 War Refugees." A three-man commission had been established, the article explained, that would decide which 200,000 would be selected from the 1.3 million displaced persons. Racial groups would be varied so that approximately half of the people would come from Estonia, Latvia, Lithuania, and Eastern

Poland. Approximately 25 percent would be Jews. Youths 16 years old or younger who had been adopted by U.S. citizens or organizations in the United States would be given first priority. Farmers would comprise the largest group of displaced persons, followed by skilled workers. Efforts would be made to scatter most of the 200,000 all over the country and not have them concentrate in New York City.[69]

"We've Been Asked — How to Hire Displaced Persons" was the theme of a question and answer scenario that *U.S. News and World Report* published in 1948. The article provided answers to bread-and-butter–type questions: How are workers selected? What must employees promise? How will private agencies help? A second part, using the same format, appeared in September 1949 about the rules for hiring displaced persons. Questions were asked such as, Is an employer bound to pay a displaced person a certain wage? Can a displaced person be fired? Who checks on the wages he actually receives?[70]

Unlike *Time* and *Newsweek*, *U.S. News and World Report* devoted most of its ten pieces on immigration in the 1950s to statistics rather than to the rhetoric used by the pro– and anti–McCarran-Walter Act forces. In its two articles in 1952, *U.S. News and World Report* employed its "We've been asked" format to summarize who was likely to come and from where in the next few years.[71] It predicted that the United States would not admit a large number of immigrants and that the quota system would remain.

The reasoning behind the recently passed McCarran-Walter Act was summarized this way: "The structure of U.S. population is set; there is no need for another mass migration." It was pointed out that the McCarran-Walter Act saved seven of ten quota numbers for British, Irish, and German people.[72]

A 1955 piece provided charts and tables explaining who was coming to the United States from which countries: 94,098 under the quota system, and 114,079 from nonquota countries such as Canada and Latin America as well as spouses and children of U.S. citizens.[73]

In 1957 *U.S. News and World Report* saw a significant increase in immigrants to the United States. It identified the number that arrived in the fiscal year that ended June 30, 1956 as the peak in the flood of foreign born arriving since 1927: 321,625. President Eisenhower was urging Congress to allow more. The State Department and the INS reported that immigrants were making a smooth adjustment to life in the United States.[74]

In its last piece of the decade, *U.S. News and World Report* showed that 325,000 immigrants had been admitted in 1957 and that altogether in the past 12 years, 2.6 million immigrants had arrived. This number did not include some 200,000 Puerto Ricans who were arriving annually.[75] None of the articles made any evaluations of how the numbers might affect the U.S. economy or society.

The five pieces *U.S. News and World Report* carried on immigration in the 1960s described legislation that would, and did, nullify the McCarran-Walter Act and the national origins quota system of the 1920s. Its first piece provided a detailed analysis of President John F. Kennedy's proposals on immigration. The essential elements involved extending to Jamaica, Trinidad, and Tobago the open-door policy as it was to all Western Hemisphere people; altering the quota system so that unused quotas from northern Europe could be used in Italy, Greece, and other countries in southern and eastern Europe; removing restrictions on the Orient; wiping out country-by-country quotas over a five-year period; raising quotas for the world, except for the Western Hemisphere, by about 10,000; and giving the president power to set aside up to 20 percent of the world quota in any year for the exclusive use of refugees.[76]

Kennedy's proposals were adopted and supported by President Lyndon Johnson. *U.S. News and World Report* carried a story on the problems facing Johnson's proposal. Most involved Senator James Eastland, who was both chairman of the Senate Judiciary Committee and chairman of the Subcommittee on Immigration Law. Senator John McClellan of Arkansas also served on that subcommittee. Both were strong opponents of liberalization of the immigration law.[77]

In a September 1965 story, *U.S. News and World Report* reported that the only issue holding up passage of a new immigration law was whether the United States should put a limit on the number of immigrants entering from Western Hemisphere nations.[78] Two other pieces in the 1960s provided detailed historical statistics on who came, when, and from which countries; who were likely to come, in what numbers, from which parts of the world; and what the provisions were of the new immigration act.

With 21 stories, immigration was one of the major topics for *U.S. News and World Report* in the 1970s. In October 1970 and again in June 1971, the magazine published graphs, tables, and trends from the 1930s to the 1970s about the number of immigrants who came to the United States and from where they came.[79] It pointed out that immigration from Asia, the Caribbean Islands, Africa, and Australia was up and European immigration was down. While noting the concerns expressed by some immigration officials that these "new immigrants might have a difficult time adjusting," *U.S. News and World Report* pointed out that a substantial number of them had professional and technical skills that were in short supply in the United States, skills that would enhance their adjustment.[80]

Beginning in 1972 and continuing until the end of the decade, almost all of the 19 stories *U.S. News and World Report* carried on immigration focused on illegal immigrants. The magazine pointed out that no one knew accurately how many illegals there were in the country, but it quoted estimates from the INS of as many as 10 million.

Three of its stories included long interviews with the then-director of the INS, Leonard Chapman, whose statements on illegal aliens sounded much like those of Francis Walker, former director when he was describing the "new immigrants" of the 1890s and early part of the twentieth century.[81] Chapman warned in each interview that the problem was very serious and getting worse. In a 1974 interview, he estimated that there were between 5 and 7 million illegal aliens in the United States and that in a few years there would be 10 million, then soon 15 million or more. They were occupying positions Americans coveted in industry and in services, he claimed. Chapman advocated employer sanctions and identification cards. In another interview conducted on December 9 of the same year, Chapman claimed that the INS apprehended 800,000 illegals over the past year. He estimated that there were probably 6 to 8 million in the United States, the majority of whom were holding jobs that were needed by unemployed Americans, including Vietnam veterans, blacks, Mexican Americans, other minorities, and legal aliens. He claimed that illegals did not pay taxes but that they used medical care, schools, and other services.

In a January 1976 interview, Chapman pushed hard for the passage of employer sanctions. He predicted that in the next three decades the new immigrants and their descendants would total 15 million, 25 percent of the total population increase. In 1975 *U.S. News and World Report* ran a piece on illegal immigrants that examined their impact on major urban centers — New York, Detroit, Miami, Chicago, San Francisco, Los Angeles, and Houston — where the immigrants were reported to be the recipients of food stamps, medical care, and other benefits.[82]

In April 1976, *U.S. News and World Report* carried a story about legal immigrants — the Asians. It was composed completely of charts showing numbers and points of origin. In the same story, sociologist Nathan Glazer was quoted as arguing that these "new immigrants" had no connection with and were a different type of people than the Europeans who had been coming for more than 150 years. These recent ones, Glazer argued, lacked the Protestant work ethic, had a Third World consciousness, and were not seeking the freedom and opportunities that motivated the movement of European immigrants. *U.S. News and World Report* concluded that scholars were divided on the answer to the question of whether the United States could absorb the new immigrant "hordes" who were arriving in the 1970s.[83]

In a piece titled "Crisis Across the Border," *U.S. News and World Report* reported that legal entries from Mexico to the United States (excluding minor children, spouses, and parents of U.S. citizens) would be cut from 40,000 to 20,000.[84]

Of the four pieces that appeared in 1977, one was an editorial that claimed that there were currently 6 million illegals from Mexico in the United States. The editorial predicted that, in the ensuing ten years, those illegals would give birth to possibly 15 million offspring. It quoted sources that placed the cost of illegals to the United States at $13 billion per year for welfare and education alone. The editorial urged employers not to hire illegals and to fire them if they hired them unknowingly. Those employers who would not cooperate should be subject to sanctions, it asserted.[85]

Of the 17 published letters to *U.S. News and World Report* about its editorial on the illegals, 10 were negative, urging tougher policies against the aliens and those who hired them, 2 were mixed or neutral in their attitudes and recommendations, and 5 were positive in that they saw the U.S. public as the major beneficiary of the illegals. The illegals worked at lower wages and the reduced costs were passed on to the consumers; or the illegals worked at jobs the U.S. laborer avoided.[86]

U.S. News and World Report finished out the decade with four stories on the boat people, who were coming mostly from Southeast Asia. It saw the U.S. policy of welcoming the refugees as part of its historical commitment to homeless people. It pointed out that on an emergency basis, the United States first admitted the Hungarians in 1956 and the Cubans in 1959 and 1960. In an editorial titled "Still a Land of Refugees," *U.S. News and World Report* urged the United States to "stretch out our hands in the spirit of humanity and for the good of our souls."[87]

In another piece, *U.S. News and World Report* described immigrants as sources of fresh ideas. It described them as a different breed than the huddled masses who once thronged to U.S. shores and said the legal immigrants of today were aggressive urbanites with considerable sophistication; they were not wide-eyed peasants.[88]

All told, *U.S. News and World Report* was enthusiastic about the prospect of having many legal immigrants from Asia come to the United States. The writers were apprehensive and saw dangers to the U.S. economy if the illegal flow from Mexico was not stopped or brought under much greater control. Mexican illegals were perceived as a drain on the U.S. economy and a social and cultural liability. Asians, on the other hand, were viewed as a positive factor to the U.S. economy and as contributing enormously to U.S. social and cultural life.

In the 1980s, *U.S. News and World Report* devoted two thirds of its 63 pieces on immigration to illegals. Many of the pieces were editorials that had negative overtones. In September 1980, editor Marvin Stone advocated creation of an employee identification card.

Such a card, Stone wrote, "could be obtained only with documented proof of eligibility and would be hard to counterfeit. Any person seeking a job would be required to show the card." Stone continued,

In this time of high unemployment, it is natural that demands again are growing for Washington to do something about illegal aliens — the multiplying legions sneaking into this country and taking jobs needed by citizens. Officials estimate there are at least 3 million illegal aliens in this country, perhaps as many as 6 million. And the influx seems endless.[89]

In December 1980, *U.S. News and World Report* carried a news story with the headline "Immigration Seen Out of Control." Reporting on a recent story by the General Accounting Office, the article quoted the INS as stating it "cannot cope with the illegal — alien population," which the accounting office said might total 5 million or more. "An illegal alien, once safely into the U.S. has little chance of being located and deported." The article also reported on a study by the Joint Economic Committee of Congress that stated "American taxpayers are spending 2 billion dollars a year caring for refugees from Cuba, Haiti, and Indochina. The piece concluded, "The study found that administrative decisions by the U.S. government encourage people to leave Indo-China for America, even when there is no threat to their lives and property. Unless policies are changed, the study said, Indo-Chinese will keep coming to the U.S. in large numbers."[90]

Of the other three pieces on immigration that appeared in 1980, one described conditions in sweat shops that "thrive on the cheap labor of illegal aliens" that have sprung up in lower Manhattan and "in the heart of Los Angeles." Workers were fearful of being deported or losing their jobs if they complained about unsafe conditions or wages below the $3.10 minimum hourly wage.[91] Another piece reported the death of 13 Salvadorans who "perished trying to enter the U.S. illegally." The article described how illegals from Mexico, El Salvador, Guatemala, Colombia, and Ecuador drown each year swimming the Rio Grande to Texas.[92]

Of the five pieces that appeared in 1981, four focused on illegals, including an editorial by Stone expressing frustration at the government's failure to deal effectively with the problems of aliens crossing our borders and entering the country illegally. "The U.S.," the editorial concluded, "is the only country that imports a poverty class".[93]

Most of the other pieces reported the recommendations of the Select Commission and Refugee Policy, which included:

Allow persons who entered the U.S. illegally before 1980 to remain in the country legally.

Boost legal immigration — now limited to 270,000 persons a year — to an annual total of 350,000.

Authorize the prosecution of persons who hire illegal aliens.

Beef up border-guard forces to cut the number of aliens who slip into the country and to stem the flow of drugs and other "illicit goods."

The commission voted nine to seven against requiring everyone to carry special identity cards.[94]

In a piece entitled, "Making It in America: Four Immigrant Odysseys," the authors described four "success stories" by recent immigrants from the Soviet Union, Uganda, Vietnam, and Mexico. Each account stressed how hard family members worked and how they wanted to "make it" in the United States.[95]

Seven of the eight pieces in 1982 focused on illegals and two were editorials by Stone anguished at the "legions of aliens" who continued to "pour across our borders each year." In Stone's words, "If newcomers show skill and initiative as workers and entrepreneurs, they often cut in on the livelihood of local people and arouse hostility; if not, they lean heavily on the public purse."[96]

Other pieces in 1982 described the new flood of Cubans and Haitians coming in; a new bill already passed by the Senate (Simpson-Mazzoli), aimed at preventing illegal immigrants from getting jobs by instituting sanctions against employers who hire illegals; and the lucrative business that had sprung up for professional smugglers who "form a vast network across the U.S. often operating in concert with middle men who supply cheap and compliant labor to American employers."[97]

"Drain and Its Benefit to the U.S." was a piece on the Soviet mathematicians who had emigrated to the United States.[98] The story reported that "in the last 10 years, nearly 70 distinguished Soviet mathematicians have immigrated to the U.S. and now teach at leading universities." Their arrival was compared with the exodus of scientists from Nazi Germany in the 1930s and the rich harvest they were for the United States.

The Sanctuary Movement was the focus of a story that characterized it as "a modern-day underground railroad" and as doing "what the church has always done in serving people who come to this country with nothing but the shirts on their backs."[99]

Marvin Stone wrote three editorials during this period on the urgency of controlling our borders before hundreds of thousands or millions of new illegal inhabitants crossed into the United States. "Although we are sympathetic and friendly and want to be helpful, there is no justice in any thought that we are obligated to take in others' poor and care for them at the expense of our own."[100] An editorial in 1984 was a plea for passage of the Simpson-Mazzoli Bill.

Stone quoted Donald Huddle, an economist at Rice University, who calculated "that unless we do something to lower the current rate of border crossings, newly arrived illegals will replace some 650,000 U.S. workers annually." The cost of helping unemployed citizens would rise by an additional $4 billion each year. Stone concluded, "If all this sounds harsh, remember that the law is to protect our own borders, as well as American workers. Congress should take note and find courage."[101]

In 1986, Mortimer B. Zuckerman took over as editor of *U.S. News and World Report*. He wrote an editorial entitled "Yankee Doodle Is Dandy" and informed his readers that he was an immigrant. Describing his own experience, Zuckerman wrote,

This helped me empathize with those earlier immigrants to America, now 50 million since 1820. Breaking with their past, they crossed the seas, most of them uprooted without the ability to speak English, without a job, the support of the community or the familiarity of custom to cushion the shock of the move. Their alienation had to be so much more complete and continuous than mine, their adjustment so much more painful, their need to improvise so much greater that their lives must have been ones of trauma after trauma. My respect for their courage and strength expanded into awe.[102]

Of the other eight pieces that year, three appeared in the same issue as the Zuckerman editorial. They characterized "America" as a land of immigrants. Two did so in statistical terms, where we came from and when the new immigrants were likely to come and from where. The other piece was the American dream retold.[103] As the author, William Broyles, Jr., wrote,

Violence, repression, persecution, and poverty may encircle their lives, but they dream of something better — of freedom. Almost 500 years old, the dream still works on the imagination like a magic name: America for each new immigrant — the dream is born again, fresh and powerful. "Come," it says, "no matter who you are and be one of us. Come and be free."

Broyles went on to say,

Today we are living in a reawakening of the immigrant experience: not since the first decade of the 20th century have so many new immigrants become Americans. Some 7 million legal immigrants are expected this decade, with perhaps millions more entering illegally. New ethnic neighborhoods are transforming our cities; new faces are turning up in our shops and factories; new languages buzz in our schools. This bubbly stem may seem strange to us, but until immigration was all but cut off in 1924 it was the condition of America.

The foreign born population in 1980 was less than half what it was in 1910.

On illegals, Broyles quoted economist Donald Huddle's estimate that for every 100 illegal workers, 65 Americans lose their jobs, but he then commented, "other studies conclude that the illegal aliens pay more in taxes than they draw in services and that they help stimulate economic growth." He concluded "Despite the costs — and even the pain — that may be caused by immigration, the benefits are incalculable. Our neighborhoods, our schools, our work places are being revived and invigorated. Each immigrant re-creates the American dream."

Illegals were the theme of other immigrant stories that year. Two focused on illegals taking jobs from U.S. workers and one on the growing violence at the border as a result of confrontations between border guards and aliens desperate to cross over.[104]

In the last three years of the decade, 8 of the 14 articles described various aspects of the illegal experience: if the trek north could be curbed; whether the Salvadorans should be granted refugee status; the plight of children who were detained and locked up when they were caught trying to cross the border; and the death of 19 Mexicans who were trapped in a locked boxcar and suffocated.

Three pieces examined the impact that the Simpson-Rodino Bill, with its employer sanctions and amnesty program, would be likely to have on illegals already in the country, and one piece described a new group of illegals: the Irish. The article stated, "Despite the enormous number of visa applications, the U.S. . . . accepts legally only 515 Irish immigrants annually. As a result, many simply come on tourist visas and never go home. The number of Irish 'illegals' in the U.S. may exceed 200,000."[105]

Another piece focused on another source of European immigrants — the nannie. The article reviewed the decision in 1981 by the U.S. Information Agency to stretch its definition of cultural exchange to include live-in babysitters, young women "who have come to be known in Europe as 'au pairs' — meaning they live 'on a par' with their host families." Two years later, the chief counsel of the United States announced that the program "was a clear violation of both the letter and the intent of the law." The decision was protested by many members of Congress, including Senators Claiborne Pell, Pat Moynihan, Jesse Helms, Ted Kennedy, and John Glenn.[106]

There was also a piece on immigrant entrepreneurs:

The American dream is alive and flourishing. But for most of today's immigrants, the trail to the top is vastly different. They are starting family businesses instead of taking factory jobs. And new ethnic networks are providing the bootstraps. . . . Today's huddled masses arrive with know how and often cash. In 1911, fewer than 2 percent of all entrants claimed to be technicians or managers, government tallies show; by 1986, the proportion has swelled to 32 percent.

For most ethnic entrepreneurs, though, the real point of running a family business is family, not business. They toil to ensure their children college educations and solid careers as doctors and lawyers, not as salesclerks.[107]

In the last year of the decade, *U.S. News and World Report* carried the fewest number of articles on immigration — two. One was on the Soviet Jews, of which the article claimed, "Gorbachev is unleashing a flood tide — a quarter million are expected next year." The numbers are causing problems in Washington, the article explains. "The President's advisors will argue that room must be left for refugees from other hot spots — China for instance — and that some of the flow must be diverted to nations such as Israel, Australia, and Canada, with room and a hunger for fresh talent."[108] The other piece described a bill passed by the Senate that would increase the number of professional and educated immigrants by allowing more people altogether. The new total would be 630,000 — 480,000 visas would go to close relations of U.S. citizens and 150,000, a threefold increase, would go to "independent immigrants" without family connections but with special know-how.[109]

NOTES

1. *Time*, September 10, 1939.
2. Ibid., October 19, 1940.
3. Ibid., March 12, 1942.
4. Ibid., June 17, 1946.
5. Ibid., June 24, 1948.
6. Ibid., April 17, 1950.
7. Ibid., October 27, 1952.
8. Ibid., January 5, 1953; July 13, 1953; August 3, 1953; February 21, 1955; July 25, 1955; August 26, 1957; January 20, 1958.
9. Ibid., January 10, 1966.
10. Ibid., October 11, 1968.
11. Ibid., May 19, 1975.
12. Ibid., July 4, 1976.
13. Ibid., September 26, 1977.
14. Ibid., November 7, 1977.
15. Ibid., October 16, 1978.
16. Ibid., October 30, 1978.

17.   Ibid., May 14, 1979.
18.   Ibid., October 8, 1979.
19.   Ibid., June 13, 1983.
20.   Ibid., July 2, 1984.
21.   Ibid., May 10, 1982.
22.   Ibid., April 25, 1982.
23.   Ibid., September 7, 1981.
24.   Ibid., August 30, 1982.
25.   Ibid., October 27, 1986.
26.   Ibid., June 16, 1987.
27.   Ibid., July 26, 1982; April 28, 1986.
28.   Ibid., January 19, May 10 and December 12, 1982.
29.   Ibid., February 27, 1989.
30.   *Life*, September 23, 1946.
31.   Ibid., July 7, 1947.
32.   Ibid., February 14, 1953.
33.   Ibid., October 21, 1954.
34.   Ibid., April 25, 1955.
35.   Ibid., May 21, 1965.
36.   Ibid., December 17, 1971.
37.   Ibid., December 6, 1978; September 21, 1979.
38.   Ibid., July 1980.
39.   Ibid., November 1980.
40.   Ibid., January 1981.
41.   Ibid., July 1981.
42.   Ibid., July 1983.
43.   Ibid., April 1989.
44.   *Newsweek*, December 4, 1939.
45.   Ibid., July 10, 1939.
46.   Ibid., December 30, 1946.
47.   Ibid., May 10, 1948.
48.   Ibid., February 6, 1950; June 2, 1952; June 23, 1952; January 5, 1953; July 13, 1953; January 7, 1957; July 15, 1957.
49.   Ibid., May 24, 1951.
50.   Ibid., September 9, 1956.
51.   Ibid., December 2, 1965.
52.   Ibid., April 2, 1979.
53.   Ibid., July 30, 1979.
54.   Ibid., August 27, 1979.
55.   Ibid., April 28, 1980.
56.   Ibid., October 9, 1989.
57.   Ibid., May 5, 1980.
58.   Ibid., January 11, 1982.
59.   Ibid., May 10, 1982.
60.   Ibid., May 31, 1982.
61.   Ibid., December 23, 1985.
62.   Ibid., November 24, 1984.
63.   Ibid., January 17, 1983.
64.   *U.S. News and World Report*, September 20, 1946; February 14, 1947; March 7, 1947; June 11, 1948; June 25, 1948; September 2, 1949.
65.   Ibid., September 20, 1946.
66.   Ibid., February 14, 1947.
67.   Ibid.
68.   Ibid.

69. Ibid., June 11, 1948.
70. Ibid., September 12, 1948.
71. Ibid., June 13, October 31, 1952.
72. Ibid., January 10, 1953.
73. Ibid., April 29, 1955.
74. Ibid., February 15, 1957.
75. Ibid., September 27, 1957.
76. Ibid., August 15, 1963.
77. Ibid., January 25, 1965.
78. Ibid., September 6, 1965.
79. Ibid., October 15, 1970; June 14, 1971.
80. Ibid., October 5, 1970.
81. Ibid., July 22, 1974; December 9, 1974; January 26, 1976.
82. Ibid., February 3, 1975.
83. Ibid., April 5, 1976.
84. Ibid., December 13, 1976.
85. Ibid., July 4, 1977.
86. Ibid., August 13, 1977.
87. Ibid., August 16, 1979.
88. Ibid., November 21, 1979.
89. Ibid., September 15, 1980.
90. Ibid., December 15, 1980.
91. Ibid., January 14, 1980.
92. Ibid., July 21, 1980.
93. Ibid., May 25, 1981.
94. Ibid., August 3, 1981.
95. Ibid., August 17, 1981.
96. Ibid., August 16, 1982.
97. Ibid., September 13, 1972.
98. Ibid., January 17, 1983.
99. Ibid., September 24, 1984.
100. Ibid., January 31, 1983.
101. Ibid., March 5, 1984.
102. Ibid., July 7, 1986.
103. Ibid.
104. Ibid., April 28, August 6, October 27, 1986.
105. Ibid., March 2, 1987.
106. Ibid., March 21, 1988.
107. Ibid., April 25, 1988.
108. Ibid., September 18, 1989.
109. Ibid., July 24, 1989.

11

The *New York Times* Editorials, 1880–1990

We limited coverage of the *New York Times* from 1880 to 1980 to its editorial page, and even that was not exhaustive. For the first 100 years we reported and commented on editorials that appeared in the first six months of the even-numbered years and in the last six months of the odd-numbered years. In the decade from 1980 to 1990, we examined every piece on immigration that appeared in the *New York Times* editorial page; thus, we included op-eds, columnists, and editorials.

1880s

Most of the editorials in the decade of the 1880s favored restrictions on immigration. The *New York Times* was especially worried about the large number of criminals, lunatics, and paupers that it believed comprised the ranks of the immigrant population. The paper's stereotyping of certain immigrant groups contrasted with its reports on U.S. policy prohibiting Chinese immigration. On this issue, the *New York Times* was more neutral. It attributed its stance to the notion that it was more a matter of concern to Americans out West than to those in the East; because easterners could not experience the westerners' sentiments, they should stay out of any disputes on this matter.[1]

In 1880, six editorials were published that discussed the issues of Chinese residents in the United States, relations with China, and the marked increase in immigration generally. Two editorials noted that a San Francisco circuit court decision had declared unconstitutional a California law that forbade corporations to employ Chinese, that the actual number of Chinese in the United States was low, and that the outcry against the Chinese was organized by a group of "creatures, who will not work and who foment dissension for sinister purposes."[2] A third editorial criticized the strong anti-Chinese attitudes of many Americans and described the emotional climate in China as antiforeigner and readying itself for war.[3]

The three editorials that discussed the overall increase in immigrants did so in a generally positive manner. The *New York Times* editors claimed that because most of the 400,000 or 500,000 men and women were skilled laborers, the nation's wealth and industrial resources would increase. The *New York Times* advocated shifting the financial burden for upkeep of immigrant services to the national government and urged prohibiting vessel owners from bringing to the United States "criminals, paupers, lunatics and other helpless creatures who must, of necessity, become an immediate charge on the public."[4] One editorial reported happily that many of the new immigrants had money with them and were heading west. The editor wrote,

> There is a limit to our powers of assimilation and when it is exceeded the country suffers from something very like indigestion. We are willing to receive immigrants just as fast as we can make them over into good American citizens, adding to our bone and sinew and increasing our productive capacity. . . . Our chief cause of anxiety concerning the swarms of newcomers is once removed by the fact that a large proportion of them are bound for the West. . . . The most casual acquaintance with the affairs of this city and with the habits of the denizens of its foreign quarters suffices to produce the conviction that we are not in need of any more aliens at present. Foreigners who come here and herd together like sheep in East-Side Tenement houses remain foreigners all their lives. . . . We know how stubbornly conservative of his dirt and his ignorance is the average immigrant who settles in New York, particularly if he is of a clannish race like the Italians. Born in squalor, raised in filth and misery and kept at work almost from infancy, these wretched beings change their abode, but not their habits, in coming to New York. . . . A bad Irish-American boy is about as unwholesome a product as was ever reared in any body politic. . . . Germans, Danes and Scandinavians are of thrifty habits and make excellent citizens.[5]

In 1882 two editorials critically discussed the newly passed Chinese Exclusion Act; and the only relevant editorial in 1884 concerned pending measures aimed at closing some loopholes in the 1882 act. The law permitted the landing of Chinese immigrants who came for purposes of trade. According to the *New York Times*, due to this provision, "many hundreds of coolies have been landed, many of whom are false traders." It concluded, "The loopholes may thus be closed for a time, but it is morally certain that should the law be amended in these particulars, new methods of ingress will be discovered by the ingenious Chinese."[6]

In 1886 the *New York Times* became more adamant in calling for greater immigration restrictions. The first editorial celebrated the fact that "our Emigrant Commissioners will soon have an opportunity to enforce the law against a cargo of very undesirable human beings . . . a party of 100 professional beggars from Malta." The *New York Times* bemoaned the fact that although these people would be prohibited from coming ashore in the United States, "they will then likely land in Canada and come across the border as the Arab beggars did a year or two ago after they had been taken from this port to Canada."[7]

Another editorial applauded "the vigilance and success with which the terrible Chinese immigrants are pursued by the U.S. government."[8] The *New York Times* reported that some Chinese laborers who had landed on the Atlantic coast and said they wanted to return home via San Francisco had disappeared. From then on the Chinese were to travel with numbered passes. A *New York Times* editor commented,

> But unless the offender paints the number of his pass on his laundry sign, when he melts into the indistinguishable mass of his fellow heathens in New York or elsewhere, we do not see that the Government will be any better able to watch him. The only adequate solution is to send him to San Francisco by express or in a registered parcel and we are surprised that the authorities have not thought of this simple device before.[9]

The remaining six editorials concerned immigrants alleged to be criminals, lunatics, idiots, paupers, and Mormons. The *New York Times* editors opined that those in the first four categories must be kept out so they would not become "wards of this country." Immigrants fitting these characteristics should not be let into the United States on bonds paid for by U.S. citizens. The *New York Times* claimed that the bonds "would probably be of no value" and should not be accepted.[10]

The practice of not accepting the bonds because of their doubted value became controversial with regard to Mormon immigrants. The *New York Times* reluctantly declared that Mormons who were not paupers, idiots, criminals, or insane could not be barred from the United States "for the sole reason that their creed is obnoxious" and the possibility they might practice polygamy. Controversy arose because although the *New York Times* said the Mormons should be treated "as other immigrants are treated," it was a generally known fact that the Mormon Church could afford and would be held responsible for payment of bonds and support of the immigrants.

When Mormons were refused entry, the Mormon Church brought the matter to court. The *New York Times* urged that it be made clear who had the final say over which immigrants were to be allowed to enter — the courts or the commissioners who worked at the ports — and what, if any, weight was to be given to the bonds. When the courts refused to try the case, saying it was the commissioners' responsibility to deter-mine who could immigrate, the *New York Times* approved but also suggested that it be "fully litigated and settled for all time" in court.

Editorials in 1888 for the most part called for better and increased enforcement of immigration regulations. Other issues discussed were the Chinese immigrants and exploitation of cheap foreign labor. Of the eight editorials about immigration in 1888, two concerned the Chinese. One reported that China was willing to agree to the United States' exclusion of Chinese immigrants with no repercussions to Americans, but the go-ahead was needed from Great Britain, who would have to agree to control its Hong Kong port. The *New York Times* predicted that if this was financially undesirable for Great Britain,

Their government will find imposing philanthropic and serious reasons for not interfering with it. We cannot, however, seriously criticize it for doing so when we reflect that the whole policy of the U.S. government for years on this subject has been dictated not by any regard for real national interests, but by a tender appreciation by the leaders of both parties of the votes of a few thousand men on the Pacific Coast who are, for the most part, inspired by a narrow and brutal prejudice.[11]

The other editorial on this topic observed that Australia was taking steps to bar Chinese from immigrating, and it hoped for a similar arrangement between the United States and China.[12]

An editorial titled "Class Legislation" called for legislation to prevent

The importation of gangs of laborers under conditions that reduce them to a condition in any degree resembling servitude or serfdom. . . . It is as important that American citizenship should not be so downgraded by immigration as that the economic needs of the country should be answered by it.[13]

The other six editorials concerned the types of immigrants that should be permitted into the United States. One piece protested the action by commissioners who, after some hesitation, let in 42 Arabs "who were generally paupers" on a $5,000 bond by the boat company that brought them. The *New York Times* quoted a report that "they are the dirtiest batch of immigrants brought to Castle Garden in years; they haven't $25 among them."[14]

Another editorial noted that the number of insane in New York had grown by 48 percent in seven years, but population growth was only 18 percent. A *New York Times* editor wrote, "This grave disparity and the rapid growth of the insane population are due to the admission of undesirable persons from abroad."[15] The editorial called for more careful enforcement of screening procedures and congressional amendments to tighten up the procedure. The *New York Times* took issue with the 1882 law for not keeping out convicts, insane, lunatics, and paupers who entered the United States via land.

The *New York Times* supported suggestions made by the Board of Charities that the law be amended to bar "shipment [of immigrants] by way of the Canadian and other exposed inland borders," that steamship companies be forbidden by law to bring to the United States these types of immigrants, that U.S. consuls at departure ports must certify the status of these immigrants, that the burden of deporting paupers after six months be shifted to the federal government, and that execution of the law be entrusted to appointees of the secretary of the treasury.[16]

Another editorial suggested that naturalization procedures must also be carefully screened to "prevent the naturalization of anarchists and of people who sought American citizenship for the protection it afforded them in their work of disturbing the politics of foreign countries." This editorial claimed,

No doubt that the chief incentive to restriction is the fact that for the first time in the history of the country grave and threatening social disturbances have occurred and that the disturbances of our peace have been almost with out exception foreigners. . . . There is a broad distinction to be drawn between immigration that does not really assimilate with the American people. The Chinese are evidently on the wrong side of this line, but not more evidently than the immigrants of some other nationalities.

On a somewhat more generous note, the *New York Times* editorial writer also commented,

It is not surprising that the national power of assimilation shows signs of indigestion and collapse under such a gargantuan feast. We must winnow the chaff . . . sentimental considerations should no longer exclusively control our policy. "America for Americans" is on the one hand as short-sighted a cry as "America, the refuge of the oppressed of all nations" is on the other.[17]

1890s

By far the most dominant immigration issue with which the *New York Times* concerned itself in the 1890s was legislation aimed at keeping Chinese laborers from coming to the United States. Other topics among the 39 immigration editorials included undesirable immigrants, illegal entry, and trends in immigration.

In 1891 the first of nine editorials on immigration for that year concerned "pauper immigrants" to the United States who came in via the Canadian border. According to the *New York Times*, because the seaport checks were becoming more stringently administered, it was likely that increasing numbers of immigrants would attempt to enter the United States via Canada. The *New York Times* applauded the New York Board of Charities for its work in returning pauper immigrants to their homes, for its information services, and for saving New York City some $2.5 million.[18]

Another editorial commented on the rising number of Italians coming to the United States. "It is therefore not strange to find some Italian local authorities beginning to worry about the great and growing exodus. The principal anxiety, however, on this side of the water, is that only the sort of emigrants may be sent that ought to be received."[19]

Five of the editorials on immigration that appeared in 1891 dealt with keeping the Chinese from illegally entering the United States. The *New York Times* blamed the smuggling in of the Chinese on several causes, including high sums of money paid to successful smugglers, the physical nature of some of the key smuggling areas, a lack of international controls, and the great expense involved in returning illegals home or elsewhere.

The outstanding issue concerning the Chinese dealt with the interpretation of a provision in immigration law that said that such illegals should be sent back to "the land from whence they came." The question was whether this phrase was to be taken literally and illegal entrants should be returned to their last departure port before they entered the United States or whether they should be returned to their homelands. The latest court decision interpreted the phrase literally and, in the *New York Times'* view, opposed the wishes of the administration. According to the *New York Times*, administration officials wanted to send Chinese people back to China because "otherwise coolies will apparently continue to slip across the border here and there all the way from Seattle to St. Albans"; however, the courts ruled this unfair, because an immigrant may no longer have been a resident of his or her homeland. The *New York Times* suggested that

Congress amend the Chinese Exclusion Act so that when people arrived through Mexico or Canada deliberately to violate the act, they could be sent directly to China.[20]

Another editorial reported that photographs would be taken of Chinese persons who were arrested for illegally entering the United States, a practice "intended to make up for . . . a defect in the exclusion laws." The *New York Times* warned, "It is to be feared that John Chinaman, under such circumstances, is inclined to be a repeater; it is further to be feared that, being peculiar in his skillful use of ways that are dark, he may in some cases defy photography."[21]

In 1893, 27 editorials were published concerning immigration, and again the predominant topic was the Chinese. In May 1983 the Geary Act required all Chinese residents in the United States to be registered with the U.S. government and to be issued certificates of residency. Without this certificate a Chinese person, under the act, could be subject to deportation or imprisonment. According to the *New York Times*, the majority of the Chinese refused to register but wished to remain in the United States. In the *New York Times*' view, this requirement was cruelly discriminatory, barbarous, and in direct violation of the U.S. treaty with China. The editors repeatedly called for this section of the law to be removed and blamed its presence on "the cowardly politicians of both parties who were afraid of losing this state or that, if they did not yield to the clamor for excluding the Chinese." They urged speedy action by the Supreme Court to try a test case to determine whether this was constitutional, expressing hopes that it would not be found so.[22]

On several occasions the *New York Times* reviewed what it perceived to be the purpose of the Geary Act, namely, to prevent further Chinese laborer immigrants from entering the United States but not to deport Chinese who were already residing in the United States. The *New York Times* was pleased when the administration neglected to enforce the law while awaiting the Supreme Court decision, and it was even more pleased when the judge who reviewed the test case found the act "so vague that he was puzzled as to the form in which the order for the deportation of Nylook should be put."[23] There evidently was no such provision, and this constituted, according to the *New York Times*, "a fine large loophole in the law through which Chinamen devoid of certificates are likely to escape freely until . . . provision for their deportation is made by the proper authorities." In other words, they could be ordered deported, but the orders would not be carried out.[24]

On this same topic the *New York Times* drew "a curious analogy" between the view of one Russian representative toward the eviction of Jews from Russia and the view of Americans who wanted the Chinese deported from the United States. The *New York Times* reported that the Russian explained,

The Jews are cleverer than the Russians. They are shrewder businessmen and keener in intellect and if they were admitted to the schools freely they would outrank the Russians in all particulars. It is because of this need of protecting the Russian citizens from the Jews, who are really immigrants, that these evictions have been made.[25]

The *New York Times* compared this view with "the antipathy for Chinese laborers on our Pacific Coast" and said that Chinese "are industrious, patient and frugal and they are not addicted to wasting their time and substance. . . . This is why they are hated by those who fear their competition."[26]

In editorializing on other immigration issues, the *New York Times* predicted that cholera outbreaks in Sweden and Norway would stimulate immigration from Scandinavia and claimed, "the Scandinavian immigration is as nearly an unmixed good as we have ever had." The *New York Times* called for immigration laws to be strictly enforced.

Whatever action may be taken with respect to the restriction of immigration generally, the government should take measures for the strict enforcement hereafter of existing laws designed to prevent the admission of paupers, lunatics, and imbeciles and other hopeless persons whose condition could easily be determined by brief inspection.[27]

Another editorial warned of health hazards immigrants could pose by bringing problems from other countries, and it called for more thorough inspections. It also warned against admitting immigrants who arrived aboard tramp steamers, which were not necessarily fit for sanitary trans-Atlantic travel and whose immigrant passengers, having been denied passage by more reputable lines, were likely to be objectionable.[28]

The "real question" regarding immigration policy, the *New York Times* said, was "whether the economic advantages of our immigration were so great that they outweigh the social disadvantages which it entails." The editors questioned whether it was time to "put up the bars" to restrict further immigration and said this was up to the U.S. citizenry to decide. However, first they must realize that "any measure that is effective in keeping out objectionable immigration must also tend to keep out some immigration that is in itself unobjectionable. If we are not prepared to reduce the total of our immigration, it is idle to discuss specific measures of restriction."[29]

In another editorial, the *New York Times* published a chart containing numbers of immigrants who had arrived in the United States from a variety of countries for the past three months and observed that there was a "decided gain in the numbers of English, Irish, Scotch and Italians, and a marked falling off in the remainder of the list. On the whole," the *New York Times* noted, "this is a change for the better in the character of the immigration movement." In the same piece, the editor remarked that immigrants arriving from Hungary, Poland, and Russia must be thoroughly inspected before entry because of the threat of disease, noting that "Immigrants from these countries are comparatively undesirable even when there is no danger that they will bring deadly and infectious diseases with them."[30]

After mid-1893, the appearance of immigration editorials dwindled, and only three more appeared in that decade. In 1895 an editorial captioned "Immigrants and Citizens" pointed out two perspectives to be considered when deciding upon immigration restriction: an economic outlook would involve an assessment of the value of immigrant labor to the United States, which the *New York Times* said was high, and a political view would involve maintaining a standard of citizenship. The *New York Times* explained that immigration law required the court to have the final say in granting citizenship and that the court must see that the immigrants are "attached to the principles of the Constitution of the United States" but that this rarely happens. "So far that the protection of suffrage is concerned, it is not a restriction of immigration that is needed; it is a restriction of judicial incapacity, perversity and unfaithfulness."[31]

The final immigration editorial of the decade appeared in October 1899 and was a review of the restrictive legislation aimed at the Chinese. Recently, three Chinese preachers had sought entry into the United States and were denied. The *New York Times* felt this to be out of line with the Chinese Exclusion Act and called for modification of the "narrow and unjust decision" that could have long-reaching effects in excluding all Chinese and not just laborers, as the *New York Times* said the law intended.[32]

1900–1909

A mix of positive and negative sentiments was expressed in the *New York Times* editorials on immigration during the opening decade of this century. Although none of the views indicated unconditional support for immigration, certain favorable opinions were expressed. Some immigrants, such as Russian Jews, Chinese, Japanese, and Germans, were seen as more desirable than others. The *New York Times* noted the passage of immigration legislature geared at keeping out such undesirables as "illiterates or those who came to the United States purely to amass a fortune and then return home with their riches."[33] In the latter segment of the decade, when immigration dropped substantially, the *New York Times* expressed concern over the slowdown, claiming, "We need immigrants as much as ever and this is a land of wide opportunities."[34]

The most consistently reiterated concern dealt with repercussions the United States was experiencing as a result of its policy regarding Chinese and Japanese immigrants and visitors. The *New York Times* termed the policies "brutal and insulting," and the editorials continually called for change and for good relations with China and Japan.[35]

Of the three editorials published in 1902 concerning immigration, two dealt with the exclusion of Chinese students. Not only was the Treasury Department's ruling on what constituted a student too strict (supposedly aimed at reducing labor competition), but treatment of Chinese visitors also was, the *New York Times* indicated, "quite inhospitable."[36]

The other 1902 immigration editorial, captioned "The Rush to America," cited a new high in numbers of immigrants to the United States. It called for more stringent regulations "in order to winnow the desirable from the undesirable" and said the current restrictions had no deterrent effect. It warned that perhaps "the assimilative powers of the great Republic shall not be equal to the task of weaving all these threads of diverse races into a homogenous whole."[37]

The two editorials that appeared in 1904 expressed similar views to those published in 1902. In quoting an editorial that had appeared in the *North American Review*, the *New York Times* gave credence to the notion that any inconveniences suffered thus far from immigration "are mere intimations of what is likely to come upon us if we raise no barriers against the flood of mongrel and polyglot accessions to our population which threaten American standards of living and American ideals generally." In this editorial, the *New York Times* described the "gross brutality" with which the Chinese were treated but concluded that "labor which is economically cheap is not necessarily socially cheap."[38] The other editorial praised a pending treaty with China that had the intent of putting "the treatment of Chinese in this country on a more human [and] decent basis."[39]

In 1906, 12 editorials discussed the Hungarian, Russian Jewish, and Chinese immigration; relations with Japan; distribution of immigration; restrictions; U.S. immigration generally; and declining immigration. On the subject of Hungarian immigrants, the *New York Times* questioned the motive of the Hungarian government in failing to restrict their emigration. "Is the Kingdom of Hungary trying to turn to our shores the paupers, wastrels and criminals of that country?" the paper queried.[40]

Soon after, the *New York Times* editorialized that we "have the land and we need the immigrants that England can't support because of its size" and that "the magnificent figures of agricultural prosperity in the United States would never have been possible without the recruits whom we have welcomed and assimilated."[41]

Three editorials called for fairer treatment of the Chinese through more reasonable restrictions on immigration. Some changes in policy were made (officials had to inform Chinese in the Chinese language that they could appeal their barred entry, and the time limit for such an appeal was extended). Apparently the Chinese were boycotting U.S. products quite effectively, and this triggered the *New York Times* to again call for fairer treatment and additionally to question Japan's influence on strengthening this boycott.[42]

Of five editorials that discussed regulations, three concerned literacy requirements, possession of cash upon entry, and an increased head tax. The *New York Times* also suggested the possibility of sending to Canada immigrants whom the United States did not wish to accept. According to the *New York Times*, the Canadian government was in the practice of enticing immigrants to their land with money: "Canada last year bought $14,428 worth of American immigrants."[43]

Another possibility the *New York Times* considered was to manipulate the distribution of immigrants, which could be achieved by setting up absorption centers in the South. "New York," the *New York Times* claimed, "receives an unjust and unfair proportion of the national burden." It distinguished between two types of immigrants: the motivated, who considered the port a way station, and the inert and helpless, who upon arrival "sit down in port."[44]

The largest number of *New York Times'* editorials about immigration in this decade appeared in 1908. Of the 14 pieces, 7 concerned relations with Japan and Japanese immigrants. The *New York Times* attempted to dispel a widespread belief that a "flood" of Japanese immigrants "threatens to submerge native workers" by citing the actual number of Japanese laborers on the U.S. mainland in 1908 at 600. By the end of 1908, a conciliatory friendship declaration had been agreed upon between Japan and the United States, and the *New York Times* urged the people of Japan and the United States to forget their grudges, because the governments had already done so. The paper interpreted this declaration to mean that "the deep foundation on which our friendship with Japan has been based and on which it rests now are beyond the reach of the disturbances that have arisen or are at all likely in the future." The editorial writer added that the base of this friendship was materialistic and that both countries had much to gain by friendship.

Immigration for the first half of 1908 dropped to one-fourth of what it was for the first half of 1907, and emigration had more than doubled. The *New York Times* was concerned about why this was happening and argued, "This surprising change makes ridiculous the proposal from [labor] sources that immigration should be checked in the interest of relieving unemployment. The need of the moment is to stimulate immigration."[45] The *New York Times* was also concerned about the increased numbers of Americans, many of whom were farmers, who were leaving the United States to become Canadian citizens. It questioned whether "the feeling of American citizenship is weakening," because although it was quite desirable to purchase land during this period of Canadian expansion, it was not mandated that landowners be Canadian.[46] The *New York Times* also considered the notion that perhaps immigration had declined "due to improvement of conditions in Russia — bad as they are," because Russian immigration had decreased markedly.[47]

Among the other themes on immigration covered in the *New York Times* editorials was one that praised German immigrants and concluded that "modern emigration prevents more wars than diplomacy." Another cited updated statistics that showed that, between 1860 and 1900, the ratio of foreign born to native born in the United States had changed very little.[48]

The most blatantly prejudiced editorial was headlined "Swarthy Americans." In it, the *New York Times* quoted a professor who had determined that the "future American type" would, as a result of "the influx of foreigners and their relatively higher birthrates" undergo "a physical reversion to a swarthy black-eyed ancestral type." The *New York Times* declared this prediction as "important, if true," and took the opportunity to warn of another of the professor's observations concerning "the criminal tendencies of the second generation immigrants."[49]

1910–1919

The *New York Times* tackled a variety of topics in the 16 editorials that appeared in the odd years of this decade. It attacked an immigration bill proposing a literacy test to screen immigrants and a ban on admitting political refugees. It questioned the effect of marriage and divorce on partners with differing citizenship. It expressed concern about immigrants who plotted against the U.S. government.

The *New York Times* responded to the contention of Harvard University President Emeritus Charles Eliot that a proposed educational test would help improve the quality of foreigners admitted to this country by claiming it was "misdirected and untimely" and would not be proof either of character or of health.[50] The *New York Times* also responded negatively to the former president's suggestion that immigrants should be tested when they apply for citizenship, saying,

Such a postponement of the test [may result in] making naturalization compulsory and deporting those unqualified for it. . . . The fact is that the separation of desirable immigrants from undesirable immigrants, except as to the extremes, is a difficult task and there is a middle ground where it is practically impossible.[51]

Responding to the economic losses incurred when immigrants left the United States with income they earned here, the *New York Times* editorialized that "reasons of patriotism and economy" should prompt Congress to require the immigration service "to aggressively supply information to immigrants to encourage them to remain in the United States."[52]

Decrying a "blanket measure" introduced by a California representative that would have applied the same restrictive immigration prohibitions, regulations, and laws that applied to Chinese to all persons of Mongolian or Asiatic races wherever they resided outside the United States, the *New York Times* warned that this final provision may lead the bill's author across the face of Europe in search of "Asiatic People." It concluded that even if the bill were to pass, "it would require a more discriminating and resourceful immigration service than Congress can ever provide, to enforce it."[53]

In an attempt at humor, another *New York Times* editorial examined the Canadian government's excuse for excluding black immigrants. The government said that "black folk could not long endure Canadian cold and would soon become public charges." Although the *New York Times* evidently agreed with that assumption ("as all Arctic animals show, white is the only wear for low temperatures, and broad nostrils in flat noses are not efficient guardians of the lungs against savagely cold air"), its point was that Canada admitted to its cold weather, a matter that Canadians had denied until then.[54]

Of the two immigration editorials that were published in 1913, one applauded the suggestion that the fingerprints of all immigrants be taken on their arrival and kept in order "to remove the criminals' only stigma of finger-printing, to provide a means of identifying every immigrant, to ease deportation procedures, to facilitate exclusion of undesirables and to save immigrants from burial in an unmarked grave."[55]

The other contested a court decision that had resulted in a $3,000 fine to a restaurant owner who imported three French chefs whom he claimed were "artists in their line" and, thus, eligible for immigration. The judge ruled that a cook cannot be an artist, and the newspaper contended that an appeal should be made "in the public interest which [the decision] imperils."[56]

The immigration topic of 1915 for the *New York Times* was a bill that, among other things, was directed at barring political refugees from entry into the United States and at imposing a literacy test on entrants. In five editorials, the *New York Times* sternly opposed the bill, which ultimately died after President Wilson's veto. The *New York Times* claimed that the

> U.S. would soon face a labor shortage, even without the literacy measure. That there is nothing in current conditions to justify compulsory reduction, and that should this bill be passed over the President's veto, it will mark reversal in a national policy as old as the nation. . . . The door [will be] closed against the ambitious and willing illiterate and against the reformer and patriot. We will admit those who have done us some good and have never disturbed anybody; we will exclude those to whom we can do good and those who have fought for freedom.[57]

After the bill died, the *New York Times* denounced politicians who may have voted for it "with an eye on constituencies, though themselves aware of its impropriety," observing, "there is hardly a pretense in any quarter that a literacy test separates the desirable from the undesirable immigrants."[58]

In 1919 the *New York Times* opened with an editorial that countered the fears expressed by the director of the U.S. government employment service, who had said that hundreds of thousands of Italian prisoners would be sent to the United States. It responded,

> Many of us might rejoice at the prospect, if prospect there were of those sound, willing and sturdy workers coming to add to the wealth of America and their own. But as Mr. Laguardia says, "Italy requires all of her people now." He has been told on good authority that Italy will restrict immigration.[59]

The other four editorials concerned "immigrants with destructive attitudes against the United States government," whom the *New York Times* said should be deported after serving their term in prison. "The war . . . has taught us that not all immigrants come here for such purposes as we have imagined and not all of them come here with the feeling of friendship for the country."[60]

The *New York Times* praised the action taken by Mayor Ole Hanson of Seattle when "foreign agitators" allegedly triggered a strike and threatened a takeover of the city's shipyard. Hanson proclaimed that "any man who attempts to take over government functions will be shot on sight." To the *New York Times*, Hanson had "defended and represented the inbred undying and ineradicable American spirit of ordered freedom."[61]

Commenting emotionally on a pending bill that would prohibit immigration for five years and would impose stricter regulations on aliens, the *New York Times* said, "the sentimental notion of America as the asylum of the oppressed has disappeared in the alarmed instinct of self-preservation." The editorial continued, "No economic or financial consideration has any standing in comparison with the imperative patriotic need of guarding against enemies of destruction."[62]

1920s

Most of the 58 editorials published in the 1920s focused on the need for legislation that would restrict immigration but, the *New York Times* editors believed, would do so fairly and humanely.

In 1920 the *New York Times* ran three editorials about Communists and deportation.[63] It criticized the secretary of labor for protecting Communist aliens subject to deportation "rather than Americans threatened by their Communistic desire to overthrow the government."[64] It supported a Utah senator's call for an investigation into the conduct of Labor Department officials who canceled the deportation warrants of 100 Communists: "The investigation is needed. It has been needed on particular and general grounds for months. There is a widespread belief that the Department of Labor is a nest of radicals." The editorial also supported a shift in the power of deportation from the Department of Labor to the Justice Department.[65]

Another editorial on Communists in the United States reviewed the labor secretary's decision that membership in the Communist Labor Party did not subject the member to deportation. The *New York Times* considered this a good ruling and explained that although the Communist Party advocated the use of force, the Communist Labor Party did not, but the editorial expressed displeasure that "some 200 alien members of the Communist Labor Party, described by the Justice Department as 'dangerous,' must now be released and continue to ornament the country to which they are a danger."[66]

Another editorial in 1920 called for a "wiser sort of regulation of immigration than we have now or than we have ever had" and charged that most of the existing regulations had been in "the interest of one or another class — usually of a class the members of which had arrived recently and sometimes of a class the members of which were not particularly notable for either their knowledge or their practice of Americanism."[67]

The *New York Times* went on record as being opposed to quotas when Congress was debating the 1921 Quota Act and again in 1924 when it debated and passed even more stringent restrictions. In most of the 29 editorials on immigration issues it published in 1924, the *New York Times* acknowledged that restrictions were needed but called the current laws unfair because they discriminated against certain races. It faulted both the 1921 and 1924 acts because they "discriminated against Italians, Poles, Russians, and Jews as well as the Japanese." Additional faults, the *New York Times* editorialized, were incurred because it violated a gentlemen's agreement with Japan, to which Japan had adhered, to restrict emigration to the United States and to willingly restrict it further, if necessary.[68]

The *New York Times* urged that some form of restriction was needed and that perhaps the "present composition of America as a whole" should be determined, rather than using as a basis for quotas the number of foreign born in the United States at a given date. "Enemies and friends of restriction alike would render greater service to their country if they looked at the entire immigration question less as antagonists or protagonists of certain groups and more as champions of a homogenous American people."[69]

The *New York Times* insisted that the purpose of restricting immigration was not to develop a "superior race." An editorial commented,

It is both natural and wise that the American race wishes to preserve its unity and does not wish to see its present blend greatly changed. It prefers immigrants who will be easily absorbed and . . . it strenuously objects to the formation of alien colonies here [and not because it] adheres to silly notions of superior and inferior races.[70]

On the topic of "Affronting Japan," the *New York Times* condemned the House of Representatives for its offensive treatment of Japan in the Johnson Bill, which excluded all Asians, except students, travelers, teachers, ministers, and businessmen, but permitted 2 percent of Europeans in proportions based on their numbers in the United States in 1890. It called this treatment by a Congress characterized by "legislative intemperance" a totally uncalled-for affront. After the bill's passage, the *New York Times* stressed that U.S. feelings toward Japan were friendly and that the ban was for economic, rather than social, purposes:

Whatever element of "inferiority" may be found, when it is considered in terms of economics, rests on the side of the whites rather than the Asiatic races. One of the principal objections has been that the Chinese and Japanese worked harder and lived more simply than the Americans and got ahead of their neighbors through diligence.[71]

In pointing out the positive aspects of the Quota Act of 1924, the *New York Times* noted that the likelihood was reduced of persons being refused admission because their quota was filled while they were on the water. The quotas were to be more evenly distributed over a ten-month period. Parents and children would not be separated because a geographic accident of birth gave the child a different nationality than the parents. In the following three years, a board would examine the composition of the white population of the United States as a whole, according to the 1920 census, and determine what proportion by birth or ancestry could be attributed to different European nations. This, perhaps, would be used to devise a new quota.

On another topic, the *New York Times* called upon Congress to find a means to admit 800 or more wives and children of immigrants who began their journey in the belief that there was legal precedent to virtually guarantee their entry into the United States. A Supreme Court decision, however, reversed the lower court's decision and resulted in the barring of these intended immigrants until the Johnson-Reed Quota Act of 1924 became effective. Congress did permit these aliens to enter the United States and the *New York Times* took the opportunity to relate the Johnson-Reed Quota Act's humanitarian considerations.[72]

In 1926 the number of immigration editorials dropped to ten. The first, titled "Again, A Racial Myth," sought to discredit any "Nordic Race" theories of superiority as a basis for restricting immigration. The *New York Times* wrote,

> The instinct that seeks to gain time for the nation to absorb the large masses of aliens with different traditions before the immigration bars are again raised must seek its justification not on the grounds of fictitious racial superiority but on the realization that too large masses of unassimilated aliens may become a danger to the social and political organization of the United States.[73]

The second editorial reviewed immigration figures and explained that the actual number of immigrants was even larger because of wives and children who were automatically admitted.[74]

The *New York Times* considered the possibility that the national origins quota system may not ever become effective because of opposition from groups whose quotas would be cut but said, "the findings of the board now estimating the national origins of the American people will help throw a clearer light on the blood contribution of the various nations of Europe to the making of America."[75]

A new issue on which the *New York Times* editorialized was the number of immigrants who were smuggled annually into the United States. The editors sympathized with the government on the difficulty in preventing such "bootlegging" and suggested an increase in border patrols. The immigration into the Southwest posed a substantial problem, according to the *New York Times*, because it was extremely difficult to control the numbers of immigrating Mexicans. The editors wondered if "in the light of immigration figures which showed that immigrants from Mexico, Latin America and Canada tended to stay while many Europeans returned to their homes, there should be an immigration restriction applied to immigrants from nearby countries." The editorial compared the social argument — that only assimilable races should be permitted to enter the country in large numbers — with the economic argument in favor of cheap labor.[76]

Furthering its humanitarian mission, the *New York Times* compared several proposals from the secretary of labor aimed at humanizing the immigration law by preventing immigrant families from being split up. It supported one suggestion that, within quota limits, special preference should be given to children and other immediate relatives of aliens residing in the United States and suggested giving the secretary of labor, or some board under his jurisdiction, greater discretionary powers to deal with exceptions.[77]

Another editorial viewed a decree allowing foreigners to own land in Japan as being indicative of Japan's progressiveness and goodwill toward other nations. The *New York Times* suggested that perhaps a treaty between the United States and Japan could be made allowing for reciprocal rights and privileges with regard to the purchase and leasing of land by Japanese in the United States and vice versa.[78]

The first of seven 1928 editorials cited similar sentiments toward immigrants held by Latin and Central American countries and the United States in wanting immigrants to

Throw in their lot with the political as well as the social life of their adopted country and completely forswear allegiance to their fatherland. . . . Both the countries of the two Americas, while recognizing the values of cultural ties with Europe, keenly resent any attempt on the part of the European governments to maintain control over their subjects who have come to America to live.

Considering this similarity of opinion, the *New York Times* said, "it would be well to consider carefully the precise relation of this problem to the general policy toward immigration of the Latin Americans."[79]

In another piece, the *New York Times* asserted that the restrictive U.S. immigration policy was not responsible for Europe's overpopulation or England's high unemployment. There were other countries in which immigrants could settle, the *New York Times* said, and the

Mere fact that the United States has closed its doors does not mean that Europe's surplus population must remain bottled up and either starve or fight.... Such pretensions in no way help the cause of the anti-restrictionists. Instead, they create international ill-will by saddling America with blame which is not justly hers.[80]

In the final editorial of 1928, the *New York Times* reported that immigrants who arrived after July 1, 1928 would be issued identification cards to simplify immigration officials' work in apprehending and investigating unlawful aliens. The *New York Times* wondered what confusion this would add to the officials' work, because it would create four classes of immigrants: those who had entered lawfully before the restriction laws became effective; those who entered lawfully since the quota system was applied; those who entered lawfully after July 1, 1928; and those in the United States illegally. Only the third group would have the identification cards.

1930s

Editorials in the 1930s noted the low numbers of immigrants due to the "coming of depression and President Hoover's orders for sharp curtailment in visas granted by our consuls abroad."[81] The characteristic emotion the *New York Times* expressed toward immigrants in the 1930s was that of sympathy. It editorialized about newly passed regulations that inconvenienced aliens by requiring them to appear twice annually in person to renew their reentry permits; it told of the plight of female immigrants who, from the upper levels of society at home, "find themselves hard put to make ends meet here"; it urged repeal of a section of immigration law that discriminated against the Japanese and Chinese by totally forbidding their immigration to the United States; and it reported on a newly formed committee that was given the charge of inquiring into the administration of immigration laws to determine whether immigrants were subjected to "unduly long detention in jails" and unhealthy quarters during deportation proceedings.[82]

It also quoted extensively from a special issue of *Social Work Today* that looked into "the so-called Immigrant Menace." The *New York Times* agreed with the magazine's editorial that cited low immigration figures and railed against "powerful propaganda [that] has been alarmingly effective in popularizing the idea that immigrants represent a destructive subversive influence in our common life."[83]

1940s

Two major themes dominated the *New York Times*' editorials in the 1940s. The first concerned the plight of the Japanese-Americans, civilian and military, who were loyal to the United States, and the second dealt with the people who had been displaced during the war and the countries to which they would be able to migrate. During World War II Japanese-Americans were subjected to doubt and mistrust by Americans who did not believe their loyalties to the United States were sincere. Civilians were placed in "internment" camps, where they would pose little threat of spying on the inner workings of U.S. war plans. Japanese-American soldiers faced "the grave danger of being captured by Japanese troops who would deal with them harshly." The *New York Times* urged extra protection for these soldiers and that Americans welcome back the Japanese-Americans upon their release from the camps. The *New York Times* did, however, support measures to screen the loyal from the disloyal.[84]

The other issue the *New York Times* repeatedly concerned itself with in the 1940s was what it viewed as the ineffective and discriminatory Displaced Persons Act. This act, according to the *New York Times*, permitted the United States to take in about 205,000 displaced persons after the war and basically screened out displaced Catholics and Jews. The *New York Times* strongly criticized the act and urged that the United States welcome these immigrants.[85]

In 1940, the *New York Times* noted that U.S. population growth of the past ten years was one-half that of the preceding ten years. This was the smallest ten-year increase in absolute numbers since 1870. The *New York Times* attributed the drop to restrictive immigration policies.[86]

Of four editorials concerning immigration that appeared in 1942, three discussed aliens in the United States in light of the war.[87] The *New York Times* agreed with the government that caution needed to be the guideline for dealing with aliens in the United States: "Those who are enemies, must be forcibly restrained, if we can't be certain what they are, they must be watched and their movement restricted." However, in the same editorial, the *New York Times* applauded gestures made by the president and the attorney general to exclude some groups of aliens from prevailing restrictions. "Many among them have been or can be most valuable to us. It is in our interest, all humane motives aside, to treat them with consideration."[88] Less than one month later, the *New York Times* acknowledged that it was a rough time for loyal Japanese-Americans but nevertheless urged "the Federal Government to keep close watch on the innocent in order to catch those who may be guilty."[89]

Soon after, the *New York Times* supported a proposal that would empower civilian review boards, already used to try Federal Bureau of Investigation suspects, to issue loyalty certificates to aliens in enemy categories. "It all boils down to the simple fact that loyalty or lack of loyalty is determined by character, not by place of birth," an editorial concluded.[90]

The final 1942 *New York Times* editorial concerning immigration questioned whether it was "right and necessary" to remove U.S. citizens of Japanese descent from their Pacific Coast homes after Pearl Harbor was bombed. This followed the Supreme Court's ruling that such action was constitutional under war powers. The *New York Times* observed that the Japanese-Americans who remained on Hawaii, unrestricted, seemed to have caused no harm.[91]

Of the three editorials published in 1946 that concerned aliens, two advocated measures to protect loyal Japanese-Americans from deportation and misguided ill will. "These citizens of ours, of Japanese extraction, deserve better of us and of the Filipinos than they are getting," claimed one of the editorials.[92]

The other topic concerned survivors of the Nazi persecution. The *New York Times* urged Americans to welcome these immigrants because "some of these people will soon be among our most useful citizens."[93]

All of the 11 editorials dealing with immigration in 1948 focused on the inadequacies of the Displaced Persons Act. The *New York Times* attacked the law, claiming it was "ungenerous, cruelly discriminating and shockingly un-American in its religious bias" and "a shocking departure from every sound tradition of American Democracy."[94] The *New York Times* insisted that it effectively barred most displaced Jews and Catholics from entry by manipulation of dates and that it made it "easier for a former Nazi to enter the United States than for one of the Nazi's innocent victims" and provided for only 205,000 displaced persons to enter the United States.[95]

Three of the 11 editorials made a special case for Baltic immigrants and called for the president to permit these people who arrived in "craft so frail [as to make] Columbus's caravels seem as luxurious as ocean liners."[96] The *New York Times* lobbied strongly for these immigrants because, it said, the Baltic states "are conquered nations, taken over by Russia without the consent of their inhabitants" and those citizens who have "managed to get out, those that have reached the United States and Canada must be by all odds the sturdiest, and most freedom-loving . . . to turn them back would be an offense against the loftiest American traditions."[97]

1950s

Editorial headlines such as "Little Iron Curtain," "Tragic Paradox," and "Nominal Totalitarians," which opened the decade of the 1950s for the *New York Times*, reflected the distaste the newspaper expressed toward the immigration policy of that period. The McCarran-Walter Act barred entry into the United States of anyone who was in any way connected with the Communist Party and members of Nazi, Fascist, or other noncommunist totalitarian organizations. This ban also applied to nominal or involuntary members of these groups, which, the *New York Times* remarked again and again, included those "genuinely supportive of democracy."[98]

The *New York Times* criticized the McCarran-Walter Act throughout the decade and supported all modifications made to the legislation during that period. Of critical interest in the *New York Times'* pieces were Europeans who wished to immigrate to the United States and who might not be permitted to enter because of constraints in the law, because of red tape, or because they may have been linked with communism.

The *New York Times* acknowledged that there was a reasonable level of fear of communism's spread because of the immigrants but termed the McCarran provisions "absurd." It repeatedly urged President Eisenhower to take a firmer stand on broadening existing legislation.[99]

In 1953 the basic thrust of the *New York Times'* editorials was to encourage passage of a bill that would permit 240,000 displaced persons above the normal immigration quotas to enter the United States in two years. Editorials on this topic appeared weekly and with strong wording such as the following:

Opposition seems a little strange except on the supposition that foreigners are not much good anyhow and that the less we see of them, the better. That argument doesn't make sense in the United States except as it might be used by full-blooded members of the native Indian tribes. . . . This nation was founded by lovers of freedom.[100]

On September 18, 1953, the *New York Times* denounced legislative provisions of the McCarran-Walter Act for having delayed the entry of a noted Latin American scholar and journalist who was an avid "champion of Democracy." "So long as the McCarran Act remains on the books, unchanged, these deplorable incidents will continue and we will discourage men and women in other countries whose esteem we should seek and cherish."[101] The *New York Times* repeatedly stated that by keeping out anticommunists who, perhaps, were once involuntarily affiliated with the Communist party, we would be letting "The staunchest enemies of Communism fall prey to the Communist wolves."[102]

The *New York Times* was not so favorably disposed toward Mexicans who immigrated illegally, whom it claimed were exploited and treated with cruelty and callousness. It supported an investigation into the "mass illegal migration by Mexican 'wetbacks,'" claiming "Only Congressional action can have any hope of imposing controls upon the annual illegal movement of more than a million aliens across our border or of checking the merciless exploitations to which these unfortunates are subject." The same editorial faulted the "all too common stereotype in our southwestern regions that Spanish-speaking Americans are in some way inferior." Additionally, it said that it was at the southern border that the real Communist threat lay — where the borders were poorly guarded and it was easy to slip by.[103]

1960s

A total of three editorials on immigration were published in the even years between 1960 and 1970, and all appeared in 1960. The *New York Times* criticized the quota system of admitting immigrants and wrote, "Our existing immigration laws are more than a generation out-of-date."[104] It characterized the McCarran-Walter Act of 1952 as "part of a long-standing effort to favor the populations of Northern Europe as contrasted with those of the Southern countries. There was a strong element of prejudice in the restrictive immigration laws that began in 1882 and were continued in legislation of 1921, 1924, and 1952." The *New York Times* concluded that "this might be a year in which it would be wise to hold out welcoming hands to those whom we can help and who can help us."

The second editorial criticized the Refugee Relief Bill, recently passed by the House, saying "it is better than nothing, but it isn't much better than nothing, and it makes a mockery of America's valued participation in the 'World Refugee Year' that ends June 30." The Refugee Relief Bill, before the Senate, permitted admission "on parole of an estimated maximum of 5,000 European refugees above regular immigration quotas for the next two years." The *New York Times* claimed that despite its high ideals, the administration did not push hard enough for liberalization of immigration law and criticized the administration for spending only $3.5 million of the $10 million Congress authorized the president to spend on refugee needs. "The fact is that with World Refugee Year nearing its end, the United States has not much to be proud of in what it is doing for the refugees."[105]

The final editorial, entitled "Two Months To Go," reviewed what the president wanted to see accomplished in the remaining two months of the legislative session. Among other issues emphasized, the *New York Times* reported that the president reminded members of the House and Congress of the need for more liberal immigration laws.[106]

1970s

The chief immigration topic during the 1970s was the plight of the refugees from Vietnam and Cambodia. The *New York Times* devoted four of its nine immigration editorials to this issue.[107]

A 1973 editorial praised the "sensible and humane" viewpoint expressed by the chairman of the New York City Board of Education's finance and budget committee in opposing the "mean spirited demand that school officials ferret out children of illegal aliens and expel them from the city's classrooms," a demand that had been made by city council committee members. The *New York Times* offered reasons why it may be a financial plus to have the children in schools and concluded, "the city's humane traditions are far better served by schools ready to teach all those who want to learn than by a policy that would be tantamount to visiting upon the children the sins of their parents."[108]

Commenting in 1979 on a conference of 60 nations that was scheduled to be held in Geneva, the *New York Times* urged the participants to "avoid more bragging about how much they are doing" and, instead, "assure the refugees decent temporary housing and demand an end to the forcible evictions from Vietnam." The conference could also inquire more closely into the causes of this expulsion policy and condemn it for what it is. "Not even Hanoi's hardened leaders are likely to be insensitive to an international finding of genocide," wrote the *New York Times*.[109]

The *New York Times* editors also urged that the organizations and nations sending food and supplies to the refugees continue despite the likelihood that much of it never reached the intended recipients. They praised President Carter for "taking the political risk of raising the monthly quota of immigrants to 14,000."[110]

On another issue, relations with Mexico, the *New York Times* urged that special efforts be made to bridge the economic gap between Mexico and the United States. "The United States has an obvious and enduring interest in Mexico's economic development" because "the flow of Mexican immigrants won't ease until Mexico prospers."[111]

The *New York Times* suggested that the United States should bend immigration and trade rules and that Mexico should ease restrictions on U.S. investments.

> Special accommodations with Mexico will be difficult to arrange [because of history and economics], but the Rio Grande will not be bridged by normal diplomacy and summit meetings. Sooner or later, the talk in Washington and Mexico City will have to turn to shared goals and dreams.[112]

In another editorial, the newspaper supported the census bureau's request to the Catholic Church that its members respond to the census questions and feel secure in the privacy of their responses. "It is especially difficult to reach Hispanics, particularly illegal aliens," the *New York Times* reported.

With the backing of the Church, perhaps more accurate population data would become available. . . . More than 550 billion a year in federal aid to local governments is distributed at least in part on the basis of population.
Perhaps half-a-million illegal aliens in New York City alone have not been counted, thus foreclosing the City from millions in Federal funds that could have been used to help them.[113]

The final 1979 immigration editorial praised the attorney general's call for an end to arrest of "undocumented aliens in their residences." The *New York Times* reported that federal immigration officers would sweep into apartment buildings and demand identification from every Chicano in sight, and those who could not prove that their status was legal were taken to detention centers. Innocent citizens and legal aliens were confronted without cause, and their residences were searched. Thousands of illegal Mexican immigrants did pose domestic and foreign problems, but this did not justify harsh treatment and abused rights, the *New York Times* commented. "If stiffer enforcement is needed, the Immigration Service can intensify its surveillance of private companies that employ aliens. It can also set up border patrols."[114]

1980s

As noted earlier, in the decade from 1980 to 1990, we selected every piece on immigration that appeared on the *New York Times* editorial page; including op-eds, columnists, and editorials. Of the 146 such pieces, 73 were proimmigrant, 40 were anti-immigrant, and 33 were neutral. Most of the attention was focused on illegal aliens and refugees.
Eight articles (five of which were favorable, two were neutral, and one was against illegal aliens) appeared in 1980. Four of the favorable articles concerned Cuban refugees and urged the United States to allow them into the country for humanitarian reasons. One editorial questioned "why the Administration has not been willing to take similar extraordinary action on behalf of the Haitian arrivals."[115] Another favorable editorial urged Texas to allow the children of illegal aliens to attend public school because it is discriminatory and ill-advised not to do so:

The Mexican-born children of illegal aliens have been kept out of school in 17 districts of Texas through prohibitive tuition

charges. No other state discriminates in this fashion. . . .
Illegal aliens are anything but freeloaders. A 1978 report by a
House committee showed that the typical illegal alien worker
in San Diego paid 17 percent of his wages in taxes, a much
larger share than was paid by citizens earning the minimum
wage. . . . Whether it be right now in the form of modest
increases . . . in public school operating costs, or . . . in terms
of social cost . . . fifteen years from now, we will pay this bill.[116]

Five of the articles in 1981 were neutral in tone. Four dealt with
Haitians. The editorials opposed the Haitians because they were
economic, not political, refugees and, thus, should not be allowed to
be gate crashers into the United States:

The United States has no good answer to the larger Haitian
problem, any more than it can answer the problem of poor and
oppressed people over the world. Millions want to come here
but America cannot take them all. . . . To let them stay would
be unjust to millions elsewhere waiting patiently to come in
legally.[117]

However, the same editorials recognized that there was a humanitarian aspect to be considered. One said, "how callous and legalistic
to have to choose between degrees of desperation, between people who
are desperately afraid and people who are desperately poor."[118]
Four editorials expressed negative sentiments against Mexican
illegal aliens. The common refrains were that we had lost control
of our borders and that illegals took jobs, strained community resources, and were violating the law by their presence.
One editorial questioned the administration's policy of interning
Cuban refugees:

Many appear to have only slightly blemished records. No one
knows for sure. The immigration laws . . . do not entitle them
to the presumption of innocence, and so the doubt works
against them. . . . When there is little recourse in law, a year is
too long to spend in a maximum-security prison — for
administrative reasons.[119]

Another article asked the readers to remember the great contributions immigrants made to the United States:

Historians, in their support of increased immigration, have
cautioned against overly restrictionist tendencies. They point
out that U.S. citizens have always been concerned about the
arrival of immigrants, but not that immigrants have always

made contributions to U.S. society. . . . One of the finalists in the annual Westinghouse Science Search for outstanding student achievement was a 16-year-old Bronx boy who completed a complicated analysis of a problem in numbers theory. . . . But this student is unusual. His name is Tan Dinh Ngo. He is a refugee from Vietnam, and a year and a half ago he spoke no English.[120]

Of the 18 articles that appeared in 1982, 10 were neutral. Five were concerned with Haitians and stressed that they were economic, not political, refugees, but the articles also stated that many Haitians had been held behind bars for more than a year and that such behavior was not humane. "It would be far more humane — and a far better deterrent — to determine the Haitians' status promptly and, just as promptly, send the ineligible ones back home."[121] Furthermore, the article continued, "some critics grant that the government has the right to detain illegal entrants, but contend that detaining only poor, black Haitians smacks of unfairness, even racism."[122]

The other neutral articles dealt with illegal immigration. The overriding themes were that there were too many illegals and they take jobs. Thus, "controlling immigration has become an important goal of conservatives and liberals alike."[123] Passage of the Simpson-Mazzoli Bill was looked upon by the *New York Times* as a "tough, fair, and human" way of dealing with the illegal immigrant problem.[124]

Three editorials were strongly against illegal immigrants. The fact that there were so many of them, the need to gain control of our borders, and the taking of jobs were the major reasons cited. Flora Lewis directed her antipathy at the Haitians. She claimed that they were not political refugees and that they had overburdened Miami:

The unlimited immigration of America's first century and a half is no longer realistic. Now the U.S. cannot avoid some responsibility for helping people nearby to make life tolerable in their own homes if we want to avoid the shameful dilemma Miami is having to face with hapless Haitians.[125]

Furthermore, Lewis wrote, "current arrivals tend to be totally unskilled illiterates, speaking an arcane language, Creole, that scarcely anyone else knows."

Later in the year, three editorials urged the Justice Department to release the 53 Haitians then being held in detention in a Brooklyn navy yard.

Eight of the ten immigration articles in 1983 focused on illegal aliens. Six were clearly against illegals, and two others were also against illegals but did not come on quite as strongly. Control of our borders, the recession, the taking of jobs, negative public opinion, and the need to take control of our own immigration policy, which had been lost to special interest groups, justified these sentiments.

In 1984, the *New York Times* featured 17 articles, of which 10 were anti-immigration, 2 were neutral, and 5 were proimmigration. One editorial was against the criminal element from Cuba, while the others were against illegal aliens on the grounds that the United States needed to control its borders and aliens took jobs from U.S. citizens. Edwin Harwood, a visiting scholar at the Hoover Institution at Stanford University, claimed that illegal aliens increased crime: "Since July 1983, service investigators have begun to concentrate on more serious violators, among them aliens involved in fraudulent visa petitions, the smuggling of drugs and aliens and other serious crimes."[126] Russell W. Peterson, president of the National Audubon Society, had environmental and population concerns:

The debate over immigration reform has failed to focus on a basic reason for such reform: world wide population growth. . . . Our population grew by nearly 2.5 million last year, much of it from immigration. . . . The environment of the United States is now under intense pressure from a steadily increasing population. . . . Environmental stress from growing numbers of human beings is intensified by the exceptionally high per-capita consumption of natural resources here in the United States. But the stresses on our soils are primarily the result of mounting food deficits world wide. . . . Providing a wide-open escape valve for the population pressures of the developing nations serves neither the interests of the United States nor the interests of long-term global stability.[127]

Peter H. Schuck, a Yale law professor, believed that the Simpson-Mazzoli law would not be effective because

Strengthening immigration enforcement without building up the rest of the administrative system would be a perverse "reform." By increasing the already large number of aliens who languish in overcrowded prisons for long periods of time, more arrests would simply shift the problem somewhere else.[128]

One editorial called for compassion and equity for the Haitians and claimed both could be achieved by adopting the Simpson-Mazzoli reform bill:

Those poor 7,200 Haitians: Is there no end to the torment and inequity they must suffer for wanting a better life in the Land of the Free? . . . Now, a new unfairness arises. . . . The Cubans are now probably eligible for permanent legal status — but not the 7,200 Haitians — and other qualified foreigners.[129]

Five of the six articles in 1985 were against illegal aliens. Anxiety about losing jobs to aliens was the major theme. Richard D. Lamm, then governor of Colorado, expressed other concerns regarding illegal immigrants, legal immigrants, and refugees and made the following policy recommendations:

Isn't it time that we ask ourselves whether the United States is running its refugee policy or is it running us? We must decide how many people we can absorb into our economy and assimilate into our culture. Congress should set a cap on the number of new immigrants we will accept in future years from all categories — immediate relatives, quota immigrants and refugees. I suggest that we hold the line at the 527,000 we are accepting this year. Increases in refugee admissions will need to be offset by fewer immigrants under our normal procedures. However, in order to avoid crowding out too many of the immigrants who now come to us under established national quotas, we should simultaneously narrow the refugee criteria to include only persons who clearly face imprisonment or execution if required to return home and their spouses and minor children . . . for our children's sake, we must ask "How much compassion can we afford?" At some point, our compassion to share what we have will destroy what we have.[130]

Thirty articles, the largest number in the sampled years, appeared in 1986, and in contrast to the previous years, the majority of the pieces were favorable to immigration. Five articles urged the repeal of the McCarran-Walter Act, passed in 1952, which barred those with ideological differences from entering the United States. The writer, Hortense Calisher, explained,

Bills have been introduced in Congress to repeal the McCarran-Walter Act, which dates from the McCarthy era and is widely regarded as a dangerous infringement of our constitutional guarantees. . . . Yet the McCarran-Walter Act, under which many writers and scholars have been stopped at our borders on the grounds of "un-American" opinions, is cited abroad as a contradiction of our flaunted preeminence in the free world.[131]

Along the same lines, an editorial stated that "the United States is strong enough to hear dissenting views, even Communist views; it's stronger for hearing them."[132]

Three editorials contained themes against illegal aliens. The need to control our borders and to be fair to those who were waiting to enter the country legally, the taking of jobs by illegals, and the fact that many of those seeking asylum were economic, not political, refugees were the reasons given for the editorials' positions.

One editorial and an article by Michael A. Ledeen, senior fellow at Georgetown University Center for Strategic and International Studies, urged the United States to allow a small number of Cubans, who were former political prisoners and whom Castro had allowed to leave Cuba, to enter the United States. Ledeen wrote,

> The immigration service is far more generous with illegal aliens than with these former prisoners, for people who attempt to enter the country illegally can be paroled if they have a parent, spouse, child or sibling who is a permanent resident of the United States ... those who have suffered so long for our common values should be able to come here and enrich us by their presence.[133]

Articles written by Arthur C. Helton (director of the Political Asylum Project of the Lawyers Committee for Human Rights), Charles Gordon (former general counsel of the Immigration and Naturalization Service), and Maurice A. Roberts (former chairman of the Board of Immigration Appeals), and Joseph Nocera (a journalist) championed the rights of refugees and asylum seekers. In their respective articles, Helton, Gordon, and Roberts pointed out that the present treatment of asylum seekers by the United States was against the U.S. ethos:

> The increasing numbers of asylum seekers languished in prison represent a sad betrayal of our melting pot heritage and our tradition of providing refuge to the poor and oppressed of all nations. Our rhetoric of compassion has broken down in practice. What's needed is a more humane policy, a policy that does not rely on prolonged and arbitrary detention. Instead of seeking to deter refugees, the United States should encourage those who seek refuge to apply for asylum while living and working at liberty. Instead of being forced to languish in prison until they give up hope and go home, they should be allowed to prepare their cases properly, with adequate access to legal counsel and we should make a good-faith effort to determine which ones qualify for asylum. ... The policy also shows a serious disregard of the right to seek refuge — a basic human right, once at the center of our American tradition and celebrated this week by the Statue of Liberty rededication.[134]

Anthony Lewis agreed. He described the U.S. experience with immigrants as follows:

> The languages and the faces have changed, but the miracle of American immigrants goes on. They come to a strange land, often persecuted and without resources. Yet they quickly make their way, grabbing the bottom rung of the economic ladder, struggling up, banding together as they adapt to American ways. . . . The human costs of current policy are heart-rendering. The cost to the American polity is also great. We are honoring a symbol this weekend while our Government forgets its substance. We and our forebearers came to this country not because there was a statue in New York Harbor, but because behind it there was the promise of liberty and justice.[135]

In an op-ed, economist Julian L. Simon stated, "the United States would benefit from admitting many more immigrants than it does now — and far more than are conceivable under existing political arrangements."[136] Immigrants create jobs and contribute to U.S. society in numerous other ways.

Thirteen of the 18 articles in 1987 on immigration were in favor of immigration, five were against it. Six articles denounced the provision of the McCarran-Walter Act that excluded individuals from the United States because of ideological differences. McCarran-Walter was considered a McCarthy-like law in that

> Passed in 1952, McCarran-Walter reflects the spirit of Joseph McCarthy; it lists 33 grounds for excluding alien visitors or migrants. . . . The most offensive bars people who would advocate economic, international and governmental doctrines of world Communism and other subversive activities. It is a clear insult to the American tradition of tolerance for dissent, and to the public's intelligence.[137]

However, Jerome Ogden, deputy assistant secretary of state for visa services, claimed that "ideological grounds are a myth" and national security is the issue:

> The idea that such a restrictive climate still exists is a myth kept alive by those who believe there should be no barrier whatsoever against people entering the United States. . . . We did not deny visas to these applicants for their abstract beliefs. We refused them because of their involvement in espionage or their personal advocacy of violence as a means to achieve political ends.[138]

An editorial warned that "not even a generous nation can afford to become a haven for millions who would like to come here to seek a better standard of living ... to grant the Salvadorans temporary refuge on the basis of Mr. Duarte's economic appeal would twist the ideal of refuge into subsidy," but within two months two other editorials urged the conferring of extended voluntary departure status for two years on undocumented Salvadorans and Nicaraguans "who might be deportable under the new law."[139]

All of the 13 articles in 1988 were proimmigration. Three urged granting additional time for those eligible for amnesty to apply:

The Immigration Service objects to dragging out the amnesty period and fears that even the possibility of an extension will discourage applicants from meeting the existing deadline. But Mr. Schumer [Rep. of N.Y.] rightly argues that society should "err on the side of humanity." Given the generous impulse behind the 1986 law and the difficulties in administering it, that approach makes sense.[140]

The bulk of the articles urged compassion for the world's refugees, including those from the Soviet Union (Armenians and Jews), eastern Europe, and Southeast Asia.

Fairness ought to be the main consideration. But often, fairness collides with the desire to respond to a highly visible plight — as demonstrated by recent decisions that seem to favor the admission of refugees from the Soviet Union while restricting entry for those from Central America. . . . Still, why bend the rules for some foreigners and not others?[141]

Of the 23 articles that appeared in 1989 and 1990, only one was anti-immigration. An editorial questioned why the refugee burden was unequally shared. It pointed out,

While the United States to its credit has accepted increasing numbers of refugees, Britain and West Germany have cut back, and Japan still does far less than it could ... regional responses [conferences] are desirable, but the responsibility for refugees is wider. Richer Western nations need to bear a major share of the burden. The overall task of taking care of the refugees will be easier when countries like Japan, West Germany and Britain do their part.[142]

The majority of the articles urged the United States to take refugees from Central America, Southeast Asia, and the Soviet Union. Anthony Lewis and one editorial claimed the McCarran-Walter Act was no longer necessary.

Reviewing the impact of the 1986 Immigration Reform and Control Act, the *New York Times* noted that the act had caused "increased discrimination by employers and the General Accounting Office is right to urge corrective measures." The article said that it was unclear on the solution of the problem.[143]

A positive view of illegal immigrants appeared in an op-ed by economist Julian L. Simon, who urged us to open our doors to more immigrants:

> Increased immigration would augment the pool of young, skilled workers who pay high taxes and use few governmental services. . . . Would doubling, say, of immigration swamp us? Not at all. Only about six percent of the present population — a bit more than one person in 20 — are foreign born, and that includes aged immigrants who came many years ago.[144]

Taken as a whole, the *New York Times* was more moderate, more even-handed than most of the magazines surveyed. In the last decade, half of its pieces were proimmigrant. On a general for-versus against-immigration continuum, the *New York Times* would place closer to *The Nation*, *Commonweal*, and the news weeklies, than it would to the *North American Review*, the *Saturday Evening Post*, and the *Atlantic Monthly* (up to the 1950s). Concerning the major issues from 1880 to 1955, the *New York Times* opposed literacy requirements, generally supported quota legislation, and opposed the McCarran-Walter Act. It expressed more compassion for the Chinese and, later, for the Japanese than most of the magazines surveyed. Its perceptions of the "new (European) immigrant" lacked the venom found in the *Saturday Evening Post*'s or *Scribner's* descriptions. In the 1970s and 1980s, the *New York Times* focused a lot of its attention on the Mexican issue, on illegals generally, and on refugees. It expressed alarm about the number who entered illegally and was fearful about the impact they would have on U.S. jobs and wages, but it also expressed concern and indignation about the treatment of illegals and their lack of rights in this country.

NOTES

1. *New York Times*, April 6, 1880.
2. Ibid., May 23, 1880; April 6, 1880.
3. Ibid., April 20, 1880.
4. Ibid., April 22, 1880.
5. Ibid., May 15, 1880.
6. Ibid., February 4, 1884.
7. Ibid., July 17, 1886.
8. Ibid., September 12, 1886.
9. Ibid.

10. Ibid., August 27, 1886.
11. Ibid., February 9, 1888.
12. Ibid., March 28, 1888.
13. Ibid., April 24, 1888.
14. Ibid., January 3, 1888.
15. Ibid., January 14, 1888.
16. Ibid., January 15, 1888.
17. Ibid., June 19, 1888.
18. Ibid., July 5, 1891.
19. Ibid., August 8, 1891.
20. Ibid., December 10, 1891.
21. Ibid., December 17, 1891.
22. Ibid., February 9, 1893.
23. Ibid., May 4, 1893.
24. Ibid., May 26 1893
25. Ibid., June 18, 1893.
26. Ibid.
27. Ibid., June 19, 1893.
28. Ibid., June 24 1893.
29. Ibid.
30. Ibid., May 29, 1893.
31. Ibid., August 7, 1895.
32. Ibid., October 23, 1899.
33. Ibid., August 7, 1904.
34. Ibid., December 27, 1908.
35. Ibid., October 16, 1904.
36. Ibid., April 7, 1902.
37. Ibid., May 4, 1902.
38. Ibid., August 7, 1904.
39. Ibid., October 16, 1904.
40. Ibid., January 3, 1906.
41. Ibid., January 6, 1906.
42. Ibid., March 4, 1906.
43. Ibid., April 2, 1906; May 4, 1902; May 7, 1906; June 27, 1906; April 17, 1906.
44. Ibid., May 8, 1906.
45. Ibid., July 3, 1908.
46. Ibid., August 1, 1908.
47. Ibid., August 24, 1908.
48. Ibid., August 31, 1908.
49. Ibid., November 30, 1908.
50. Ibid., January 14, 1911.
51. Ibid.
52. Ibid., February 9, 1911.
53. Ibid., April 18, 1911.
54. Ibid., April 28, 1911.
55. Ibid., October 25, 1913.
56. Ibid., December 6, 1913.
57. Ibid., February 9, 1915.
58. Ibid., February 6, 1915.
59. Ibid., January 16, 1919.
60. Ibid., January 19, 1919.
61. Ibid., February 11, 1919.
62. Ibid., June 9, 1919.
63. Ibid., March 22, 1920; May 7, 1920; June 3, 1920.

64. Ibid., June 3, 1920.
65. Ibid., March 22, 1920.
66. Ibid., May 7, 1920.
67. Ibid., May 11, 1920.
68. Ibid., January 15, 1924.
69. Ibid., January 29, 1924.
70. Ibid., April 15, 1924.
71. Ibid.
72. Ibid., June 10, 1924.
73. Ibid., July 30, 1926.
74. Ibid., August 24, 1926.
75. Ibid., October 10, 1926.
76. Ibid., November 10, 1926.
77. Ibid., December 11, 1926.
78. Ibid., November 11, 1926.
79. Ibid., February 12, 1928.
80. Ibid., June 23, 1928.
81. Ibid., December 5, 1931.
82. Ibid., November 20, 1931; September 9, 1931; August 4, 1931; June 28, 1933.
83. Ibid., December 10, 1939.
84. Ibid., January 14, 1946.
85. Ibid., April 8, 1946.
86. Ibid., October 13, 1940.
87. Ibid., February 11, 1942; March 3, 1942; April 6, 1942; April 18, 1942.
88. Ibid., February 11, 1942.
89. Ibid., March 3, 1942.
90. Ibid., April 6, 1942.
91. Ibid., April 18, 1942.
92. Ibid., January 14, 1946.
93. Ibid., May 22, 1946.
94. Ibid., July 21, 1948.
95. Ibid., August 31, 1948.
96. Ibid., August 3, 1948; December 1, 1948; December 11, 1948.
97. Ibid., December 11, 1948.
98. Ibid., March 16, 1951.
99. Ibid., February 24, 1951.
100. Ibid., July 10, 1953.
101. Ibid., September 18, 1953.
102. Ibid., July 27, 1953.
103. Ibid., March 27, 1955.
104. Ibid., March 18, 1960.
105. Ibid., April 12, 1960.
106. Ibid., June 7, 1960.
107. Ibid., July 5, 1979.
108. Ibid., June 16, 1973.
109. Ibid., July 5, 1979.
110. Ibid., August 29, 1979.
111. Ibid., September 28, 1979.
112. Ibid.
113. Ibid., November 15, 1979.
114. Ibid., December 1, 1979.
115. Ibid., April 6, 1980.
116. Ibid., August 2, 1980.
117. Ibid., October 28, 1981.

118. Ibid.
119. Ibid., May 2, 1981.
120. Ibid., March 4, 1981.
121. Ibid., January 5, 1982.
122. Ibid.
123. Ibid., August 19, 1982.
124. Ibid., March 18, 1982.
125. Ibid., February 11, 1982.
126. Ibid., January 27, 1984.
127. Ibid., May 4, 1984.
128. Ibid., September 24, 1984.
129. Ibid., February 20, 1984.
130. Ibid., December 15, 1985.
131. Ibid., October 25, 1986.
132. Ibid., November 13, 1986.
133. Ibid., July 18, 1986.
134. Ibid., July 3, 1986.
135. Ibid.
136. Ibid., January 28, 1986.
137. Ibid., December 15, 1987.
138. Ibid., January 10, 1987.
139. Ibid., April 30, 1987.
140. Ibid., February 9, 1988.
141. Ibid., December 19, 1988.
142. Ibid., April 16, 1989.
143. Ibid., April 3, 1990.
144. Ibid., May 10, 1990.

12

The Miracle of Immigration: Summary and Concluding Remarks

The first part of this chapter summarizes each magazine's coverage of immigration issues for the time span of the survey. The second reviews the *New York Times* editorials, and the last part offers some general observations about the media and public opinion vis-à-vis the immigration issue.

NORTH AMERICAN REVIEW

The majority of the 50 articles that the *North American Review* published about immigrants between 1880 and 1940 favored restricting their entry, largely because the types of people who wanted to come were different than those who came earlier. Their differences, in the opinions of most of the *North American Review*'s writers, would make them less likely or less able to assimilate into U.S. society and more likely to contribute to the population of lunatics, paupers, criminals, and subversives. Writers who disagreed with these views argued that although the immigrants from the 1880s onward were coming from different countries than did the ones who came earlier, they were making and would continue to make important and useful contributions to the economic, cultural, and social life of their host country.

Like many of those who wrote for the *Atlantic Monthly*, contributors to the *North American Review* were often public officials and statesmen whose views influenced and helped formulate official policies on immigration. Senators Chandler and Lodge, John Weber (U.S. commissioner of immigration), Prescott Hall (secretary of the Immigration Restriction League), and Congressmen Geary and Young were among the magazine's contributors.

Until the 1920s the *North American Review* was even-handed on immigration. Quite often it ran two articles in the same issue, one favoring and the other opposing immigration; one praising the contribution immigrants had made to the social and economic development of the country, the other damning them because they were a drain on the resources of the country and contributed disproportionately to the insane, criminal, and pauper population. The damnation was always directed at the current crop of immigrants, those from southern and eastern Europe, who were described as semibarbarous, illiterate, and breeders of crime and mental illness.

The *North American Review* carried more essays on immigration between 1880 and 1910 than any of the other magazines. The articles often contained statistics on where immigrants had come from during different periods, estimates of the value of immigrant labor to U.S. society, and appraisals of how immigrants had been received in earlier periods.

During World War I, the *North American Review* questioned the loyalty of certain immigrant groups. It also published pieces such as "The Crux of the Immigration Question" that argued that the United States had always been ambivalent about "newcomers" and that each generation believed that those coming currently were inferior, were likely to be charges upon the state, and were less capable of becoming loyal, useful U.S. citizens. The Puritans and Pilgrims of New England held those views about Quakers, Episcopalians, and Catholics; the English held them about the Germans and Irish; and the latter held them about the eastern and southern Europeans.

Beginning in 1920, the *North American Review* adopted a more one-sided stand on immigration. For the first time in the 60 years of the survey, it urged a total ban on immigration. During the 1920s the *North American Review* vied with the *Saturday Evening Post* in representing the strongest anti-immigrant position. The founding fathers (Washington, Adams, and Jefferson) were cited as supporters of immigration restriction, and the readers were reminded of their Nordic heritage. Data from the army intelligence tests were published to show that immigrants from southern and eastern Europe had minds "scarcely superior to the ox."

In the 1930s, the decade before the magazine's demise, the *North American Review* carried only two articles on immigration. The last one was by an economist who disputed the Malthusian assumptions and argued that immigrants expanded employment opportunities and improved conditions of employment. By then, however, more people were leaving than entering the United States and little space was devoted to immigration in any of the magazines.

SATURDAY EVENING POST

Overall, the *Saturday Evening Post* stands out as the most anti-immigrant magazine in the survey. Its prorestrictionist position, its attacks on the character and quality of southern and eastern

European immigrants, and its praise of Nordic superiority and racial homogeneity began to appear in the second decade of the twentieth century, reached its peak during the 1920s, and changed drastically in the 1960s.

From the 1890s through 1910, the thrust of the articles in the *Saturday Evening Post* ranged from encouragement of more immigrants and praise for the contribution that immigrants had made to the development of the country to mild concern about changes in the level of skill that the recent immigrants were bringing and the countries from which they were coming. In the decade of the 1910s, the *Saturday Evening Post* supported congressional efforts to enact literacy requirements and urged the exercising of greater selectivity in the types of persons who would be admitted to the United States.

During the 1920s the magazine published 53 articles about immigration, all of which were anti-immigrant and prorestrictionist. It described the Quota Act of 1924, which was more restrictionist than the Quota Act of 1921, as the "Second Declaration of Independence." The immigrants arriving from southern and eastern Europe were characterized as the dullest and dumbest people in Europe, the dregs of the earth, and the magazine warned that the United States was becoming the dumping ground for the world's riffraff as a result of its willingness to permit them to enter. It claimed that the Italians, Jews, Poles, Russians, Greeks, and others would erode, destroy, and mongrelize U.S. society. They had higher rates of insanity, crime, and other forms of deviance than people from other parts of Europe, the *Saturday Evening Post* declared.

Although more people emigrated from the United States than entered as aliens during the 1930s, the *Saturday Evening Post* advocated suspending all immigration for at least two years and deporting many of those already in the country. The United States was overpopulated, according to the magazine. It also advocated extending quota limits on Western Hemisphere countries. The *Saturday Evening Post* warned that Mexicans were reconquering the Southwest by their illegal entry. When Bruno Hauptman was charged and convicted of the kidnapping and slaying of the Lindberg baby, the *Saturday Evening Post* publicized Hauptman's illegal alien status and warned that there were thousands, perhaps millions, more like him in the country.

The *Saturday Evening Post* supported the McCarran-Walter Act in the 1950s on the grounds that the United States needed to restrict immigration because the country was overpopulated and more people would severely lower current standards of living; because the writers believed that many of the displaced persons who sought entry had pro-Communist subversive political views; and because the national origins quota system prevented an upset in the balance among the racial and national groups already in the country.

Suddenly, and without a backward glance at its history, the *Saturday Evening Post* ran an editorial in 1960 that advocated changing the immigration law because the quota system was discriminatory. It said, in effect, that we are a nation of immigrants and current formulas are prejudicial because they favor one group (the northern Europeans) over all others.

After the *Saturday Evening Post* resumed publication in 1971 (after a two-year lapse), it ran an editorial that compared blacks in South Africa to illegal Mexican immigrants in the United States and decried the failure of both societies to provide them with civil rights. There were no articles on immigration in the *Saturday Evening Post* during the 1980s.

LITERARY DIGEST

Even though more space is devoted in this book to the *Literary Digest* than to any of the other magazines, given the nature of the publication, it is difficult to characterize the magazine's position and views on immigration. Its editors' interest in the topic is attested to by the number of editorials and stories it excerpted from newspapers and magazines throughout the country. Although most articles favored restrictions, had an anti-eastern and -southern European bias, favored literacy requirements, and supported the Quota Acts, it is nevertheless difficult to distinguish whether the pieces were excerpted because they dramatized the mood and policies of the day or because they most closely agreed with the views of the editors of the *Literary Digest*.

Reading through the *Literary Digest*, we find immigrants described as arriving in hordes in an unending flow. The immigrants were described as having low intelligence and morals, as lacking in energy and talent, and as diseased and beaten people. Early in the 1880s, most of the newspapers quoted favored exclusion of the Chinese. Later in the decade, however, support for Chinese exclusion was more likely to be limited to newspapers on the West Coast, in California especially. The big-city northeastern dailies were critical of the West Coast press and California politicians for their anti-Chinese stance and favored abrogating the Chinese Exclusion Act. During the first decade of the twentieth century, the issue of Japanese immigrants and the West Coast's reaction to them came to the fore, and the Chinese issue drifted to the background. Newspapers and officials in California favored prohibiting Japanese immigration completely.

Literacy requirements and immigration restriction were the *Literary Digest*'s main immigration stories in the 1910s. When a literacy requirement was finally enacted in 1917 over four presidential vetoes, a cross section of newspaper opinion supported the Congress. A minority of the press, concentrated primarily in the Northeast, sided with President Wilson in opposing the Literacy Act.

Toward the end of the decade and continuing into the 1920s, the role of the American Federation of Labor (A.F. of L.) in the movement to restrict immigration was given a lot of publicity. During the debate over literacy requirements, the support of the A.F. of L. was noted on the floor of the House, and the newspapers claimed that the A.F. of L. support for the bill was a major factor in its passage. Several years later, the A.F. of L. was also widely cited for its support of a bill that would halt immigration completely for several years.

During debate on the 1921 and 1924 Quota Acts, the division of newspaper opinion between the northeastern dailies and much of the rest of the country, as reflected in the *Literary Digest,* became even sharper. Most of the papers in New York City, Boston, Philadelphia, and Washington, D.C. opposed the Quota Acts; the newspapers in all other parts of the country supported the measures and referred to them as "the most important single piece of legislation" and "as the United States' Second Declaration of Independence." The foreign language press, according to the *Literary Digest*, was unanimous in their opposition to the bills.

By the 1930s the immigration issue had receded into the background; the attention it received was tied to its effect on the economic depression and unemployment problems. In 1930 the *Literary Digest* reported that editorial opinion around the country supported a proposal by Senator David Reed, coauthor of the Johnson-Reed Quota Act of 1924, to suspend all quotas plus nonquota Philippine immigration for two years because, in the senator's words, "Every arriving alien who comes here to earn a living in times like the present either displaces someone now at work or becomes in some degree a public charge." As the decade wore on, even the big-city northeastern newspapers supported and demanded greater government action against aliens who were entering the country illegally. The "gate crashers," as they were frequently called, were perceived as the greatest threat to the U.S. labor force. The *Literary Digest* folded in 1937.

HARPER'S, SCRIBNER'S, ATLANTIC MONTHLY, AND THE NATION

Harper's, *Scribner's*, *Atlantic Monthly*, and *The Nation* appealed to much the same educated middle and upper middle class readership as did the *North American Review*. All four magazines began publishing prior to the Civil War, and three of the four have continued to the present. (*Scribner's* folded in 1939.) Of the four, the

Atlantic Monthly devoted more space to immigration than the others; *Harper's*, the least. *The Nation* adopted the most consistently favorable stance toward immigration; *Scribner's* held the most consistently restrictionist views.

Harper's coverage of immigration, especially up to the 1940s, contained mainly first-person, literary-biographical accounts, as opposed to analytical essays or position pieces. During the 1940s and 1950s, *Harper's* coverage focused on refugees and on the positive qualities of immigrants: a strong work ethic, diligence, literacy, and a low propensity for crime. The one article it printed on the McCarran-Walter Act described it as "the most restrictionist piece of legislation ever enacted."

After a hiatus of some 30 years, *Harper's* returned to the immigration theme with five pieces in the 1980s. Two of these pieces picked up on the loyalty theme. *Harper's* attacked the Reagan administration for denying visas to persons seeking entry to the United States and for excluding U.S. citizens from obtaining government-sponsored speaking engagements abroad for ideological reasons. In three pieces on illegal immigrants from Central America, it urged that they be granted political refugee status.

In 1931 *Scribner's* warned that "New York City was being taken over by Oriental looking foreigners." During World War I, it published results of the army mental tests and concluded that immigrants should be excluded from U.S. society because of their low intelligence and high propensity for crime. It supported the 1921 and 1924 Quota Acts. *Scribner's* last piece on immigrants in 1940 warned that the European refugees were bad risks for the United States and posed a special threat to U.S. academia.

Francis Walker was for the *Atlantic Monthly* in the 1890s what Kenneth Roberts was for the *Saturday Evening Post* in the 1920s: the leading protagonist against the new immigration. In addition to Walker, other important academic and public figures who espoused restrictionism were economist W. Jett Lauck (who also contributed to the *Saturday Evening Post*) and theologian Reinhold Nebuhr. During World War I, the *Atlantic Monthly* carried three anti–German-immigrant pieces, but most of its anti-immigrant fervor from the 1890s until World War II was directed at the eastern and southern European immigrants. In 1978, the *Atlantic Monthly* focused on the current most unpopular group of immigrants — the Mexican illegals. It described the conditions under which they lived and the complexity of the problem. The three pieces in the 1980s showed support for admitting more immigrants as political refugees, be they from Southeast Asia or Central America.

Unlike the other three magazines in this subcategory, *The Nation* was and is a weekly; thus, it had greater opportunity to publish more pieces on immigration over the same time span than did *Harper's* or the *Atlantic Monthly*. Although the more than 70 articles that appeared in *The Nation* between 1880 and 1990 do not represent a fourfold increase over the monthlies, they do provide a lot of material for analysis of *The Nation's* views on immigrants. As we noted earlier, more than any of the other magazines in the survey, *The Nation* was consistently proimmigrant. In the 1880s it opposed proposals for prolonging the period of naturalization on certain types of immigrants. In the 1890s it opposed congressional efforts to impose literacy requirements. In the 1900s it called for more immigrants to settle in the South, and it attacked President Theodore Roosevelt for his support of a Japanese exclusion treaty. In the 1910s it claimed that the presence of immigrant laborers probably raised rather than hurt the position of U.S. workers. It also attacked the new proposals for literacy requirements and urged repeal of the Chinese Exclusion Act and gentlemen's agreement on Japanese exclusion. Even in the 1920s, when restrictionist sentiment seemed all-pervasive, *The Nation* opposed both the 1921 and 1924 Quota Acts. In the 1930s *The Nation* expressed concern about the European refugees and the failure of the United States to admit more of them. Following World War II, the magazine strongly supported liberal policies vis-à-vis the admission of displaced persons. *The Nation* devoted more space (14 articles) and was more consistently opposed to the McCarran-Walter Act than any other magazine in the survey.

In the most recent period, from the 1960s through the 1980s, *The Nation* turned its attention to illegal Mexican immigrants and voiced opposition to such proposals as identification cards and employer sanctions. It also strongly endorsed the Sanctuary Movement and especially urged the granting of refugee status to the Haitians. In 1979 it carried a review of the work of one of its former editors, Carey McWilliams, who showed that the United States had treated Chinese and Japanese immigrants badly and was in the process of doing so with the current cohort of Mexican immigrants. *The Nation* characterized the Simpson-Mazzoli Bill as legitimating "an approach to immigration that has its roots in racism and xenophobia." According to *The Nation*, "No area of government action defines the character and destiny of our nation, who and what we are, more directly than our handling of immigration."

CHRISTIAN CENTURY, COMMENTARY, AND COMMONWEAL

The opportunities for overlap on immigration coverage among the three denominational magazines in our survey are less than one would expect among the major news weeklies or intellectual monthlies because the time span of their publication and the frequency of their appearance are more varied. The Protestant *Christian Century* is the oldest of the three and the only weekly, but it published fewer pieces than did the Catholic *Commonweal*. The Jewish-affiliated *Commentary* had by far the fewest number of articles on immi-gration for the same time span. Of the three, *Commonweal* was the most consistently proimmigrant.

In the 1910s and 1920s the *Christian Century* supported literacy requirements and quotas. In the 1930s and 1940s it expressed concern about refugees and argued for the elimination of the formal exclusion of immigrants on the basis of color. Its silence during the years of debate over the McCarran-Walter Act is rather surprising because of its prorefugee, antidiscrimination stand in the 1930s and 1940s. The *Christian Century* gave little space to immigration in the 1950s and 1960s. It devoted more space to the issue in the 1970s and focused primarily on Mexican immigrants. In the 1979 Christmas issue, it predicted that the moral issues of the 1980s would be the ways in which the United States treated Mexicans who entered illegally and U.S. treatment of those seeking refugee status from Haiti and Central America. In the 20 pieces on immigration that the *Christian Century* carried in the 1980s, 17 were critical of U.S. policy vis-à-vis the Haitians and the Central Americans. It also endorsed the goals of the Sanctuary Movement as a true message of Christian values.

In the 45 years of *Commentary*'s publication, it carried four articles on immigration, three of which focused on matters of assimilation and acculturation as perceived by two social scientists and one theologian. One piece was directed at policy; it condemned the Congress and the Eisenhower administration for not moving faster and more effectively on removing displaced persons out of the camps in Europe.

From its founding in 1922, *Commonweal* was critical of U.S. immigration policy. It opposed the ban on Asians, it favored a more liberal policy vis-à-vis refugees, and it deplored the 1921 and 1924 Quota Acts. After *The Nation*, *Commonweal* carried more articles critical of the McCarran-Walter Act than any other magazine in the survey. Following the 1950s, *Commonweal* cut its coverage of immigration but maintained its position that immigrants are good for the country and refugees should be welcomed. It wrote favorably about Mexican immigrants, the legal ones as well as the illegals, and it likened public attitudes toward the Mexicans in the 1970s to those exhibited against the southern and eastern Europeans almost a century earlier. Illegal immigration, the Sanctuary Movement, and the justifications for granting refugee status to the Haitians and immigrants from Central America were the themes of *Commonweal*'s pieces in the 1980s.

READER'S DIGEST

Immigration was not a high priority issue for the *Reader's Digest*. From its founding in 1922 through 1990 it included 26 pieces on immigration, the first of which did not appear until 1938. Although the *Reader's Digest* was founded early in the decade in which the media gave a lot of attention to immigration, *Reader's Digest* did not reprint any of the debate. In the main, the pieces on immigration that appeared in the *Reader's Digest* before and in the decade following World War II favored restrictionist policies. The articles advocated that U.S. interests should come first, that immigrants are a drain on the socioeconomic and cultural systems and assets of the society, and, most important, that the United States had done its share of absorbing immigrants in earlier decades; it was now up to other countries of the world to accept refugees and displaced persons.

An article in the late 1950s and another by historian Oscar Handlin in 1966 were two of the four proimmigrant pieces that appeared in the *Reader's Digest* during the 68 years of its publication. In the 1970s two articles focused on illegal immigrants from Mexico, which the *Reader's Digest* saw as a major problem. The articles recommended passage of employer sanctions, the use of alien identification cards, and an increase in appropriations to the border patrol force. In the 1980s, after carrying two pieces that applauded the industriousness and work ethic of Cuban and Korean immigrants, the *Reader's Digest* included four articles that warned of the dangers of immigrants taking jobs away from U.S. citizens and generally placing too great a burden on the U.S. economy and society.

THE NEWS WEEKLIES

Although the amount of coverage varied considerably among the weeklies, there was a good deal of overlap in the issues and topics covered in each decade among the four news weeklies. In the 1930s, and even more so in the 1940s, they focused on refugees and displaced persons. How many persons the United States should admit and from which countries they should come were the major themes. The debate surrounding the specific components of the McCarran-Walter Act monopolized the immigration stories in *Time, Newsweek,* and *Life* in the 1950s. *U.S. News and World Report* also discussed the McCarran-Walter Act but in a larger context and with a statistical-historical background that described how many immigrants had arrived from which countries during earlier decades and how the quota system affected the flow of immigrants. All of the weeklies carried fewer stories on immigration in the 1960s than they did in the 1950s, but almost all of them were about the Hart-Celler Act and how it rectified many of the policy errors made into law in the McCarran-Walter Act. As in its treatment of the McCarran-Walter Act, *U.S. News and World Report* provided longer, in-depth analyses accompanied by charts and graphs containing statistics going back 50 years.

The 1970s and 1980s had two major immigration themes: the legal and illegal Mexican immigrants, and the refugees from Southeast Asia and Cuba and those seeking refugee status from Haiti and the Central American countries. All of the news weeklies found the prospect of absorbing refugees from Southeast Asia more attractive and less complicated for the United States than the absorption of Mexican immigrants. The latter, especially illegal aliens, were viewed as a liability and a drain on the U.S. economy.

THE *NEW YORK TIMES*

Coverage of the *New York Times* is not as exhaustive as coverage of the magazines because, for the first 100 years, only the editorials were examined and we sampled rather than included all of the editorials. For the decade between 1980 and 1990, all of the editorials, the op-eds, and the columnists that appeared in the editorial page were included. All told, some 350 editorials were reviewed.

The *New York Times* did not have a consistent stance on immigration for the entire period. At the beginning of the period surveyed, it favored restrictionist policies more than it did at the end of the period. In the 1880s the *New York Times* emphasized the problems of digesting the huge numbers of persons seeking to enter the United States. It described immigrants from southern and eastern Europe as undesirable, unwholesome, clannish, and ignorant. It also advocated careful screening of persons with subversive political views.

The *New York Times* carried twice as many editorials on immigration in the 1890s as it did in the 1880s, concerned mostly with finding more effective ways of keeping illegals out. It provided a ranking of more- and less-desirable immigrants. The English, Irish, and Scottish were on the desirable or positive end, and immigrants from Italy, Poland, Hungary, and Russia were on the negative end.

The next decade witnessed a shift toward more favorable views of immigrants generally and of Russian Jews and Japanese specifically. The Chinese and Germans were also included on the plus side of the immigration ledger. The *New York Times* championed the cause of the Chinese and also attacked U.S. policy toward the Japanese. It believed that the government's policy toward both groups was "brutal" and "insulting" and against the best interests of the United States. Most of the magazines surveyed favored literacy requirements as a means of restricting immigration in the decade that witnessed passage of such requirements. In the opinion of the *New York Times*, immigrants with alien political beliefs should be barred, not immigrants who could not read or write.

The 1920s marked the high point in the number of editorials devoted to immigration. Again, in contrast to almost all of the magazines surveyed (*The Nation* was the exception), the *New York Times* did not support the 1921 and 1924 Quota Acts. Its editorials recognized a need for restrictive legislation, but they claimed that the proposed laws would discriminate against Italians, Poles, Russians, Jews, and Japanese.

The *New York Times* ran editorials that sought to discredit Nordic race superiority and warned against using race as a basis for immigration restriction. It continued, however, to urge barring and deportation of politically radical aliens. Anticipating future policy by some 40 years, the *New York Times* urged adoption of restrictions against immigrants from Western Hemisphere countries.

Although it opposed the national origins basis for the 1921 and 1924 Quota Acts, the *New York Times* favored immigration restriction generally and pointed out that the United States was not responsible for Europe's overpopulation. There were other countries to which immigrants could go, and Europe should find some way other than emigration for solving its economic and population problems. The *New York Times* saw no reason for U.S. guilt about this issue.

Immigration was not a high-priority issue in the 1930s. The half-dozen or so editorials in our sample during that decade noted the sharp drop in the numbers coming to the United States. The *New York Times* continued its attack against U.S. policy barring Japanese and Chinese immigrants.

Internment of Japanese-Americans and the plight of displaced persons were the two major themes in the *New York Times* editorials during the 1940s. On the first issue, the *New York Times* took the position that the government must keep close watch on the innocent in order to catch those who may be guilty, but it questioned the removal of U.S. citizens of Japanese descent from their homes on the Pacific Coast and their internment in camps. It did not, however, condemn the practice. After the war it urged protection against deportation of Japanese-Americans on a class basis. On the second theme, that of the admission of refugees and displaced persons, the *New York Times* urged liberalization of U.S. immigration policy. It declared the 1948 Displaced Persons Act inadequate and discriminatory against Catholics and Jews.

The *New York Times*' antipathy toward the 1948 Act paled in contrast to its distaste for the McCarran-Walter Act. The *New York Times* criticized the bill throughout the decade and supported all efforts at modification and repeal.

There were only three editorials on immigration during the years surveyed in the 1960s. Each criticized the McCarran-Walter Act and linked it to the Quota Acts of 1921 and 1924. The *New York Times* viewed those acts as part of a long-standing racially discriminatory policy against southern and eastern European immigrants and in favor of northern European immigrants.

The plight of refugees from Southeast Asia was the major theme of the *New York Times* editorials in the 1970s. The *New York Times* commended President Carter for increasing the U.S. monthly quota to 14,000 and urged other countries to open their doors.

Illegal immigration from Mexico was the other theme in the *New York Times* editorials. The newspaper's editors praised Attorney General Benjamin Civiletti for calling a halt to raids on illegals in their homes and declared that the United States should handle the problem of illegals by more stringent and closer scrutiny of business firms that hire illegal aliens. It also supported the census bureau's request for the support of the Catholic Church in getting Hispanics generally, and illegal aliens particularly, to cooperate with census takers. The debate on illegals continued on the editorial page of the *New York Times* throughout the 1980s, as did the newspaper's concern about U.S. treatment of those seeking refugee status. It expressed compassion for the Haitians but did not support granting them refugee status. It also expressed positive and negative sentiments vis-à-vis the illegals. On the one hand, the *New York Times* urged control of our borders and expressed a concern that illegals take jobs from U.S. citizens. On the other hand, it acknowledged that illegals work hard, pay taxes, and use few government services.

Looking back and comparing the *New York Times'* 110 years of editorials on immigration with the magazines surveyed, none, except *The Nation*, had as consistently positive a record as did the *New York Times*. *Commonweal* in its much shorter history joins *The Nation* in being more proimmigrant than the *New York Times*.

CONCLUDING REMARKS

It is something of a miracle that so many immigrants gained entry to the United States between 1880 and 1990. Going back to recapture the tone of the debate in the print media, examining the bills proposed and passed by Congress and the statutes enacted into federal law, and reviewing the national poll data lead to wonderment and bewilderment at how more than 40 million people gained admittance during a century and to a country that at best was ambivalent toward them and at worst erected barriers to their entry.

The large majority of the magazines surveyed (and they represent a cross section of the industry) were always ambivalent about how many foreigners ought to be allowed to come to our shores. In the time span of the survey, there were always more people who wanted to settle in the United States than the magazines thought ought to be permitted; and they seemed always to be coming from the wrong countries. When the largest influx of immigrants was coming from eastern and southern Europe, the magazines bemoaned the loss of the sturdy, independent, hard-working northern and western Europeans. When the direction shifted and the neighboring southern countries of the Western Hemisphere were the major sources of origin, the European immigrant of yesteryear took on a rosy glow. When the migration pattern shifted across the Pacific and the countries of Asia became the major exporters of immigrants, the collective wishes were to halt, or at least limit, immigration of people whose backgrounds and experiences were different; they could never assimilate into U.S. culture.

During the 110 years covered by this survey, the most important messages that the majority of the magazines communicated were the desire to reduce sharply the overall numbers who wanted to come from anywhere and to exclude persons from certain countries and regions. There were a few exceptions. *The Nation* most consistently and for the longest period and *Commonweal* for the shorter period during which it was published were the deviant voices. They opposed restrictions in principle and toward whichever categories of people they were directed, and they praised the contributions that immigrants made to the economy and culture of the nation.

The magazines, however, did not function in a vacuum, nor did they appear to be the leaders or molders of the restrictionist movement and of anti-immigrant sentiments. Congress, for more than a quarter century, persisted in passing literacy requirements that it believed would effectively restrict the least desirable of the immigrants from gaining entry: those from southern and eastern Europe who were primarily Catholic and Jewish, poor, unskilled, uncultured, and purportedly unassimilable. Finally, after four presidents vetoed various versions of a literacy requirement, the Congress, because it had the support of two-thirds of its membership, was able to enact such a statute. It was also during this period that the Chinese Exclusion Act was passed and continuously extended and the gentlemen's agreement was arranged between the United States and Japan that effectively excluded Japanese from becoming citizens.

The idea of establishing quotas on potential immigrants from different countries gained enough support to become the centerpiece of immigration legislation during the 1920s and through the 1950s. It was not until the mid-1960s that a major change occurred in U.S. policy and, to a large extent, in the opinions expressed in the magazines. Refugees from Communist regimes in Cuba, Southeast Asia, and the Soviet Union were the biggest benefactors of those changes.

The government and the majority of the magazines shared positive beliefs about the importance of accepting refugees above immigration quotas and of the positive impact such policies would have on domestic as well as foreign policy. Neither in content nor in style did any of the magazines in the 1960s and 1970s capture the rhetoric or substance of the anti-immigration positions assumed by the *Atlantic Monthly*, *Scribner's*, and the *North American Review* in the 1890s and early 1900s or by the *Saturday Evening Post* in the 1920s.

The majority of the U.S. public, however, has remained doubtful and unpersuaded as to the wisdom of the changed policy and the benefits of generosity toward immigrants. None of the national polls in the 1960s, 1970s or 1980s showed that most Americans advocated or desired a more liberal stance vis-à-vis immigration. If public opinion polls dictated immigration policies, the restrictionist legislation of the 1920s and 1950s would have remained in place and it is unlikely that the refugee programs would have been enacted. Especially among persons of lower socioeconomic status, immigrants represent a threat to livelihoods and to standards of living and competition for scarce resources. Poorer Americans fear that more immigrants mean fewer jobs; lower rates of pay; fewer opportunities for mobility; more competition for housing, schools, and social services; and fewer opportunities for their children in higher education.

Once again, it is extraordinary that more than 40 million immigrants gained legal entry to the United States between 1880 and 1990 in light of the public's, the print media's, and the legislature's attitudes, opinions, and policies vis-à-vis immigration. Perhaps the movements of peoples from one part of the world to another do not lend themselves to the same type of control by majority rule as do other social practices and events. Perhaps special interest groups — in the early period, steamship companies, for example, and later, industry and commerce — were able to exercise greater influence than the more passive majorities. Perhaps the selective influence and actions of various ethnic groups, religious organizations, and other lobbyists at crucial times were able to offset the less mobilized, negative sentiment of the public, as witnessed by the enactment of refugee statutes beginning in the late 1950s. The role of the presidents should also be noted in their vetoes of more stringent literacy requirements and quotas and in their use of executive powers on the issue of refugees.

It is not clear precisely how important or effective any or all of these factors have been, but taken together, they are much more congruous with the fact to be explained — the number of immigrants who came to the United States — than are the public's attitudes and the print media's opinions and positions vis-à-vis immigration.

Appendix A: Profiles of the Magazines Surveyed

NORTH AMERICAN REVIEW

The *North American Review* is the oldest magazine in the survey. Founded in 1815 by a group from Harvard University, it was, according to Frank Luther Mott, "Harvardian, Bostonian, Unitarian" but with visions of being a magazine of national interest.[1] Like other magazines of its time, the *North American Review* was an eclectic collection of features on travel, science, and local politics as well as stories from British publications. It was, however, primarily a literary magazine. By 1880, its editors and contributors included Harvard tutors, Boston lawyers, and the grandsons of John Quincy Adams. Seven different editors edited the *North American Review* from 1880 until its demise in 1940. The first was Allen Thorndike Rice, a wealthy young Bostonian who edited the *North American Review* through its peak circulation period. The last was Joseph Hilton Smyth. Smyth was arrested in 1942 and accused of acting as an agent of the Japanese government. Critics charged that he had received financial support for the purchase of several magazines, including the *North American Review*, to make them over as a voice for Japanese propaganda.

Circulation of the magazine rose from 7,600 in 1880 to a peak of approximately 75,000 around 1892 and then leveled off to approximately 25,000 until its decline in the 1930s when circulation was approximately 3,000. It was never a "popular" magazine in the tradition of the *Saturday Evening Post*; rather, it drew its readers from the educated middle class. Frank Mott wrote of the magazine in 1938: "It is unquestionably true that the *North American* is regarded by more people, in all parts of the country, as at once the highest and most impartial platform upon which current public issues can be discussed, than is any other magazine or review."[2]

SATURDAY EVENING POST

The *Saturday Evening Post* was also established well before 1880. Its opening publication date is not certain but is generally thought to have been around the 1820s. The early *Saturday Evening Post* was founded as a combination weekly newspaper and magazine, a format it retained during most of its 150 years of publication. In 1897 Cyrus H. K. Curtis bought the magazine from the estate of A. E. Smyth. Curtis's $1,000 investment gave him the rights to the title and tradition of the magazine; and within 20 years, circulation was well over the 1 million mark. When he purchased the magazine, Curtis hired reporter George Horace Lorimer as editor, a post Lorimer held for 40 years.

Curtis and Lorimer developed a combination of literary attributes that kept the magazine popular for almost 75 years. Their primary aim for the magazine was entertainment. Fiction accounted for a large percentage of its content, but the magazine also covered social issues of the day. After World War I, Lorimer began to cover the world's problems. He initiated the fight for restricting immigration in his editorials and continued it on the feature pages. Quoting Wood about Lorimer:

[He felt] further immigration had to be limited in volume and that the possibilities and desirabilities of different races had to be analyzed. Henry H. Curran and Kenneth Roberts presented the subject in a series of *Post* articles. According to W. W. Husband, then Commissioner General of Immigration, the articles by Roberts were responsible for the passage of the restrictive Immigration Act of 1924. Curran became Commissioner of Immigration at the Port of New York.[3]

Upon Lorimer's resignation in 1936, his protege, Wesley Stout, became editor. Stout resigned after the *Saturday Evening Post* was charged with anti-Semitism in 1942 and was succeeded by Ben Hibbs, editor of another Curtis publication. Neither Stout nor Hibbs had the personality or acumen of the original team, and the *Saturday Evening Post* began a steady decline. Its last issue appeared on February 8, 1969. At that time it was still owned by Curtis Publishing Company, with William A. Emerson as the editor. The magazine reappeared in a new format in 1971 with Cory Ser Vass as editor and publisher.

When Curtis purchased the *Saturday Evening Post* in 1897, its weekly circulation was approximately 30,000. Circulation continued to rise and reached 2 million by 1920, 3 million by 1930, and 6 million before its final issue.

LITERARY DIGEST

Daniel Boorstin has described the *Literary Digest*, founded in 1890 by the book publishers Isaac Funk and Adam Wagnall, as attempting to fulfill the needs of its turn-of-the-century readers to get more information more quickly. The *Literary Digest* and another contemporary weekly published by Funk and Wagnall are described as: "weekly eclectics that surveyed editorial opinion and condensed and arranged it for the information of readers."[4]

Literary Digest enjoyed its peak period of popularity from 1910 to 1930. From 1933 until its final publication in 1937, the magazine had five editors, none of whom was successful in fighting the competition of the new weekly news magazines, *Time* and *Newsweek*.

Financial difficulties within the *Literary Digest* coupled with the embarrassment of a public opinion poll predicting a landslide victory for Alfred Landon in the presidential election of 1936 expedited the end of the *Literary Digest*, which was once second only to the *Saturday Evening Post* in weekly circulation. In 1938 it was incorporated with *Time* magazine.

HARPER'S

Only three magazines, *Harper's*, *The Nation*, and the *Atlantic Monthly*, span the entire 110 years of this survey. *Harper's* was founded in 1850 by Harper & Bros. Publishing Company and was seen as a vehicle for advertising company products and stimulating readers' interest in fiction.

While the *Saturday Evening Post* was perceived as the magazine of middle America, *Harper's* was considered the magazine for those of higher status. Throughout its history, it was designed to appeal to the educated middle class.

Based on the results of readership surveys conducted after World War I, *Harper's* began "to devote the magazine to the interpretation and discussion of the modern scene."[5] Articles written by public figures were included, along with pieces by leading authors. Some of the works of the most influential authors of the time, such as Charles Dickens, Mark Twain, and Thomas Wolfe, were published in *Harper's*. Now added to these names were Bertrand Russell, Henry Steele Commager, and Daniel Boorstin.

Before the 1900s, *Harper's* led most other magazines in circulation totals. With the rise of mass media, however, it was overshadowed by the *Saturday Evening Post* and the *Literary Digest*. *Harper's*, however, has maintained its appeal to the audience for which it was initially intended: the educated, professional middle class.

SCRIBNER'S

According to Mott, a fourth "quality" magazine was *Scribner's* magazine, the other three being *Harper's, Century Illustrated*, and the *Atlantic Monthly*. The original *Scribner's* had a somewhat confusing beginning. It was started in 1870 by two religious New Englanders, Dr. Josiah Holland and Roswell Smith, with the assistance of a loan from book publisher Charles Scribner. Holland and Smith's original intent was to publish a magazine that would criticize U.S. society from a Christian standpoint.[6] In 1880 Smith bought out Holland, and in 1881 Scribner's son sold Smith the remaining stock on the condition that Scribner's name would not be used for five years.

Smith continued publishing the magazine but changed its name to *Century Illustrated Monthly Magazine*. Five years later the book publishers, Charles Scribner's Sons, began a new magazine, *Scribner's* magazine, with Edward Burlingame as editor. The premier issue was January 1887, and from the start it competed with *Harper's* and the *Atlantic Monthly* for readers from the new middle class of U.S. society.

Burlingame's philosophy was to present "popular topics with literary treatment."[7] The emphasis was on the literary, although articles on travel, the technology of industry, biographies, and autobiographies were also featured. Stories of the poor by Jacob Riis were featured in the beginning years, as were articles on psychology by William James. Edward Burlingame continued to edit the magazine for 27 years, and these were the peak years for *Scribner's* circulation.

By 1925 *Scribner's* showed a greater emphasis on public affairs. Beginning in January of that year, each issue had two or three articles on contemporary concerns.[8] When Alfred Dashiell assumed the editorship in 1930, he adjusted the content to attract the young intellectuals of the left. The more conservative writings of Theodore Roosevelt were replaced by those of Clarence Darrow, John Dewey, and Malcolm Cowley. The fiction of Bret Harte was replaced by that of F. Scott Fitzgerald. According to Mott, this had a disastrous effect on the circulation, as old subscribers dropped and were not replaced by new ones. In 1939, *Scribner's* ceased publication.

ATLANTIC MONTHLY

The *Atlantic Monthly* is another literary magazine that appealed to a limited audience and was published during the entire 110 years of this survey. From its beginning it attracted a readership consisting of business and political leaders. Early contributors included Ralph Waldo Emerson, James Lowell, and Harriet Beecher Stowe. The

Atlantic Monthly wrote about matters of interest to, and in large measure reflected the opinions and beliefs of, the educated upper middle-class Anglo-Saxon population of the United States.

In 1909 Ellery Sedgwick purchased the magazine from Houghton Mifflin Publishing Company and became owner-editor. Under Sedgwick's management the *Atlantic Monthly* showed a sense of the "profound importance of the economic, social and political changes in contemporary life, all of which it reflected with dignity and frequently with literary charm."[9] Although the *Atlantic Monthly*'s emphasis was primarily on belles-lettres, it also covered social issues such as the civil rights movement, the Vietnam War, and, more recently, new technologies and development in Third World nations.

THE NATION

In 1880 the *London Daily News* described *The Nation* as "represent(ing) the best section of American politics and society."[10] *The Nation* is a weekly magazine that was founded in 1865 by Frederick Law Olmstead. He established the magazine as "an American weekly paper which should enlist as contributors men of scholarship, brilliance, and independence."[11] Irish reporter E. L. Godkin was its first editor. Godkin has been described as an editor "so powerful (that) . . . clergymen, educators, politicians drew on his editorials, and what he had to say filtered down from these opinion-makers, as they would be called today, and eventually were understood by the electorate, who translated much of what he advocated into political action."[12] The magazine was liberal, and most of the time its editorial views opposed the popular opinions of the day.

The Nation had its highest circulation in the 1920s and 1930s and again in the 1950s with about 40,000 readers. It has had a series of editors after Godkin that included Oswald Garrison Villar, Freda Kirchwey, Carey McWilliams, and, currently, Victor Navasky. All of them carried on in Godkin's tradition, continuing to offer strong opinions and to cover politics, literature, science, drama, music, art, and business.

READER'S DIGEST

Reader's Digest offers another example of the popularization of magazine formats designed to provide more information more quickly. Founded in 1922 after much discouragement and with little support, it has grown to represent the United States around the globe. DeWitt and Lila Scheson Wallace started the magazine in a basement apartment with a charter subscription list of about 1,500 members. *Reader's Digest*, with offices around the world, now has a circulation that is many times that of its nearest competitors. The Wallaces' original notion was to select articles from magazines of the day, condense them, and present the results in an easy-to-read format. This plan, however, was not readily accepted by potential financial backers and did not become a reality until the Wallaces accepted a friend's advice to obtain mail-order subscriptions.

The magazine's format and philosophy have changed little over the years. Some original writings were introduced in the 1930s, but even today, much of the material is condensed from other sources. Advertising appeared in *Reader's Digest* in 1955.

The Wallaces and their magazine were influential in representing the U.S. dream and individual success. Through the *Reader's Digest*, the Wallaces served as propagandists for the United States in foreign countries. It is largely due to *Reader's Digest*'s successful example that nonfiction articles now play a dominant role in U.S. magazines.[13] *Time* magazine credits the Wallaces with having influenced the individual, the magazine industry, and the education of the people of the United States.

CHRISTIAN CENTURY

Distinctly different from the previously described magazines, the *Christian Century* was first published in Iowa in 1884 as the *Christian Oracle*, under the guidance of the Disciples of Christ Church. In 1891 its base shifted to Chicago, and by 1900 its name had been changed to proclaim that the twentieth century would be the "Christian Century." Charles Clayton Morrison was owner and editor for 39 years, from 1908 to 1947. His influence on the journal's editorial policy was threefold: he advocated a union among Protestants in the United States, world peace, and the separation of church and state.[14] His ideals were reflected in the magazine's nondenominational and liberal policy. The editorial staff further reflected the nondenominational nature of the *Christian Century*, as its members belonged to a variety of Protestant denominations, including Methodist, Baptist, Lutheran, Presbyterian, and the Disciples of Christ.

As did *Harper's*, *Atlantic Monthly*, and *The Nation*, the *Christian Century* included among its contributors some of the social, moral, and political leaders of the day, such as Paul Tillich, Albert Schweitzer, Jane Addams, Norman Thomas, Paul Douglas, and Harold Stassen. On its editorial feature pages the *Christian Century* has addressed social issues such as prohibition, Indian rights, organized labor, civil rights, and world government. Although its circulation has never been large (38,000 at its peak in 1950), the ideals and concerns of the *Christian Century* have been read by professionals interested in U.S. Protestantism and U.S. ideals.

COMMENTARY

Commentary is the youngest magazine in the survey, having been founded in 1945 by the American Jewish Committee. In Volume 1, Number 1, the American Jewish Committee explained sponsorship of *Commentary* as a desire to enlighten and clarify public opinion on problems of Jewish concern, to fight bigotry and protect human rights, and to promote Jewish cultural interest and creative achievement in the United States. *Commentary*, in its view, would be a "journal of significant thought and opinion on Jewish affairs and contemporary world issues."[15]

Commentary has remained under the sponsorship of the American Jewish Committee and the guidance of two editors — Elliott Cohen (1945–1959) and Norman Podhoretz (1959 to the present). Its contributors have included such influential thinkers as Hannah Arendt, George Orwell, Norman Mailer, James Baldwin, Gunnar Myrdal, and Mary McCarthy.

COMMONWEAL

Commonweal describes itself as "A Weekly Review of Literature, the Arts and Public Affairs." It was founded by Roman Catholic laymen in 1924, and its first editor and moving force was Michael Williams. Williams was a journalist and writer who wanted to begin "an intellectual Catholic weekly" like the then-highly influential *New Republic* and *The Nation. Commonweal* was considered a "highbrow" review, and early subscribers numbered a sparse 3,000.

> The editors of the *Commonweal* believe that nothing can do so much for the betterment, the happiness, and the peace of the American people as the influence of the enduring and tested principles of Catholic Christianity. To that high task the *Commonweal* is dedicated.[16]

Commonweal has often been critical of the established church. Never a magazine of mass appeal, its circulation has, nonetheless, been competitive with *The Nation, Commentary*, and *Christian Century*.

TIME

Time magazine was founded in 1923 by Henry P. Luce and Britton Hadden, one year after *Reader's Digest* appeared on the market. Theodore Peterson points out the parallels:

> Both the Reader's Digest Association, Inc. and Time, Inc. were founded by, and in their earlier years staffed by, persons

without previous magazine experience. Both companies were established on relatively small investments, a circumstance made possible in part because their publications did not originate editorial material but merely condensed, simplified, and brightened up material which had first appeared in other publications. Both companies were among the largest magazine publishing enterprise in the world in 1957.[17]

After Hadden died in 1929, Luce continued as editor-in-chief until he retired in 1964. As chief stockholder, he continued to have a strong influence on the magazine, and in his will he requested that his beneficiaries carry on in the tradition of a "journalistic enterprise."

The readership of *Time* has always been characterized as middle class and well educated. Originally to be titled *Facts*, *Time* was designed to summarize the news in such a way that it could be read within one hour.[18]

LIFE

Life magazine was among the most successful of Time, Inc., ventures. Founded in 1936, it offered a new concept: the news in picture form.

A *Life* magazine had originally been established about 1882 by several Harvard students. It was a magazine of literature and humor. During the years of World War I, its circulation reached a peak of a quarter of a million. When Luce wanted access to the title "Life," the magazine's circulation had declined to about 70,000. Luce thus had little problem buying the magazine to use the name "Life" for his newest venture.[19] *Life* covered national and international stories of politics, disasters, and theater. The story was told with photographs, and although more text was gradually added, it remained a photojournalistic magazine.

Life's circulation was almost always second only to that of *Reader's Digest*, and it survived the competition of television and motion pictures for many years. The magazine eventually folded in 1972 but began publishing again in 1978, but without its one-time broad readership. Its current editor is Jason McManus.

NEWSWEEK

In 1933 Thomas Martyn, a former foreign editor of *Time*, published the first issue of *Newsweek* magazine. Martyn's idea was to present each week's news in a magazine, the cover of which displayed seven descriptive photos, each representing a different day of the week. And unlike *Time*, *Newsweek* (the title spelling was transformed about 1937) would publish by-lined columns in an effort to separate opinion from fact. The magazine focused on three-dimensional coverage, "consisting of the news itself, the background to the news, and interpretations of the significance of the news."[20]

Newsweek's circulation generally has remained half that of *Time* and slightly more than that of the weekly news digest *U.S. News and World Report*. In 1950 the readership of *Newsweek* was identified as college graduates who owned their home and two cars. Eight of every ten were in business, and of those, 45 percent were executives.

U.S. NEWS AND WORLD REPORT

United States News, like *Newsweek*, was first published in 1933. David Lawrence, a philosophical conservative and personal friend of President Woodrow Wilson, founded the magazine to report national news in the style of *Time* magazine.[21] It was a magazine for "people in business, industry, finance, government, and the professions."[22] In 1946 Lawrence began *World Report* to cover and analyze international news. It merged with *United States News* in 1948 to become *U.S. News and World Report*.

The magazine's circulation is about half as large as that of *Time* and slightly less than that of *Newsweek*, and its audience is primarily those influential in business and government.

NOTES

1. Frank Luther Mott, *A History of American Magazines 1741–1905*, vol. 2 (Cambridge, Mass.: Harvard University Press, 1938), p. 223.

2. Ibid., p. 255.

3. James Playsted Wood, *Magazines in the United States* (New York: The Ronald Press Co., 1949/1956), p. 159.

4. Mott, *American Magazines*, vol. 4, p. 64.

5. Mott, *American Magazines*, vol. 2, p. 404.

6. Arthur John, *The Best Years of the Century* (Champaign, Ill.: University of Illinois Press, 1981), p. 24.

7. Mott, *American Magazines*, vol. 4, p. 718.

8. Ibid., p. 728.

9. Ibid., p. 513.

10. N. W. Ayer, *American Newspaper Annual* (Philadelphia: American Newspaper Annual, 1910), p. 261

11. Mott, *American Magazines*, vol. 3, p. 331.

12. John Tebbel, *The American Magazine: A Compact History* (New York: Hawthorne Books, Inc., 1969), p. 113.

13. *Time*, December 10, 1951, p. 75.

14. Alfred Roger Goebbel, *The Christian Century: Editorial Policy: Positions 1908–1966* (Champaign: University of Illinois Press, 1967), p. 16.

15. *Commentary*, vol. 1, no. 1, 1945.

16. Rodger Van Allen, *The Commonweal and American Catholicism — The Magazine, The Movement, The Meaning* (Philadelphia: Fortress Press, 1974), p. 5.

17. Theodore Peterson, *Magazines in the Twentieth Century* (Urbana: University of Illinois Press, 1956), pp. 210–11.

18. Robert T. Elson, *Time Inc.: The Intimate History of a Publishing Enterprise 1923–1941* (New York: Atheneum, 1968), p. 66.

19. Ibid., p. 291.

20. Peterson, *Magazines*, p. 303.

21. James Ford, *Magazines for Millions* (Carbondale: Southern Illinois University Press, 1969), p. 136.

22. Ibid., p. 138.

Appendix B: Organized Opposition to Immigration

An important component of the anti-immigration opinion in the United States is the hundreds of organizations that have adopted negative positions about the numbers and types of immigrants who are allowed to enter the United States. For many of these organizations, immigration is not their major or primary issue; rather, it is imbedded in their larger concerns about population stabilization and/or environmental issues. The Federation for American Immigration Reform (FAIR) is the major anti-immigration organization, operating with an annual budget of $1.7 million and a membership of some 50,000 supporters. Immigration is FAIR's only business, and its platform covers a wide range of immigration issues. Basically, FAIR advocates setting a ceiling on immigration at roughly 300,000 per year. (As of the 1990 Immigration Act, that is less than 40 percent of current levels.) FAIR contends that immigration contributes to higher social welfare costs, overpopulation, and resource depletion.

The Immigration Reform Law Institute (IRLI), which is the legal offspring of FAIR, files amicus briefs in suits dealing with illegal immigration and suits against the Immigration and Naturalization Service. IRLI was formed in 1986, after FAIR had successfully lobbied Congress to pass the Immigration Reform and Control Act, which imposes penalties on employers who hire illegal immigrants. FAIR is often the sponsor of national public opinion polls concerning immigration. Executive Director Dan Stein works closely with the media in publicizing the results of the polls, which show that less than 10 percent of the people in the United States favor increases in immigration levels, that the large majority are worried about illegal entries, and that at least a sizeable plurality support national identity cards and activities that would strengthen our southern borders.

Larger in membership than FAIR and operating with a $2.2 million budget, the American Immigration Control Foundation

(AICF) assumes more extreme anti-immigrant positions than FAIR. It believes that immigrants take U.S. jobs, go on welfare, and waste law enforcement resources. It faults immigration for weakening the incentives of Third World nations to adopt population control policies; it accuses Third World nations of allowing excessive population growth with the intent of exporting their excessive numbers to the United States. AICF has argued that people from authoritarian countries appreciate freedom but that they lack the heritage and the habits to maintain it. AICF has lobbied consistently against the passage of any bills that would increase immigration or provide amnesty to illegal aliens.

The Rockford Institute, under the presidency of Allan Carlson, advocates much the same position as AICF. In its magazine *Chronicles: A Magazine of American Culture*, it has stated that immigrants are a threat to U.S. cultural norms. Immigrants cannot comprehend certain intangible notions of U.S. politics, art, literature, religious morality, and work ethic. The *Chronicles* has accused liberal elites of bringing in new immigrants and aliens to bolster their power base in the underclass.

Although smaller in its number of active supporters and budget than either FAIR or AICF, the Center for Immigration Studies (CIS) is also a broad-based anti-immigration organization that holds present immigration policies responsible for the existence of Asian organized crime rings. CIS has published studies on the negative effects of immigration on public education, housing, and job opportunities for U.S. workers. In the past, it has criticized U.S. immigration policy as "complicating the pursuit of more traditional political, security and trade concerns" with such countries as Cuba, Vietnam, and the Soviet Union.[1]

The most extreme anti-immigrant message is spread by the National Association for the Advancement of White People (NAAWP), whose chairperson is David Duke and which reports a membership of some 40,000. The NAAWP warns that Hispanic immigrants are engaged in a secretive "irredentist" movement to seize the U.S. Southwest and give it back to Mexico. The NAAWP also claims that most immigrants from non-European origins are not assimilable into white U.S. culture. It favors a return to the pre-1965 national origins system, whereby immigrants are permitted to enter as a national origins percentage base equal to the proportion of people from a given country already living in the United States as of a certain time period. The NAAWP advocates bringing home all the military forces stationed overseas and employing them on the Mexican border to catch illegals.

U.S. Citizens, Inc., worries about immigrants imposing upon citizen rights in the areas of political representation, public services, and natural resources. It charges immigrants with seeking affirmative action units and utilizing civil rights laws in order to secure unfair advantages.

These organizations provide a flavor of the platforms assumed by the major generally anti-immigrant groups in the country. They view immigrants as threats to U.S. culture and ideals and as competitors for jobs, housing, and educational opportunities. They believe that immigrants take undue advantage of our welfare system and that they do not understand how to live in a free society. They believe immigrants threaten population stabilization and depletion of our natural resources.

There is a subset of anti-immigration groups whose primary focuses are the closing of our southern borders to illegal aliens and the repeal of amnesty programs for illegals already in this country. Among such groups are U.S. Border Control, Coalition for Freedom, Alliance for Border Control, Light up the Border, Council for Inter America Security, and Americans for Immigration Control.

A direct mail solicitation entitled "Repeal Illegal Amnesty for Aliens," distributed by Americans for Immigration Control, and signed by Meldren Thomson, Jr., former governor of New Hampshire, stated,

> One tax expert estimates that right now the average tax payer pays $259 a year just to support illegal aliens now in the U.S. Illegal aliens cost you tax dollars when they get food stamps, welfare benefits, medical and medicare payments, free bilingual public schooling and social security benefits — illegal aliens take 3.5 million jobs from Americans.[2]

The U.S. Border Control views aliens as a key factor in drug smuggling, crime, and terrorism; it is also opposed to the granting of amnesty. Light up the Border states that it is against illegal aliens but is not generally anti-immigrant. The founder, Muriel Watson, argues that all too often the illegals are victims. They are exploited by working for wages below the minimum, and they are frequently attacked and robbed by Mexican "bandits" as they cross the border.

The Coalition for Freedom is concerned that public services are being wasted on illegal aliens, primarily in the areas of public education, welfare, hospital care, and prenatal care. It also warns that millions of refugees are flooding and will continue to flood our southern borders as a result of communist revolution and tyranny in Central American countries.

In a letter to one of the authors, Audrey Bergner, chair of the steering committee for Alliance for Border Control wrote:

> We are a nation which has blended the traditions, languages and cultures of hundreds of countries to evolve our own

typically American — and distinguishable from all others. It is predicated upon many things but primarily *a common language, a shared heritage, and a belief in Jeffersonian precepts*. These things which bind us together as a united people, are now being destroyed by those who demand bilingual education, minority quotas for jobs and scholarships (regardless of ability or skill).

Do we believe in Legal Immigration? You bet. Every one of us is the child of immigrants. Do we oppose illegal immigration? Absolutely. No state, no nation, can absorb a million and a half illiterate, unskilled people of a different culture, speaking a different language every year and still survive as a unified nation.[3]

The organizations that favor closing our southern border and deporting illegals and oppose amnesty usually steer clear of general legal immigration issues such as numbers and criteria for admission, for example, skills versus family unification.

Still another category of anti-immigrant organization is those for whom immigration is a by-product of their central concerns: population stabilization and preserving the environment. These groups include Zero Population Growth, Californians for Population Stabilization, Population Crisis Committee, Sierra Club, Population Environment Balance, and Negative Population Growth (NPG). NPG's primary objective is to achieve negative population growth for the United States and immigrant control is an important part of that strategy. NPG states that zero net migration should be the cornerstone of U.S. immigration policy. Annual net migration (immigration minus emigration) should no longer be allowed to contribute to U.S. population growth. Zero net migration means that total immigration should never exceed emigration in any given year. To achieve zero net migration, NPG advocates tallying illegal immigration and reducing legal immigration so that it does not exceed an overall ceiling of 100,000 a year, as NPG estimates emigration at about 100,000 a year. According to NPG, immigration is an environmental and resource issue. "Each additional immigrant, regardless of his or her personal qualifications and merit, swells our numbers and further increases the already dangerous level of environmental pollution. In addition, most immigrants have low skills and are illiterate. They add nothing positive to the labor market."[4] About illegal immigration, NPG holds this view: "Illegal immigration constitutes a massive and criminal invasion of our country. It is inconceivable that any other country would allow its laws to be violated, with almost complete impunity, by millions of illegal aliens each year."[5]

Population Environment Balance has assumed much the same stance on immigration as has NPG, but for Population Environment

Balance, the major focus is the environment. In the words of its executive director, Rose Hanes,

> The realities of our resource use and the vulnerability of our environment need to be considered when determining the number of immigrants that we allow into our country.... If we are to take seriously our problems regarding deteriorating infrastructures, overburdened public facilities, budget deficit, and strained social services, we must question the numbers of immigrants we add to our unskilled population base. Most immigrants are relatively unskilled and compete with our own unemployed and underemployed for jobs.[6]

Population Environment Balance estimates that approximately 200,000 Americans leave the United States in a given year; therefore, it recommends that an equal number, 200,000, should be allowed to enter, and refugees should be included in that ceiling.

The Sierra Club, with its membership of half a million and an annual budget of $29.9 million, shares the sentiments of NPG and Population Environment Balance. Sierra Club's executive director has stated,

> The Sierra Club has long believed that an end to population growth in each nation of the world is an essential part of environmental protection. This applies both to "developing" nations with rapid growth rates as well as "developed" nations with high resource consumption.... The Sierra Club believes that the number of immigrants to the U.S. should be determined within the context of a national population policy trending the U.S. towards stabilization by the middle of the next century.[7]

Californians for Population Stabilization (CAPS) believes that the state of California is presently beyond "carrying capacity," that is, it cannot sustain any more human beings in its environment.[8] CAPS expresses the fear that new immigrants will exacerbate the problems of smog, water shortages, overcrowding, high real estate costs, traffic jams, and public education.

The Population Crisis Committee perceives immigration as a serious economic drain on the United States. Immigrants take jobs from poor people and force them onto welfare. Many immigrant children, according to the Population Crisis Committee, are illiterate or cannot speak English and will not be able to find jobs and will end up on welfare.[9]

These, then, are the major organizational voices in the debate over U.S. immigration policy. Their values are remarkably homogeneous.

For somewhat different reasons, they are all anti-immigration. Are there any organizations who are avowedly proimmigration? Yes — the American Enterprise Institute, a conservative think tank; CATO, a libertarian think tank; and the Reason Foundation, another conservative think tank, all support raising the ceiling for the number of immigrants permitted to enter each year and expanding the definition of political refugees. They also argue that immigrants are good for the U.S. economy.

The American Jewish Committee, the U.S. Catholic Conference, Cuban American Nation Council, Lutheran Immigration and Refugee Service, the Indo-China Resource Action Center, the Polish American Congress, Irish National Caucus, La Raza, and the Organization of Chinese Americans are among the religious-ethnic groups that are generally proimmigrant but are more likely to become involved in the debate when specific issues are under consideration, such as the number of visas to be allocated for family unification as opposed to special skills, or when refugee status is at risk or about to be granted for a particular ethnic community. None of the organizations cited have made immigration its reason to be or a centerpiece of its existence in the way that FAIR has defined its mission. There is no single "address," for example, that the media turns to for proimmigrant information or positions in the way that FAIR is available to make the case for anti-immigration.

NOTES

1. Quoted from testimony by Rose M. Hanes, executive director, Population-Environment Balance, Inc., before the U.S. House of Representatives Committee on the Judiciary, Subcommittee on Immigration Refugees and International Law, September 27, 1989, p. 3.

2. Americans for Immigration Control, "Repeal Amnesty for Illegal Aliens" (Direct Mail Solicitation, 1991), p. 1.

3. Letter from Audrey W. Bergner to Rita J. Simon, July 23, 1990.

4. Negative Population Growth, "Zero Net Immigration" (Washington, D.C.: The NPG Forum), p. 2.

5. Ibid., p. 1.

6. Hanes, op. cit., p. 3.

7. Letter from Michael L. Fischer, executive director, to Rita J. Simon, October 10, 1990, p. 2.

8. Statement by Barbara Alexander, executive director.

9. Statement by Dr. J. Joseph Speidel, executive director.

Selected Bibliography

Anderson, Annelise, *Illegal Aliens and Employer Sanctions: Solving the Wrong Problem* (Stanford, CA: Hoover Institute, 1986).

Borjas, George J., *Friends and Strangers* (New York: Basic Books, Inc., 1990).

Cafferty, Pastora San Juan, *The Dilemmas of American Immigration: Beyond the Golden Door* (New Brunswick, NJ: Transaction Books, 1983).

Chiswick, Barry, *The Gateway: U.S. Immigration Issues and Policies* (Washington, DC: American Enterprise Institute, 1982).

Crewdson, John, *The Tarnished Door* (New York: Times Books, 1983), pp. 95–96.

Easterlin, Richard A., et al., *Immigration* (Cambridge, MA: Belknap Press, 1982).

Fermi, Laura, *Illustrious Immigrants* (Chicago: University of Chicago Press, 1968).

Glazer, Nathan, *Clamor at the Gates* (San Francisco, CA: ICS Press, 1985).

Glazer, Nathan, and David Moynihan, *Beyond the Melting Pot* (Cambridge, MA: MIT Press, 1970).

Handlin, Oscar, *The Uprooted* (New York: Grosset and Dunlap, 1951).

Harwood, Edwin, "American Public Opinion and U.S. Immigration Policy," *Annals of the American Academy of Political and Social Sciences,* 487 (September 1986): 201–12.

Higham, John, *Strangers in the Land* (New Brunswick, NJ: Rutgers University Press, 1955).

Hutchinson, E. P., *Immigrants and Their Children* (New York: Wiley, 1956).

___, *Legislative History of American Immigration Policy 1798–1965* (Philadelphia: University of Pennsylvania Press, 1981), p. 624.

Johnson, Donald Bruce, *National Party Platforms: 1960–1976*, Vol. II (Urbana: University of Illinois Press, 1978), p. 760.

Kirkpatrick, Clifford, *Intelligence and Immigration* (Baltimore, MD: Williams & Wilkins, 1926).

Kraut, Alan M., *The Huddled Masses: The Immigrant in American Society* (Arlington Height, IL: Harlan Davidson, 1982).

Kritz, Mary, *U.S. Immigration and Refugee Policy* (Lexington, MA: Lexington Books, 1982).

Lamm, Richard D., and Gary Imhoff, *The Immigration Time Bomb: The Fragmenting of America* (New York: Dutton, 1985).

Lieberson, Stanley, *A Piece of the Pie* (Berkeley: University of California Press, 1981).

Mott, Frank Luther, *A History of American Magazines, 1741–1905*, Vol. 2 (Cambridge, MA: Harvard University Press, 1938).

Muller, Thomas, and Thomas J. Espenshade, *The Fourth Wave: California's Newest Immigrants* (Washington, DC: Urban Institute, 1985).

North, David S., and Allen La Bel, *Manpower and Immigration Policies in the U.S.* (National Commission for Manpower Policies, Special Report No. 20 February 1978).

Passel, Jeffrey S., "Undocumented Immigration," *Annals of the American Academy of Political and Social Sciences*, 487 (September 1986): 181–200.

Peterson, Theodore, *Magazines in the Twentieth Century* (Champaign: University of Illinois Press, 1958).

Portes, Alejandro, "Illegal Immigration and the International System: Lessons for Recent Mexican Immigrants to the United States," *Social Problems* 26(4) (1979): 426–38.

Portes, Alejandro and Reuben G. Rumbant, *Immigrant America* (Berkeley: University of California Press, 1990).

Reimers, David M., *Still the Golden Door: The Third World Comes to America* (New York: Columbia University Press, 1985).

Samora, Julian, *Los Mojados: The Wetback Story* (Notre Dame, IN: Notre Dame University Press, 1971).

Simon, Julian, *The Economic Consequences of Immigration* (Cambridge, MA: Basil Blackwell, Inc., 1989).

Simon, Rita J., "Immigration and American Public Policy," *Annals of the American Academy of Political and Social Sciences*, 487 (September 1986).

___, *Public Opinion in America: 1936–1970* (Chicago: Rand McNally, 1974), p. 7.

Sowell, Thomas, *Ethnic America: A History* (New York: Basic Books, 1981).

Tebbel, John, *The American Magazine: A Compact History* (New York: Hawthorn Books, Inc., 1969).

U.S. Immigration Policy and the National Interest: The Final Report and Recommendations of the Select Commission on Immigration and Refugee Policy, March 1981.

Wood, James P., *Magazines in the United States* (New York: The Ronald Press Company, 1949/1956).

Index

About the Authors

Rita J. Simon is Professor of Justice, Law, and Society at The American University. She is the author or editor of more than twenty books, including Praeger's *Transracial Adoptees and Their Families*, *Intercountry Adoption*, and *Adoption, Race and Identity* (with Howard Altstein, 1987, 1990, and 1992), *The Insanity Defense* (with David Aaronson, 1988), *Women's Movements in America* (with Gloria Danziger, 1991), and *Rabbis, Lawyers, Immigrants, and Thieves* (forthcoming, 1993).

Susan H. Alexander is Assistant Professor of Sociology at Lycoming College.